YO-BRN-190

Readings in the Theology of the Church

PRENTICE-HALL INTERNATIONAL, INC., *London*
PRENTICE-HALL OF AUSTRALIA, PTY. LTD., *Sydney*
PRENTICE-HALL OF CANADA, LTD., *Toronto*
PRENTICE-HALL OF INDIA PRIVATE LIMITED, *New Delhi*
PRENTICE-HALL OF JAPAN, INC., *Tokyo*

EDWARD J. DIRKSWAGER, JR.

College of St. Thomas
St. Paul, Minnesota

Readings in the Theology of the Church

Prentice-Hall, Inc., *Englewood Cliffs, New Jersey*

LIBRARY OF CONGRESS CATALOG CARD NO.: 73–97921
PRINTED IN THE UNITED STATES OF AMERICA: 13–761957–X
CURRENT PRINTING (LAST DIGIT):
10 9 8 7 6 5 4 3 2 1

Preface

It has become increasingly obvious to all thoughtful men that the present age is a time of tension and reevaluation in Roman Catholic theology. Many members of the Catholic community and a number of members of other Christian communities are not aware of the profound ramifications of contemporary Catholic thought. Nowhere is this more evident than in ecclesiology, that is, in the attempt to arrive at an authentic understanding of the Christian community as Church.

Since the Second Vatican Council and especially since the release of the encyclical of Pope Paul VI entitled *Humanae Vitae* in 1968 we have witnessed the publication of a large number of articles and books on questions related to the nature of the Christian Church. *Readings in the Theology of the Church* has been edited to provide the educated man, whether he be Catholic or not, with some insight into the tensions facing the Christian in his attempt to fathom the issues confronting the Christian community as Church.

This selection of articles is an attempt to present some of the seminal ideas in the contemporary theology of the Church. The selections are arranged in a logical fashion but they do not present a synthesis nor do they represent a uniform point of view. The volume was not designed to answer questions, however, it was designed with the following questions in mind. Why is there a need for a Church? (Implicit in this question—What is meant by Church?) What is the real difference between the Christian Churches? Does any contemporary Church evidence Christ's love? What are the biblical and historical foundations of the Church? What is meant by authority and infallibility? What is meant by doctrinal development? Why is cult necessary for the Christian? What is the place of the Eucharistic celebration in the Church? What does the future have in store for the Church?

This volume is not an apologetic for any particular point of view. The articles chosen are meant to serve as the *beginning* of a discussion of the issues involved and are not to be taken as apodictic solutions to the issues raised.

In an attempt to bring this series of articles to as wide an audience as possible, the editor has translated the Greek and Latin phrases in the texts of the articles when the authors themselves do not do so. These translations are placed in brackets in the text. Footnotes are often an obstacle to the general reader, especially if the notes contain references to foreign language material. Nevertheless the editor feels that many will desire to consult the documentation for some of the statements made. To obviate difficulty for the general reader, the editor has placed all footnotes at the end of each article.

The editor wishes to thank the original publishers of the articles that appear in this volume for their permission to reprint the material here.

Edward J. Dirkswager, Jr.

Contents

Readings in the Theology of the Church

INTRODUCTION

ANNA MORAWSKA

Secular Awareness and the Dark Night of the Church

This article is an introduction to many of the current tensions in Christian theology. The author attempts to describe the attitudes and questions of the contemporary Christian. Some of the central issues raised in this article can be ascertained by trying to answer the following questions. What does the author mean by "secular" values? Was the present revolution in Catholic Christianity caused by the Second Vatican Council or by the "secular" world? Has renewal in the Church since Vatican II "outdistanced" the Council? Are we undergoing a crisis of the whole traditional form of institutionalized religion? What are the implications of the "new Christian awareness"? Can we rightly call our age "the dark night of the Church"?

Anna Morawska is a well-known Polish writer. Some of her essays have appeared in *Cross Currents*.

The most crucial event of the Council seems in retrospect to be the recognition of the secular world, of its values and its mentality, and in a deeper theological sense of the eschatological significance of its historical processes and developments. This recognition, which occurred on various levels, has far-reaching consequences—more so, perhaps, than was expected, and in any case needing clear and dispassionate evaluation.

Reprinted from *Cross Currents,* XVII, No. 1 (Winter 1967), pp. 34-40, with the permission of the publisher.

In the first period of *aggiornamento*, the whole question of bridging the gap between the Church and the world and of re-establishing genuine contact between two ways of living and of thinking was seen mainly as a matter of slight readjustments of language, liturgy, and structures, and of a few declarations of good will and commitment to the most pressing "secular" concerns. These readjustments and commitments were to be made by the various national hierarchies in accordance with the conciliar blueprints.

Soon, however, this vertical pattern of renewal proved impracticable. The idea that the Church not only is reformable after all, but actually needs reform badly, and that at least some typically "secular" thinking has been proven right (both of these things implied, if not openly admitted in the conciliar proceedings), produced a sort of chain reaction in the Catholic world at large. The first result, therefore, of the still timid attempt at a reconciliation with the secular world was an outburst of the long-repressed secular aspirations and resentments of lay Catholics themselves. Their emancipation and far-going "revisionism" soon outdistanced the Council and went its own way, confronting ever more fundamental aspects of the Christian tradition.

Such evolution in the growing circles of the Catholic avant-gardes had its own internal logic. In the light of modern "secular" values, now openly professed—such as freedom of individual conscience, democracy, intellectual honesty, etc.—the current Catholic ecclesiology posed problems which could not be solved without reference to the very foundations of Catholic belief. What was first meant to be a renewal of the Catholic Church was thus bound to move on to a second stage, to a new investigation of such issues as the meaning and character of Revelation, faith, and ministry. Thus, already during the third session of the Council, when the Fathers were still involved in the juridical intricacies of collegiality, Catholics outside the aula (or at least the Catholic elites) were asking questions of a quite different order: Who is Christ for us today, in the light of all we know and experience? What really is Christian tradition, and what does it say? What sort of evidence and what sort of truth are to be found in the Bible? Because of the existence of the mass media and the critical and inquiring mood created everywhere by the Council, all these questions, at least in the form of a growing anxiety, were present in very large circles of lay Catholics and lower clergy by the end of the Council, and part of subsequent tensions is perhaps due to this difference in experience and concerns between the Church authorities, still thinking in terms of the classical pattern of ecclesiology and struggling to preserve their continuity, and some of the most committed Catholic avant-gardes, trying to understand and reformulate the fundamentals of the Christian tradition itself.

In the postconciliar years, the renewal continued to develop on these two levels. While for some of the faithful the issues raised by the Council and the practical measures undertaken by the bishops, in accordance with conciliar instructions, seemed too advanced, other groups, preoccupied by the problems—and ensuing conflicts—of a far more basic order, were gradually losing intellectual contact (to say the least) with their bishops, and experiencing a growing frustration at what they felt to be the utter irrelevance of the institutional Church in its present form, including the official attempts at renewal.

The outline of the new vision of biblical faith as a "secular" commitment to God "acting in the midst of our life" was thus created, and the renewal itself was again bound to move on to what may be considered a third stage, which consisted in a new and far more radical criticism of the historical Church. The centrifugal tendencies manifested themselves and grew stronger, as moral conflicts caused by the obvious contradiction between the new vision of Christian commitment and all forms of institutionalized religion were becoming more and more generalized and acute. The gap between the genuine and, in part at least, truly creative Catholic thinking and official Church theory and practice, which seemed to be bridged at the beginning of the Council, was thus created again, and is still growing. The resulting confusion—more or less successfully coped with by the typical believer—is considerably increased by the fact that the progressives (including many gifted and committed intellectuals, leaders of lay movements, etc.) are far more articulate than conservatives or moderates, and their ideas and problems are bound, sooner or later, to reach a wide Catholic public.

In this situation, the most urgent postconciliar question is surely what to do about this gap. Can it be bridged soon? If so, how? If not, what can be done to reduce the dangers it creates for unity and charity, without, however, limiting freedom?

Whatever the final answers may be, it seems helpful and perhaps by now possible to try to evaluate some of the general directions the "new Church" (or, as some say, the "new new Church") has taken in the postconciliar years, and to face squarely the questions they raise and the prospects they open. In other words, it seems worthwhile to repeat the preconciliar experience of an inquiry into the actual status quo of our Church and its possible developments. Let us ask ourselves as honestly and clearly as we did before the Council: Where are we today, and where do we want to go from where we are? What do we think of and expect from the postconciliar period?

Each inquiry has to have some framework to keep within, if it is not to be diluted in generalities. The above general description of the development of Catholic self-awareness in the conciliar and postconciliar years is in itself such a framework, meant to be either used, or questioned. Was the "revolution" caused—if not planned—by the Council really a "secular" one? How and why has the subsequent renewal "outdistanced" the Council?

Some further hypotheses to start with could be formulated as follows.

Although the Catholic avant-gardes (not to speak of the rank and file) are still very far from a clear and unequivocal synthesis of their vision of Catholic faith, some of its general features can be discerned and seem to have some measure of irreversibility. They create, however, very serious problems if not contradictions in the very fabric of Catholic Christianity and result in what is sometimes called an acute crisis of structures. Indeed, it may be even more than that: perhaps it is a crisis of the whole traditional form of institutionalized religion.

Or is it? Let us have a look at some more specific issues.

It can be said that the dominant feature of the new Christian awareness in all its various forms of expression is a strong conviction that the God of Christian tradition is truly Lord of history. This is not simply a pious metaphor, but has very important consequences for the whole vision of faith and Christian mission. Perhaps the most radical thing about the so-called radicals of renewal is simply that they have admitted these consequences sooner and indeed more radically than the others.

The belief in the "Lord of history" means that God has revealed himself through historical, "secular" events, that what was actually revealed was his salvific will concerning the concrete, historical world at large, and not only in regard to the Churches or our individual souls. It means that God's workings towards this salvific end are still occurring "in the world" (that it to say, everywhere), in all human striving for the good and in historical developments aimed at more human relationships and deeper community, which are foretastes of the Kingdom.

Such a view seems to many Christians the only one which is tenable—at least for the time being. First of all, it is in harmony with the new planetary self-awareness, and it should be noted that this self-awareness is not experienced merely as an abstract intellectual construction but as the highest human value. It would thus be psychologically impossible, if not blasphemous, to imagine God and his acts as somehow "below" this highest value and ideal, and no speculative casuistry can overcome this basic relationship of man to what he considers to be Absolute. All such casuistry can do, and indeed tried to do for a long time, is to make the whole idea of God utterly irrelevant to man's genuine values and vital concerns.

What is more, modern biblical criticism, which tends to show Revelation as very deeply embedded in and sustained by quite secular events and processes, has helped to create a situation in which not only the sense of values but also a purely intellectual honesty, simply forces one either to believe in God working in the secular world at large and by means of this world, or not to believe in him and his acts at all.

All this, however, produces a major shift in the understanding of quite basic Catholic tenets. Does the mission of the Church consist in "converting" people, in the sense of "giving Christ" to them, or in recognizing the acts and presence of "Christ incognito" wherever and however they occur? In other words, does the Christian mission consist primarily in commitment to all truly human community and its good strivings, wherever they are to be found?

And what sort of commitment should it be? The Catholic Church is faced today with two quite contradictory kinds of expectation. On the one hand, it is said that it should effectively support the good secular causes, such as peace, or development, but to do this in the modern world, the Church must keep the advantages of large-scale organization. This means that it must remain what we call a "power," or a "pressure group," and the more centralized and institutionalized it is, the better for the effectiveness of its actions. On the other hand, however, it is precisely its "power" and "institutions" that are most bitterly criticized, and some groups tend to see the true Christian Church "outside the walls of Ur" in informal, small communities, whose commitment may be genuinely Christian, but whose actual influence must remain limited and indirect. Should the Christian mission, then, consist in an "effective charity," in large-scale actions, in transforming the social structures, which can be done by economic and political means only? Or is it to be a mission of "pure sign," of heroic witness? It is difficult to exclude either of these two forms of Christian presence. But the choice is a very practical one, since it determines the structures of the Church we look forward to, and therefore must be somehow made.

Another crucial question is: How do we recognize God's acting in history? If it is understood that God operates through historical processes, secular movements, etc., then God must be obeyed. But how to discern those genuinely divine "signs of the times" in actual life? Was not, for example, reasoning similar to this used to justify a commitment to Nazism?

Further, does the Christian mission really begin and end in such "horizontal" commitments? What, after all, is faith? If it is essentially the consent to God's will, as met in actual existence in the form of its constant appeal to our "being for others," does it have to express itself at all in some clear religious convictions? Do we have to think the word "God" at all to say "yes" to God? Or can he be absent in individual experience, or even in the experience of whole generations, without preventing their life from being truly Christian?

If we answer in the affirmative, we should admit that the Christian message is actually no more than an interpretation of world history and of the experience of each individual life, a history and an experience which occur anyway, whether the interpretation is preached and accepted or not. If so, however, and if an act of faith is possible without the actual preaching of the Gospel, why—indeed, how—preach it?

And what does "preaching" mean? Is it a matter of some demythologized presentation of our message of love and hope? If so, how far can this demythologizing go? Or is perhaps the commitment to true human community a "preaching of the Gospel" in itself? Does "being Christian" mean, quite simply, a vocation to give special witness to love and hope, which are acting and are being realized in the world anyway? Would this be similar to the way monasteries were a special witness to Christianity in earlier centuries?

Here again we have to think of some answers, although a clear choice does not seem easy. For it is again a very practical question of structures, or at least of admitting openly the existence and desirability of very varied structures within the one Catholic Church.

The emerging "secular" self-awareness, as described above, is sometimes said to be merely a shift of emphasis in the traditional Christian vision, and it is rightly stressed that such shifts have frequently occurred in the course of history, and should not be overdramatized. It seems, however, that as far as the Catholic Church, and particularly Catholic ecclesiology today is concerned, this recent shift creates very serious problems, and quite a few open or latent conflicts now occurring are due to the fact that some questions are open and perhaps bound to remain open for some time yet.

It seems better, in any case, to state them honestly. We are, for instance, constantly brought back in recent years to the fundamental fact that in many ways the world teaches (and has always taught) the Church, and that only too often the world was right as against the Church. As a matter of historical fact, have not the most "revolutionary" Council documents belatedly borrowed many of their basic truths from "the world"? In all frankness, have not our basic convictions on human equality, liberty, solidarity, or justice developed and asserted themselves in constant struggle with the current teachings of the Magisterium, at least the so-called ordinary Magisterium, though some more formal definitions also need far-going "reinterpretations"? In the light of the belief in God's acting in the whole world, there is nothing very alarming in this discovery in itself. But don't we badly need a reinterpretation of the Catholic doctrine of infallibility, of the holiness of the Church, of the character and biblical grounds of Church authority in general, before the contradiction between the obvious and the formally stated (and still binding in conscience) proves too much of a burden for too many Catholics?

This is only one example and, no doubt, the most drastic. But there are many other points in Catholic ecclesiology which either have to be reinterpreted in the light of the new vision of faith and of historical and sociological facts, now all too clear to everybody, or will inevitably constitute latent sources of tension and moral conflicts for growing numbers of Catholics.

The more "secular" our ideas of the acts of God and of the Christian mission are, and the more manifest are the ensuing centrifugal tendencies in the Church, the more important seems the role of liturgy as the vital center of spiritual "réssourcement" in the now purposeful diaspora, and as the central, most meaningful symbol of Christian identity. Here again, however, questions are raised.

Is our liturgy meant to be a sign available to all mankind, or a sort of secret discipline, the only specific "otherness" of Christians? Does it really serve either of these two possible purposes in its actual form? Is liturgy primarily a worship of Christ's presence in the depth of human community and of the world's strivings toward its fullness, and a solemn act of saying a trustful "yes" to human destiny, as assumed and sanctified in hope by Christ? If so, does it really and meaningfully express this? If not, how should its other meanings be stated so as to be integrated in the actual vision of the Christian faith?

And can we answer all these questions at all without dealing with the whole "crisis of metaphysics," of which the horizontal or "secular" vision of our faith is a symptom? If, in the actual experience of many of us, we can follow the Lord only as he acts "in the midst of our life and of history," and if that is what we think the Bible tells us to do, does not all talk about "the supernatural" turn into purely philosophical speculation, very valuable in its own right, but irrelevant to the living faith? Did it not in actual religious praxis turn into an individualistic, insurancelike hedge against eschatological contingencies and against the (possible) anger of (possibly existing) "Power"? And if it did, don't we also have to rethink our doctrine, our understanding of liturgy, and indeed all our current assumptions?

But can we? Isn't more at stake here than just the structures of the institutional Church? Is this really an "end of religion"? Do we want it, and can we stop it if we don't?

These are only some of the open questions, by no means all of them. They seem enough, however, to start with. If we agree that the common source of the whole present "revolution" is the recognition of the Christian significance of the secular sphere, including even the so-called dechristianization, we might realize that this recognition not only creates problems, but opens up tremendous prospects for the unity of all mankind, centered on one common faith and hope. A unity which, to our knowledge at least, could not be achieved in any foreseeable future by way of "conversions" to particular Christian Churches in their present form of institutionalization.

This dazzling and, let us admit, uncertain, prospect has, as we have seen, tremendous costs for the Churches, as they are here and now, and, first of all, for millions of unsophisticated human beings, for whom these Churches do still symbolize adequately the best they hope for and aspire to. Can we and should we try to avoid these costs altogether? Or should we rather choose to assume knowingly the unavoidable period of uncertainties, and for some even of a "dark night"? Roman Catholics, in particular, were never brought up to face dark nights, and still less perhaps to assume the experience of apparent discontinuity or even breakdown in their own Church. Must we and can we stand this test now?

EDWARD SCHILLEBEECKX, O.P.

The Church and Mankind

The author of this article attempts to build a foundation for a discussion of the relation between Christianity and authentic human existence. The author claims to find a tendency in mankind toward community, a claim that the reader is asked to evaluate. It is important to ascertain exactly how the author uses the terms "ecclesial," "Church," "People of God," and "Body of Christ." Is Christianity as fellowship and brotherhood antithetical to Christianity as Church? What is meant by "implicit" or "anonymous" Christianity? What is the purpose or mission of the Christian community?

Edward Schillebeeckx, O.P., is a Professor of Dogmatic Theology at the University of Nijmegen, Holland. He is the author of many articles and books. One of his recent books is *God—The Future of Man.*

The Problem

In our age we have become aware, more than in the past, that our salvation comes about within the one reality that is ours, within the scope of our own life in this world. Everywhere there is evi-

Reprinted from "The Church and Mankind," in *Concilium,* Vol. I, *The Church and Mankind,* ed. Edward Schillebeeckx, O.P. (Glen Rock, N.J.: Paulist Press, 1965), pp. 69–101; *Concilium,* January 1965, *Dogma,* Vol. I, no. 1 (Burns and Oates Ltd., London), pp. 34–50, with the permission of *Concilium.*

dence of a reaction against any kind of religious practice which is alien to this world. Christianity had come to be regarded as something added on to life here on earth with its sorrow and joy, its fear and hope, its activities and moments of recollection. Many Christians used to practice their Christianity as a superstructure erected on top of their normal lives. Frequently they would look upon this life as merely matter, without religious significance in itself, for the occasional exercise of Christian virtues. Life's own significance had, in their eyes, nothing to do with Christianity.

Real religion, they held, was only practiced within a church edifice or by saying a few prayers at home—in other words, at the periphery of life. As a result, many Christians gave the impression that Christianity was an ideological superstructure, or a special department where people talked about forgiveness, redemption, the cross, and resurrection, while life in this world waited outside. The human problems of life on this earth failed to get from them the attention they received from nonbelievers to the benefit of mankind.

At present, there is a strong emerging realization that adherence to faith is not a mere structure superimposed upon human and secular relationships, which would in fact be what they are, with or without Christianity, and so would be unaffected by faith. Consequently, reaction against ghetto-Catholicism and ghetto-Christianity is characteristic of present-day religious awareness among both Catholics and Reformed Christians. Service to a world which is growing into a closer unity; the ethical commitment imposed upon Western man by the advanced position which the West enjoys in contrast to the rest of the world, particularly the underdeveloped countries; the plans for a dynamic blueprint to set up a society upon earth that shall be worthy of men—all this is seen, also by the religious man of today, as the concrete, even the principal way in which he purposes to give form to his religion and to Christianity.

Hand in hand with this new religious awareness there is opposition to an exotic religious vocabulary. Religious ideas have to be couched in "profane" words, in language that springs from the profound realities of human existence. People want their Christianity to be less explicit and prefer it to work implicitly, almost incognito, toward salvation within their secular human relationships.

This current phenomenon, however, has one drawback. Many believers are at a loss as to what to do about the Church as an objective reality. Sociological researches draw attention to the fact that some kind of faith in God as the basis of all existence, and faith, too, in the Man Jesus, who by his life has shown the meaning of God's love for men, actually exist in persons who had "practiced" earlier in their lives but do not belong at present to any Church: they also show that precisely these persons no longer find any room in their belief for the "Church."

They could only accept the Church—and with enthusiasm—if Church meant no more than the establishment of a community among men, the real expression of the community that human fellowship ought to build up in the world. There is talk of "Christianity without a Church," a Christianity in which fellowship and brotherhood appear as the essence of Church.

The lines of our essay take two directions. We inquire first into the increasingly "ecclesial" tendency in the world, or rather in mankind; and second, we inquire into the tendency within the Church to sanctify the secular. On the one hand, the human fellowship in Christ is surely the heart of the Church as a phenomenon: St. Thomas calls sanctifying grace *gratia fraterna*, the grace that establishes brotherhood. On the other hand, as believers, we cannot help admitting that the Church is a community *sui juris* [in its own right], or rather, *juris Christi* [through the grace of Christ]. But *ipso facto* we then create a certain distance between the Church and mankind. There are boundaries between the Church and humanity, and yet they are fluid, not hard and fast. Into the implications of this we now propose to inquire, for the sake of a mankind that grows away from the Church and for the sake of faith in the Church as founded by Christ.

I
The Unity of Mankind and the Communion of Saints

Mankind's specific unity from an anthropological viewpoint must formally (*formaliter*) be based, not on its biological substratum, but, by its very nature, on a community of *persons*, a *communio*. It can only be built on a value-appeal, the community-building force of truly human values. This means simply that human unity has its origin in oneness of vocation and destiny.

Communio among all men is the immanent human expression of this single vocation. Human unity in its essence is not a mere datum: it is a task to be carried out. This task, we know from Revelation, is in fact the response to a free and gracious act of God. The *koinonía* or community which he wills is also his gift. By his absolute self-communication to men he at once reveals himself as their highest value and reveals mankind to itself as his People, the People of God. By the granting of his grace God constitutes mankind "the People of God." Communion among men is the reflection, immanent in mankind's history, of man's transcending communion with the living God: the God-willed unity of mankind is therefore nothing less than the *communio Sanctorum*, the community of mankind sanctified.

Not only is the fact of this community an undue gift to men, but the manner of producing it also has its origin in a sovereign, free act of God. The history of salvation in both the Old and the New Testaments, even though the outlook of the ancient Near Eastern peoples plays its role in them, makes this fact clear: God did not intend "abstract" fundamental values to be the basis on which human unity was to be realized. He intends to gather all men into a holy community of persons on the basis of values that were expressed in living persons as in prototypes.

Time and again someone is chosen from among ourselves to be the means of salvation in forming the "great gathering" of men from the diaspora, the People of God.[1] The manner, not due to men, in which God establishes a community among them is that of representative or vicarious mediation: for the sake of one man, whom God freely calls for the purpose, salvation—or destruction—is brought to many. In the Old and the New Testaments, time and again, the representative function whether of one man or of a limited collectivity is essential for salvation or destruction: Adam, Noah, Moses, the twelve Patriarchs, "Israel," the "King," the Servant of Yahweh, Jesus.

In the Bible the establishment of a community through mediation implies that election and universal mission coalesce into one. Thus, however gradually and hesitantly, Israel did at last become aware of her election to be an example to all peoples—of her election for the service of all men. In the Old Testament conception it is to Yahweh's redemptive covenant with Noah after the Flood that the totality of mankind throughout history owes its existence. And in connection with that covenant a catalog is drawn up of all the nations existing in the world as conceived by the ancients (Gen. 10).[2] Again, in Abraham "shall all nations be blessed" (Gen. 12:3; 18:18; 22:18). His election, too, is God's ratification of universal salvation.

The notion of mediatorship shows us that men are dependent upon one another and that God in bringing his transcendent salvation means to preserve the structure of human fellowship. Through men he wants to bring salvation to men. The notions of "the first-born among many brethren" (Rom. 8:29), which embraces prototypical religious fellowship, and of "God's first-born son" (Ex. 4:22), in which divine choice and service to the neighbor are united, are led up to throughout the Old Testament. They suggest the fundamental notion that salvation is a gift conveyed through man's fraternal service to others according to God's election. Even Israel, the People of God, is, when chosen, "God's first-born son" (*loc. cit.*): Israel is personified, initially, in the vicarious figure of the King, who is therefore eponymously called "Son of God (e.g., 2 Sam. 7:14; Psalm 2:7), and ultimately in the figure of the coming Messiah and Son of Man, "the Son of God" *par excellence.*

Jesus is not merely one of us—he represents "Israel, the Son of God," but in an incomparably deeper sense: in a uniquely transcendent manner he is "the Son of the Father." Nevertheless, he is our fellowman "taken from among men" (Heb. 5:1), "born of a woman" (Gal. 4:4). Election and fraternal service, "Son of God," servant of God and men—these ideas find their highest fulfillment in Jesus. And so it is in him that the "great gathering" of all men around God, *he ekklesia toû Theoû* [the community of God] (1 Cor. 11:22; 15:9) is formed into a mutual *communio* of men with Christ as their center—a "Church of Christ," *hai ekklesiai toû Christoû* [all the churches of Christ] (Rom. 16:16). Scattered mankind becomes in Christ unified mankind (Eph. 2:15) founded on the "eschatological Man,"[3] the *eschatos Adam* [final Adam] (1 Cor. 15:45). He is a vivifying Spirit (*loc. cit.*), not merely man, but a man who "gives life" to his fellowmen.

Mankind, then, has received salvation through the fraternal service of one chosen from among ourselves—Jesus Christ, the Elect of God, the Son of the Father. This fact of Christ, which took place in our history and in our secular and human affairs, has had a real effect on human history. Mankind's new fundamental but real unity and new structure as a community rest upon God's universal saving will. This will is not an actuality that is simply beyond history; it has manifested itself visibly within history in the "objective redemption," that is, in the personal life of Jesus, representative man, Son of God, appearing among us in our history.

In one Man—the *homo principalis* as Irenaeus says,[4] i.e., he who stands at the wellspring of the new mankind, which *ipso facto* he has gathered into a community—in this one Man all men have already ascended through the passion to the glory with the Father.

Thus the history of Israel, which is a component of, and imbedded in, human history, takes on a new meaning. For human history, wherever it is made, has in this manner found grace with the Father and is already conclusively accepted by the Father in the *Eschaton*, Jesus Christ. For the Father has established Jesus who humbled himself, as the glorified Christ, the "Son of God in power" (Rom. 1:4) at his own right hand. Consequently Christ is at once the Alpha and Omega of human history in its entirety (Apoc. 1:8; 21:6; 22:13). As such, he is the key to history, not only in an exclusively transcendent manner beyond time and space, but his humanity now glorified is a truly historical humanity that has reached its consummation at a real point in history. In Jesus, history is finally and conclusively perfected with that kind of perfect achievement that persists in eternity. As representative, first of Israel, and so of mankind, he is the prototypical moment of mankind's history; this moment has already been inserted in eternal glory. And so our Lord, although in a dimension that exceeds our experience, gives our human history its final immanent meaning. Every historical human event wherever occurring, even in areas called "profane," can thus be understood only through the eschatological Man, Jesus Christ.

II
Dialectical Tension Between "Mankind" and the Church

Christ has bestowed a new religious meaning upon mankind in principle and in the concrete (i.e., integrated in our own history). Nevertheless, between mankind "gathered" into a collectivity in principle and its actual manifestation in Christ there exists a certain distance. This distance and tension are embodied in Christ's Church. For it is in the Church, by free assent to the grace of justification, by acceptance of God's Word in faith, and by admission to baptism in the name of the Holy Trinity, that mankind's new religious meaning takes on the form that establishes an historical, visible, concrete community. When a man is incorporated into the Church, Christ's triumphant grace becomes a plain, historical, recognizable fact.[5] The result is that, at least from the ascension until the Second Coming, there is a certain distinction and dialectical tension between humanity redeemed in principle, at its source, and the Church.

In a series of articles of progressive subtlety, A. Vögtle, a Catholic biblical exegete, has demonstrated that Jesus, at least in his public teaching, nowhere manifests an intention of selecting from Israel a specific group of persons in order to form them into a separate community.[6] By his public preaching of God's dominion and by his call to repentance he plainly intended to gather not a remnant only but all of Israel and make of it the new Israel, the eschatological People of *God*. Sectarianism was alien to him. Radically he pursues the path of the history of salvation as Paul will afterward copy it: salvation is announced first to Israel, and then, according to the divine design, via Israel to the whole world.

Jesus' call of "the twelve" from among the group of disciples is clearly explained as a parable in action[7] that his contemporaries could not mistake: in "the twelve," the twelve Patriarchs of Israel are represented—a further proof of Jesus' purpose to win all Israel for the kingdom of heaven. Actually, however, all Israel does not adhere to his doctrine, but on the contrary, opposition to his activities grows ever stronger. Chiefly because of the massive dimensions the opposition assumed and as he sees the historical event of his death approaching and the violent form it is to take, Jesus begins within the limited circle of the disciples to interpret its meaning and to explain it in the light of the prophecy in Deutero-Isaiah: his death is to be an expiation "for the many"—that is, for all—and God has arranged it so beforehand. Not before his death and resurrection,[8] and only in connection with them, is he to speak to his disciples of "the Church which he is going to build upon the Rock" (Peter) (Matt. 16:18f.; see John 21:15–17).

This implies that the redeemed People of God will become after Jesus' death and resurrection an *Ecclesia Christi*—an historical, visible gathering or congregation of men around Christ, in visible communion with the "Rock" and the twelve apostles. This situation gives Jesus' community a special ecclesiastico-social structure, which as such does not coincide with the social structure of secular society.

We see, then, that on the one hand, in his public preaching Jesus never speaks of a Church with forms of organization, and that he lays down obedient acceptance of his message of salvation, here and now, in the *kairos* [golden opportunity; God's salvific will for man as expressed in the signs of the times] of the present moment, as the sole condition for entering the kingdom of God. And on the other hand, it is in the light of his death as an expiation for all men that he speaks of the founding of his Church. This he presents as a postpaschal event: "I *shall* build my Church." Holy Scripture, then, clearly connects the messianic suffering—Jesus' "going away"—with the postpaschal realization of the Church.

The Church is God's People with a special qualification: the People of God who through Jesus' death and resurrection become through the Spirit the Body of Christ—*soma Christoû*—the Body of the *Lord*. On earth this Body is built as "the Church" upon Peter, the Rock. The return to the Father—the vertical theme of Jesus' public preaching—becomes in the light of his death, explained to his apostles as reconciliation, after Easter and Pentecost also a horizontal theme: the building of a mutual community around the Rock. It becomes, consequently, a clear theme of a mankind redeemed with the purpose of an ecclesial brotherhood, a communal Church with its own initiation, its own cult, especially the sharing of the eucharistic table, a community guided and accompanied by a ministering office. Thus the death and glorification of Jesus, the Christ, have made access to this brotherhood, the sacramentally and historically visible Church, a condition for entrance into the kingdom of God.[9] The *communio* of believers gathered about its bishop (in communion with the Rock)—this *is* salvation, the Church of Christ. Precisely in this *koinonía* must the Father's absolute self-communication through the Son in the Holy Spirit find that historically visible realization, which is in truth the sign of all mankind's vocation. Hence the Church is not just a *koinonía*, a communion or sharing of grace with Christ, the fruit of his redemptive work, but it is also an institution for salvation to which the keys that make entrance possible into the kingdom of God have been entrusted. In contrast to Jesus' "Woe unto you, scribes and Pharisees," who bar the entrance to the kingdom (Matt. 23:13), Christ gives Peter the keys that open the gates.

III
The Basis of the Dialectical Tension

There is, then, a distance or interval between mankind, fundamentally and historically redeemed, and the community of Jesus built upon the Rock, which is the Church or body of "practicing Christians." To understand this distance we must first remember the connection laid by Holy Scripture between the messianic death—Jesus' "going away"—and the Church, which is only postpaschal and therefore a new reality, new even in comparison with that universal reality which is the People of God.

From our point of view the death of Jesus is mankind's rejection of him: Israel's rejection through its representative, the Sanhedrin; the Gentiles' rejection of him in the person of Pilate, and even the rejection by the hierarchy of the future Church in the persons of the apostles who ran away, and of Peter, who denied him. In his death Jesus stands alone, crushed by "the sins of the world"; alone in his surrender to the Father for the service of his fellowmen. That which achieved this reconciliation was, therefore, also the cause of Jesus' factual absence—the absence, in other words, of the source of grace. From our point of view, the breach of the covenant of grace was made complete by his death: mankind has banished from the world "the coming of God's kingdom" in Christ and so has expelled it from the *communio* of men.

Every death, of course, means bodily absence and the breaking off of relations with the dead as fellowmen. In the case of Jesus, however, it is a matter of the death of the only one who could bring redemption. From our point of view, this removal of Christ, the Man of grace, is therefore irrevocable. For the renewal of his relations with us through the resurrection is certainly not owing to us, not even to Christ's humanity as such. Only by understanding the profound importance of his death can we fully appreciate the basic saving significance of his resurrection, which, on account of the sacrifice that had been offered, made possible the sending of the Holy Spirit and the building of the Church. In the resurrection, which was a grace of the Father, the redemptive work of Jesus triumphed. But this triumph implies that henceforth our salvation depends upon someone who is absent from our experience, Jesus Christ.

We may justly conclude from this that the final state of our condition as it was created by original sin is "a situation in which the *privation* of supernatural grace can *only be removed sacramentally*, a situation in which man found himself ever since, and, because of the breach of the covenant with God, was made complete through man's rejection of Christ." [10]

Jesus himself connects his going away with the coming of the Spirit and the building of his Church. In his Body, the Church, wherein the Holy Spirit dwells, he intends to remain as the source of all grace. Hence, this Body, the Church, becomes the condition or the embodiment of our restored relationship with Christ and our entrance into the kingdom of God. Christ, absent from the universal human community, is made present again through the resurrection in the Church, his Body on earth.

The weighty consequence of this fact is significantly expressed by St. Thomas: "The grace of Christ comes to us not through human nature but through the *personal action* of Christ himself." [11] In present-day terms this means that the source of Christ's grace is not fellow-creaturehood in and by itself, but fellow-creaturehood with Christ, who, while absent since his death from the horizon of our experience, means to remain present among us, but postpaschally, in virtue of the Spirit of God, in his Body, the Church.

As the Body of our Lord, the Church forms the living link with Christ—horizontally, with the Jesus of history, who arose and appeared to the apostles; vertically, with the Lord of glory, thanks to the Spirit that dwells in the whole community of the Church in its hierarchical function, its preaching, its sacraments. Because of Christ's fellowship with us the universal human fellowship, too, takes on a deepened meaning, and the boundaries between mankind and the Church begin to blur.

IV
Fluidity of the Boundaries Between the Church and Mankind

The history of salvation, then, deals with one covenant that has passed through two phases, or a twofold *dispositio* [disposition or economy]. An absolutely new situation has been created in the plan of salvation by Christ's death and resurrection. Now the further question arises: What is the relationship between the universal People of God, coextensive with mankind, and the Church, in which the People of God has become the Body of our Lord?

The *locus theologicus* [theological locus] of all reflection on the faith and, consequently, of the theology of the relationships between the Church and the world, is the historical advent of salvation in Jesus Christ: the man Jesus who is to us the absolute and gratuitous presence of God. In Christ and through him, human existence has become the objective expression of God's absolute communication of himself to man and, by the same token, the objective expression of the human response to that total divine gift. As a corollary of that fact, the human condition in its historical setting has become the concrete matter and space of the historical manifestation of man's God-related life in Christ. The human existence of Christ, taken with all its determinisms and all its human implications, is the *personal* life of God, the Son.

This means that the entire temporal dimension and the unabridged reality we call profane can be assumed into a God-related life, given that in the Son the Eternal has presented itself personally within temporal and terrestrial realities. The very definition of the hypostatic union is exactly that. This also reveals the fact that thanks to Christ all of human history is swathed in God's love; it is assumed into the absolute and gratuitous presence of the mystery of God. The worldly and the temporal remain worldly and temporal; they are not sacralized but sanctified by that presence, that is, by the God-centered life of Christ and of his faithful.

Everyone will agree that our human existence is immersed in unfathomable mystery, although the way of saying so may vary infinitely. In her Revelation-through-the-Word, the Church merely clarifies for the benefit of all mankind the reality of the mystery's absolute presence in Christ; it proclaims that this mystery has drawn closer to us, not only in some mystical and interior intimacy, but also through the medium of a palpable and visible historical reality. The whole kerygma and all of Christian dogma can be summarized in that fundamental affirmation: beginning with the Trinity, the incarnation, the life of grace, but also including the Church with her ministry, worship, preaching, sacraments, as well as collective and individual eschatology.

Word-revelation, of which the Church is the herald, only unfolds the implications of that absolute and gratuitous presence which, as revelations-reality, is already present in the lives of men, even prior to their historical encounter with the phenomenon "Church." Moreover, the free acceptance of the mystery's absolute and gratuitous presence is the very substance of what we call theologal or God-related faith. To believe is to have confidence in this mystery thus present; it means trusting in him in spite of everything and under all circumstances. That affirmation strikes me as of the utmost importance because what is implied is that the acceptance of real human existence, concretely taken with all its responsibilities, is in truth an act of God-centered faith: for Christ has shown us, by living it, that human existence taken concretely—not in the abstract—was for him, precisely in his human condition steeped as it was in the mystery, the objective expression of his communion with the Father in the *Dynamis* of the Holy Spirit and for the benefit of his fellowmen.

Here is what this brief analysis shows us:

1. Within the Church of Christ the absolute and gratuitous presence of the mystery becomes an explicit epiphany, historically and humanly observable—both as a reality and as a task to be accomplished.

2. This concentrated ecclesial manifestation of God merely explicates

that which in fact and at its own level is going on in all of human existence, even if the subject is not aware of it, namely, the gratuitous presence of the mystery, which is an active, an operative presence.

From this viewpoint, the incarnation teaches us that the entire human reality may ferry divine grace and can be assumed into a God-centered life. Day-to-day human life with its worldly concerns for human advancement is the area wherein normal Christian life must develop; the explicit and ecclesial expression of that selfsame communion with God shall indeed be the fountainhead and the driving force of the expression of Christian life in the world. St. Paul told us as much in a masterful though negative manner: "Neither death, nor life, nor angels, nor principalities, nor things present, nor things to come, nor powers, nor height, nor depth, nor any other creature will be able to separate us from the love of God, which is in Christ Jesus our Lord" (Rom. 8:38–39). What does it all mean if not that Christianity is upheld by faith in the absolute and gratuitous presence of God within Christ as well as by the fact that we must accept human history and our entire earthly life as a reality steeped and swaddled in God's love? Improving the world whenever we improve ourselves, we are always in the presence of and beneath the wings of the mystery who gives himself freely.

While respecting the worldly and earthly significance of the reality we call the world, this outlook gives it a profoundly theological meaning. This is what the world is: the profane, earthly, and temporal reality with structures all its own, with its special and immediate end, but which, in Christ, is assumed into the absolute and gratuitous presence of God. In saying this one should beware of imagining the world as some static, immobile reality. Planet Earth is the material given to man with which to fashion a human world, a dwelling place worthy of man. Of course man's world has the mark of the creature upon it; moreover, as everything else common to man, it is a world wrought by sin. The construction of the world and the promotion of peoples remain a finite task, the work of men, and as such it shares in the ambiguity of all that is human. This world is creature, non-God. To say this is to affirm the secularity of earthly tasks. Indeed, creation is a divine act that situates realities within their respective spheres; and contrary to the mythological legends held by the contemporaries of ancient Israel, the Bible refers to that divine act, in Genesis, as desacralizing and unmystifying the world, handing it over to itself, into the hands of man for God's glory. This means that as a result of the divine act of sustained creation, the history of mankind will assert itself as the progressive and prolonged desacralization of earthly structures and functions.

But that is only one facet of a far richer and more profound reality: since God created so as to bestow himself to man and to be, he himself, present in a gratuitous and redemptive manner, in our brother, Jesus the Anointed. This means that in the plan of salvation the concrete world, by definition, is an *implicit Christianity;* it is an objective, nonsacral but saintly and sanctified expression of mankind's communion with the living God; whereas the Church *qua* institution of salvation, with her explicit creed, her worship and sacraments, is the direct and sacral expression of that identical communion—she is the *separata a mundo* [set apart from the world].

To speak of the relationships between the Church and the world does not mean therefore that a dialogue is to be launched between the strictly Christian dimension of our human life and its distinctly non-Christian dimension; nor is it a question of conducting a dialogue between the religious and the profane, between the supernatural and the natural or intraworldly—it is rather a dialogue between *two complementary, authentically Christian expressions* of one and the same God-related life concealed in the mystery of Christ, namely, the *ecclesial* expression (in the strict sense of the word) and the *worldly* expression of that identically same life, internalized within human life through man's free acceptance of grace. In other words, the *implicitly* Christian and the *explicitly* Christian dimension of the same God-related life, that is, of human life hidden in God's absolute and gratuitous presence.[12] In that context, this is what is meant by implicit Christianity; it is the human, earthly, and profane reality assumed in its secularity into the God-related life which it proceeds to express objectively, even when that God-related life remains anonymous and implicit. Earthly reality will at the same time share in the first fruits of eschatological grace and in the advent of the kingdom of God. Within that God-centered life, albeit anonymous, the construction of the world and the promotion of peoples, those two great hopes of mankind on earth, become an activity which is not only intentionally but intrinsically relevant to the kingdom of God.

It is evident that the ultimate eschatological perfection of all earthly values completely transcends the temporal construction of this world, precisely because it is an absolute and gratuitous perfection; but nevertheless, by virtue of its assumption into God-related life, harbinger of the *vita venturi saeculi* [life of the coming age], the world of earthly values will participate in that mystery of eternal life, as we are told by the dogma of the resurrection of the flesh and by the kerygma of the new earth.

Unequivocally, God loves man; and the being called man is not some abstract "human nature" but a flesh-and-blood being who, together with his fellowmen, takes the fate of the world and of mankind into his own hands; he is a being who, by humanizing the world humanizes himself. It is this historical, real being whom God loves. Every single human and worldly reality is therefore implied in God's absolute and gratuitous presence. This conveys a sense of the eternal and, therefore, of the irrevocable to the construction of the world and the promotion of the advancement of peoples.

Although it is solely due to his *capacitas gratiae* [capacity for grace] that man is the object of grace, the very being who, upon transcending his own self is assumed into theologal intimacy with God and shares in the eternal life—that being is none other than man, all of man as he really and historically exists, committed to this world.

In the past, a dualistic anthropological conception misled Christians into considering grace and redemption as a matter for God and the soul of man to deal with, so much so that the whole range of earthly life and of human responsibility for the terrestrial future of mankind seemed to be relegated to the fringe of Christianity; one ran the risk of disregarding the truly Christian value of building the world and of promoting the advancement of peoples, thereby relinquishing the chore to those who called themselves non-Christians. How easy it is to discern in that behavior one of the many factors through which the institutional Church alienated men from herself.

When we connect now the things which were said about the

one signification of the Church with that which is called "implicit Christianity," we arrive at new explicitations [*sic*] concerning the relation "Church and World."

The acts of Christ in glory are the acts of the whole Christ, the integral Christ in and with his Body, the Church. Hence, what the Church as such does, is done also by the glorified Christ together with the Spirit, his Spirit. What is Christian, therefore, is also ecclesial: the qualifications are inseparably and organically united. However much Jesus, as the Lord, transcends his Body, the Church, his immanence in the Church is coextensive with his transcendence. He transcends the Church through his immanence in it. That he transcends the boundaries of his Body, the Church, means that his free self-giving reaches out from within the Church to all who are not yet visible members of the Church. This implies that he is active among those who have not yet been historically confronted with the Church, but also that this activity of his is equally an activity of his Body, the Church. The bond with Christ, forged by this activity is, even when not explicitly seen as such, *ipso facto* an equally strong bond with the Church. Consequently, the Church represents the source of redemption also for that portion of mankind that has not yet experienced and availed itself of her in her peculiar historical form.

Seen in this perspective, the real interval separating the Church as such from mankind becomes less pronounced. The Church is actively present even where her adequate ecclesial form has not yet appeared. The contrast between the Church and mankind cannot be equated with an opposition between Church and non-Church. There is, moreover, much in her own life that is "nonecclesial," just as in the collective life of mankind there is much that is ecclesial. In the strict sense, of course, the Church is mankind insofar as it willingly places itself under Christ's influence through faith and baptism, and "helps its unbelief" at the common table of the Eucharist.

Perhaps it is better not to give the name "Church" to that portion of mankind that is anonymously Christian and in which the Church is anonymously present. This phenomenon might be called a "pre-Church"; but even against this, various objections might be brought. In the proper sense of the word, the Church is the saving revelation, the explicitly Christian realization of our Lord's activity among all mankind—the *koinonía* of men with one another in the acceptance of God and baptism in Christ, which is the efficacious sign of the call of those not yet in the Church.

On the other hand, anonymous Christianity—and its existence must be taken as a fact—not least because of its hopeful trust in the triumphant grace of Christ's redemption ("I have overcome the world") is an anonymity that inwardly demands a fitting sacramental visibility. Because the worldwide activity of Christ's grace is carried out in and through the Church, since his "going away" is related to the Church's postpaschal reality as the Body of our Lord, in virtue of the Spirit of God, this very grace is essentially "Church founding." Where the Church is at work as grace—and as such it is coextensive with mankind and therefore with universal fellowship—something of the *Corpus Mysticum* [Mystical Body] is brought to visible realization, though in a veiled manner. Because this grace takes on particular, historical, visible forms in the Church, its appearance bears witness to the fact that wherever it is operative (and that is wherever human history is in process of realization), it has an inward leaning toward historical manifestation, i.e., toward ecclesial explicitness.

This process can be observed in human history. Beyond the pale of the concretely situated, real Church, this grace will express itself, as a result of the unrecognized bond with Christ and his Church, in widely varying human interpretations—whether in other religious forms, or in so-called secular institutions, whose explicit form is inadequate to express their true purpose. Failure to grasp the proper meaning of this deepest feeling latent in the restless life of mankind is no indication that the difference between mankind and the Church is merely one of "knowing explicitly" and "knowing implicitly." For it is only in self-expression that man reaches full self-consciousness. Whatever is experienced without being recognized is a fragile datum until it finds its way to authentic self-expression. And this is more than a question of mere knowledge.

Without the God-given ecclesial form and expression of this deepest core of life in Christ, this experience remains a "light hidden under a bushel," a flickering flame ready to be quenched by the weakest draught. The properly ecclesial milieu is where the word of God's forgiveness is heard, where baptism is administered and the Eucharist celebrated, where there is the faith that nothing can separate us from the Lord and that for men there is no absolute solitude because God is with us. This milieu, which believers, the faithful, jointly constitute, is vitally necessary for the breakthrough of what grace effects silently and anonymously in human life. But the Church's special importance as a sign and revelation demands that she return again and again to the sources of biblical authenticity and show herself in forms that clearly and simply manifest her authenticity.

Thanks, therefore, to Christ's historical coming there is in living humanity a kind of built-in compass pointing to the Church. Her missionary activity is merely the counterpart of this. This pointing to the Church, or mankind's need of her in the concrete, and, on the other hand, her going out to mankind, are both visible forms of the one operative salvation which our Lord is in the Spirit of God, *Pneuma Theoû*. In both, Jesus the Christ visits his messianic community that he acquired upon the cross to prepare for himself his eschatological bride without spot unto the glory of God the Father.

The anonymous Church that is the work of Christ's Spirit and of his Body, the explicit Church vitally joined to him, will become manifest through the Spirit, as his Body, incorporated through baptism into his death and resurrection, as a visible sign both of the eschatological Man, Jesus Christ, and of what human life is concretely—namely, a deep and painful suffering, an existence ending in death, coupled with the unquenchable hope that this is not the last word about mankind. In Christ's *kenôsis* [emptying or humbling of himself] and *hypsôsis* [exaltation]—in his final humiliation and exaltation—the destiny of human life is exemplified. The enduring struggle for life in mankind, hoping against all hope, is the nameless echo of this fact: there is here more than mere secularity, even though it is expressed perhaps in a purely secular fashion.

The boundaries between the Church and mankind are fluid not merely in the Church's direction, but also, it may be said, in the direction of mankind and the world. The present-day process toward desacralization and secularization points to the fact that what was earlier felt to be a specialty of the Church—helping those of slender means, works of charity, and the like—has nowadays become "desacralized" as state relief measures for humanity within a secular vision, and is now an accepted feature of mankind at large. What had earlier taken the form of specific activities of the Church, in its precise sense, has now become in many ways an accepted expression of man's life in and for the world.

This osmosis from the Church to the world knows no final point on earth because here below the old aeon and the new continue to coexist. The fact that the communion of men coincides with the communion of saints is, when manifest, a heavenly, not an earthly fact. The blurring of the boundaries between the Church and mankind can never abolish the dialectical tension between the two. This tension, however, does not destroy either the dynamic of the world's tendency to become ecclesial or the Church's tendency to sanctify the secular. The latter process, however, is a holy secularization arising from the transcendent community with God in Christ. Whoever forgets this would have the Church in the long run dissolve into something like UNO or UNESCO.

All this has been expressed by St. Paul in his own way and in the framework of his ancient world picture. Christ by his death and glorification has fulfilled "all things"—"all things in heaven and on earth," "visible and invisible," all created reality (Eph. 1:10; Col. 1:16–20). H. Schlier, the biblical exegete, in his commentary on Ephesians comments rightly upon this point:

> There is no sphere of being that is not also the Church's sphere. The Church is fundamentally directed to the universe. Her boundaries are those of the universe. There is no realization of Christ's dominion without the Church or outside her, no "fulfillment" apart from her. The way in which the universe grows toward Christ is the way the Church grows. There are areas, to be sure, that are opposed to "fulfillment" through the Church; but ultimately the reason is that they are filled with themselves.[13]

St. Paul says this plainly: "God has placed all things under his feet, and has given him, exalted above all, as Head to the Church, which is his Body, the fullness of him who fulfills all in all" (Eph. 1:22f.). It is through the Church that the fulfillment of all existence and all reality is achieved.[14] Eschatologically, Church and mankind coincide fully.

V
Unity of Creation, Redemption, and Growth of the Church

The Church and mankind, then, are coming closer together; and yet the undeniable boundary remains between them because of Christ's postpaschal "building of the Church upon the Rock."[15] It now remains to clarify a dogmatic insight in which creation and the bestowal of grace, redemption, and the building of the Church are all seen together in the sublime unity of God's covenant with men.

Grace is God's absolute self-communication to men; it is the personal sharing of life with God—Father, Son, and Holy Spirit. That even in the pre-Christian era grace could only be trinitarian, we only know in the light of the historical mystery of Christ. It is in him that this fundamental aspect of the whole life of grace first becomes explicit. There is a close connection between him and grace. The fact that the trinitarian character of grace, imparted before his coming, remained implicit and anonymous leads to the question whether the anonymous character of this trinitarian grace is not due to the fact that man's existence was originally orientated to Christ, and that this obviously had to remain implicit. An analysis of the trinitarian character of grace as well as of its postponed revelation in Christ shows that its original conferment and God's establishment of mankind as his People were the consequence of man's creation in view of Christ. "Adam's" creation was implicitly directed toward Christ, and because of this, grace was bestowed upon him.[16] In other words, human existence in the concrete is itself a messianic prophecy pointing to him who is to come. The task to form a true *communio* among men as the essential task of a community of *persons* is a prophecy of the coming of Christ's Mystical Body, the Church. Thus, by another and perhaps more radical way we come to a conclusion at least materially the same as that of Karl Rahner who speaks of mankind in its entirety as the (faithful or unfaithful) People of God, and considers membership of this People a constitutive element of our concrete humanity.[17] Therefore, in the concrete, every free human act is one that works toward salvation or perdition. But it seems to me that the manner in which we arrive at this insight sheds a clearer light on mankind's objectively new situation since the death and resurrection of Christ.

Surely this new situation makes it obvious that salvation is conferred upon the People of God, not as such, but insofar as it has become the Body of Christ. This implies that since the appearance of the mystery of Christ in history at least the faithful People of God, in virtue of his sole saving power at work in his Body, the Church, becomes the expression of a *desiderium ecclesiae* [ecclesial orientation]. The basis of this should be clear from what has been thus far presented here, but it may help to clarify it further.

Creation in view of Christ, which includes the gift of grace, means that since creation all mankind carries within itself and anonymously this ecclesial orientation as a grace that is accepted or rejected. We may say, then, that it is always within and for a People of God that man's religious life is fulfilled, whether this People be mankind as yet unspecified or Israel, in which messianic humanity began to manifest itself more clearly, or the People of God redeemed by Christ, with its features sharply drawn and constituted as the Church.[18] The human community, insofar as it is created with this orientation toward Christ, is an early rough draft of the Church that is to come. But it is no more than that. For the appearance of Jesus in history and his exclusion from the human community created a completely new situation. It is as the Risen One that he built his Church and set it visibly among men as a community with its peculiar sacramental community structure, with its hierarchical function, with its service of the Word.

This absolutely new fact in salvation history restricts the universal application of this reality of God's People as coextensive with mankind. On the other hand, this new fact lifts that reality into a new dimension and turns its implicit acceptance into a *votum ecclesiae* [Church-in-intention]. The anonymously Christian portion of mankind now becomes for the first time a true *votum ecclesiae*, precisely because of Christ's universally operative action *in* the Church to the benefit of all mankind.[19]

Christ's Church, then, is not so much the last phase of the interior development of God's People as it comes into ever clearer view in visible form, although this aspect cannot be denied. Rather, Christ's historical redemptive work with its postpaschal fruit, the Church, recapitulates in his death and resurrection the People of God created from of old in view of him, and *constitutes* that People as the *votum ecclesiae*. Hence, we can say: *Extra ecclesiam nulla salus*—apart from Christ and his Body there is no salvation.

At the same time we must say that the Church here on earth has not yet reached the perfection of what she ought to be. This was acutely formulated by Origen: "*Ho kosmos tou kosmou he ekklesia*": man's world brought to actual perfection, to order—to peace and *communio*—this is the Church.[20] The Church carries within herself the principles and the incipient reality of this peace in virtue of the fact that she, the fruit of Christ's redemption, is his Body in this world.

In and through that Body he, now in glory, carries on his universal activity in the Spirit. The Church in human history, then, is, as token for all the world, the forerunner of eschatological salvation. Hence, her apostolic duty; hence, the constant demand daily to orient herself anew at the wellsprings of Holy Scripture, especially at this time when the face of the world and of man is fundamentally altering.

VI
The Church as Fellowship To Be Realized

The blurring of the enduring boundaries between the Church and mankind can also be explained more clearly through the Church's inner structure. In the one Church of Christ we may distinguish two different, though not opposed, dialectical aspects: the one, of the Church as a community guided by the Spirit of God active in the apostolic office of the episcopacy throughout the world; the other, of the same Church guided by the Spirit of God active in every individual's conscience.

This latter activity of the Spirit, and hence of individual Christians, also effects the building of the Church, especially in the midst of the world and of ordinary everyday things. This is where they are to be found who have not yet joined the Church community explicitly. Here, too, the building of the Church retains a kind of hidden character. Because this is a nonhierarchical activity, which is just as much the work of the Holy Spirit in Christian consciences, there really is an active building of the Church by her members in the midst of the so-called profane world, where the hierarchical Church is not present. A genuine, but even more veiled manifestation of this reality, moreover, is the genesis of the Church in the world that is Christian without the name. It can be recognized for what it is only in the light of Christ and the visible Church.

If, therefore, we would inquire into the pregnant characteristics that mark out the anonymously Christian Church which, because of what she is, longs for the moment when she can appear in her own ecclesial manifestation, we should not consider the fellowship or brotherhood among men in general, but with the special qualification which Jesus himself indicated. This qualification is love, a love that reaches out to the *mikroi*, the little ones, and to the *elachistoi*, the least of men, to help them for the reason that Jesus calls them "My brethren" (Matt. 25:31–36). It is in respect to their practice of this love that Church members and non-Church members alike are to be judged at the end of time (Matt. 25:35–45): "What you have done to the least of my brethren, you have done to me" (Matt. 25:40). "I was hungry and you gave me to eat; I was thirsty and you gave me to drink; I was a stranger and you welcomed me" (Matt. 25: 35f.). "What you have failed to do for the least of these, you have failed to do for me" (Matt. 25:45).

In modern terms this might be expressed thus: your failure to help the underdeveloped countries is failing Christ himself. The help you extend to them, not from political motives, but out of pure brotherhood and fellowship, is authentic Christianity. Self-sacrifice to the extreme was the messianic act by which Christ founded his Church. Where men follow in his footsteps on the way of self-sacrifice, without even knowing perhaps whose steps they are, they are working to establish the Church, the community in Christ. The parable of the Good Samaritan teaches us, with a certain amount of sarcasm directed at those who are "in the Church," that everyone who assists anyone whom he finds in need and helps him superabundantly, with the luxury of extravagant love, is actively establishing the *koinonía*. He makes of the man he helps, his neighbor and brother.

The activity that establishes the Church which is, even without the name, Christian, goes outside and beyond the limits of the official Church, which is sociologically situated and clearly visible in history —the Church of those who acknowledge Christ and share the table of the Eucharist. This activity exceeds the official Church's limits even in such a way that this superabundant love, however clearly visible in the Church's saints, is not historically and *per se*, necessarily realized by practicing Christians. And yet the Church is truly established only where love makes men brothers, because the active love that establishes her is the core of her being. It was to preserve that core that Christ established an official hierarchy, which he assists in a special manner in order to preserve his People in one community of love and hope founded upon one faith in him. Ultimately, however, the Church is not a matter of this hierarchy but of the People of God and the active love that establishes her. And for her, the hierarchy, although in the *modus* of Christian authority, has a function of service.

Outside the visible community of Jesus, then, the establishment of the Church is accomplished primarily by surrender to one's fellowmen in unselfish love. Concretely, our fellow-creatures are a token of God's grace, a sacramental sign of his saving will. Such they are only because created in Christ and for the sake of him who is the constitutive sign of God's saving will. The universal sacramentality of fellow-creaturehood is not destroyed because of the perfect sacramental form of Christ's fellow-creaturehood, nor is it, so to say, translated into the formal structure of the visible Church. On the contrary, because of the appearance of the Man, Jesus Christ the Son of God, in history, the sacramental power of the grace of fellowship can be realized in its full meaning now for the first time. It is realized in him and for him. The general sacramental feature of fellowship is made concrete only in the community that is called the Church. And the seven sacraments, the preaching, the worship, the hierarchy's guidance—all these are but the highest point of crystallization of the stake the Church has in our fellowmen.

The Church, therefore, will appear as a sign among men, actually drawing and inviting them, only when the love of her members for humankind becomes concretely and historically visible here and now, and is no longer confined to those particular climactic moments in which at present Christ places his grace in a concentrated manner. It is just during the Second Vatican Council that out of the deliberations on the nature of the Church there has come a desire to include in the schema a consideration of the active presence of Church members in the world. The schema which is shortly to become the Constitution, *De Ecclesia* [the Dogmatic Constitution on the Church], cries out from the heart for schema xvii.

On all these grounds we cannot relegate the Church's significance for the unchurched to some kind of "representative function" that would dispense them from the superabundant love and redeem them by "substitution," that is, by the overflowing love which is at least present in Christ's Church. In an authentically Christian perspective, vicariousness and mediation never stand for substitution, but for a prototypical reality which gives of its abundance *in order that* others, by virtue of the grace they have received, may be enabled themselves to achieve what had already been done by the prototype. In this sense the Church exists in the strength of Christ's Spirit for the good of all men. But equally, the operation of Christ's grace among men through the Church must retain a visible form, especially in its apostolic activity. In the Church's confrontation with mankind in history her members must be living examples and "types" of this overflowing love and manifest their willingness to give up their personal lives in the service of others.

VII
Secular and Sacral Realization of the Church's Holiness

The problem posed at the beginning of this essay has found some answer, it is hoped, in the course of our investigation. There is obviously going on throughout mankind a process of bringing things into the Church, and in the Church, correspondingly, there is a process of secularization that conveys sanctity. Within the inviolable limits set by the Word, the sacrament, and the office—and all those are forms of *service*—the boundaries between the Church and mankind are blurred. It is in the positive encounter with Christ in his Church that the most complete form of Christianity that may be realized is objectively offered to us.

The Church, then, must be a really habitable home, and her mission is to bring this to pass in every age in ever differing ways. Complete religion has an explicitly Christian and ecclesial practical expression. Because of this, Christianity, however involved it is in our everyday cares and tasks and all our secular activity, has a special sacral space set apart from secular developments and from culture, within which we grow in intimacy with God. Here we are simply together with God in Christ. Now, on a merely human level silence forms a part of discourse and social intercourse, though in and for itself it has no meaning; it has meaning only as a function of fellowship. It is necessary in order to make contact between men human and to keep it so—to humanize it. It is silence that makes speech personal. Without it, dialogue is impossible. But in a revealed religion, silence with God has a value in itself and for its own sake, just because God is God. Failure to recognize the value of mere being with God, as the Beloved, without doing anything, is to gouge the heart out of Christianity.

Our whole immersion in the world of men and things penetrates also into our communion with God, not as mere distraction, but essentially. We cannot tell God that we love or desire to love him except with words, concepts, and pictures taken from our human environment. Moreover, our communion with God is not individualism, for our prayer would be insincere—not prayer at all—if we did not pray: "Our Father, . . ." or if in our prayer we forgot God's kingdom and our fellowman.

Christianity means not only communion with God in the concrete milieu of Christ in his Church, but also *working* with the living God, with the Father "who is ever active" (John 5:17) both in the Church and in the world. Religion is primarily personal intercourse with God—the living God, who is the Creator of men and things, all of which he offers to us for humanization. Therefore, our living relationship with our neighbor and with the world is not only cultural, but also religious.

Agape embraces God and men. Love of God cannot and must not be separated from love of men. Christian love for the neighbor means that we—God and I—love *my* fellowman. While in natural human love, God is present only in silence as the transcendent Third, my Christian *caritas* toward my fellows is just as much love, but a love lived in communion with God. And so the Christian loves his fellowman with the same love as that with which he loves God and with which both he and his fellowmen are loved by God. In Christ alone do we learn the proper meaning of "being a man for the sake of others," although secular and human experience will teach us how we must express this fellowship in concrete situations.

But, however ecclesial the explicit expression of religion and Christianity may be, the working out of our Christian character must needs take shape in the ordinary daily dealings in and with the world and our fellowmen. The sincerity of our personal dealings with God, of our Christianity and ecclesial status must therefore be tested constantly by the authenticity of our fellowship, our genuine love of men. The source of this Christian love of the neighbor, however, lies in our personal assimilation of those ways of dealing with God which Christ himself has given us: hearing the Word of God, familiarity with Holy Scripture, the common celebration of the Church's sacramental liturgy. In our world, then, authentic Christianity has both a *sacred* and a corresponding *secular* milieu. In everything he does, by acceptance or refusal, man brings about salvation or perdition.

We must be close to God, not merely in church, in prayer and the sacraments, in Scripture reading—in a word, in the sacred forms of religion—but also in our secular and human relationships and in our everyday tasks. Then we may say with serenity that there are different ways of being Christian. Some will bring their interior relationship with God to fulfillment chiefly in sacral forms, thereby stressing the fact that the Church is "not of this world." Others will express their Christianity particularly in secular activities, in "secular sanctity," and so will stress the fact that the Christian faith is not an ideological structure superimposed upon human life.

But these are emphases of the one Christian life which is immanent in this world precisely because it is transcendent. For what has been said here about the universal relationship between mankind and the Church is also valid for the individual Christian. The unrecognized genuine witness of the Christian in this profane world finds the source of its strength in that explicit Christianity which is shaped by active participation in the life of the Word and of the Sacrament of "Christ's Church."

Footnotes

[1] See J. Scharbert, *Heilsmittler im Alten Testament und im Alten Orient* (*Quaest. Disp.* 23, 24, Freiburg im Breisgau, 1964).

[2] See G. von Rad, "Das z. erste Buch Mose" in *Das Alte Testament Deutsch,* Vol. II (Göttingen, 1949), pp. 119f.

[3] See, among others, E. Peterson, "Die Kirche," *Theologische Traktate* (Munich, 1951), pp. 409–28.

[4] Irenaeus, *Adv. Haereses,* V.21.1 (*PG* 7.1179). *Principalis* (*archaios*) in *Adv. Haer.* means "standing at the point of," and is used in connection with Irenaeus' theory of recapitulation. Christ stands at the new beginning of all things.

[5] See, among others, K. Rahner, "Kirche und Parusie Christi," in *Catholica,* XVII (1963), pp. 113–28.

[6] A. Vögtle, *Das öffentliche Wirken Jesu auf dem Hintergrund der Qumranbewegung* (Freiburger Universitäsreden, N.F., 27, Freiburg im Breisgau, 1958, pp. 5–20, esp. pp. 15ff.); "Ekklesiologische Auftragsworte des Auferstandenen," in *Actes du Congrès internationale catholique des sciences bibliques à Bruxelles* (1959), pp. 892–906; "Jesus und die Kirche," in *Begenung der Christen,* ed. Hoesle-Cullman (Frankfurt am Main, 1960), pp. 54, 82; "Der Einzelne und die Gemeinschaft in der Stufenfolge der Christusoffenbarung," in *Sentire Ecclesiam,* eds. Daniélou and Vorgrimler (Freiburg im Breisgau, 1961), pp. 50–91; see also, "Die Adam-Christus Typologie und der Menschensohn," in *Trierer Theol. Zeitschrift* (1951), pp. 209–28. See also note 7.

[7] See A. Vögtle, *Das öffentliche Wirken Jesu,* p. 15; F. Braun, *Neues Licht auf die Kirche* (Einsiedeln, 1946), p. 71; A. Fridrichsen, "Messias und Kirche," in *Ein Buch von der Kirche* (Göttingen, 1951), p. 33; see K. Rengstorf, *Theologische Wörterbuch zum Neuen Testament,* Part II, pp. 321–28, s.v. *dodeka.*

[8] See A. Vögtle, "Messiasbekenntnis und Petrusverheissung," in *Biblische Zeitschrift,* N.F. Vol. 1 (1957), pp. 257–72 and Vol. II (1958), pp. 85–103. The connection between Peter's confession at Caesarea and Christ's promise of the *Ecclesia* is called secondary, i.e., it is an "arrangement" of Matthew or of the Matthew tradition.

[9] Mark 10:40 and Matthew 20:20–23; Mark 14:25; see Luke 22:16, 18.

[10] P. Schoonenberg, "Natuur en zondenval," in *Tijdschr. v. Theol.,* Vol. II (1962), pp. 199–200; see also, E. Schillebeeckx, *Christ, the Sacrament of the Encounter with God* (New York, 1963), pp. 40–46.

[11] *Summa Theologica,* III, q. 8, a. 2, ad 1.

[12] It is obvious that in so saying I speak of the state of implicit Christianity as such, realizing that the individual can shut himself away from grace. God is the sole judge of man's conscience. One does not therefore affirm that all non-Christians are by the mere fact implicitly Christians, just as one does not maintain that every member of the Church is an authentic Christian. Nevertheless the redemptive grace of "Christus Victor" is more powerful than the fragility of human freedom.

[13] H. Schlier, "Die Kirche nach dem Briefe an die Epheser," in *Die Zeit der Kirche* (Freiburg im Breisgau, 1956), p. 69.

[14] Schlier has the following acute comment on this passage in Saint Paul: "The Church is the *Pleroma* of Christ. This means the plenitude, fulfilled by him and in its turn fulfilling, of him who has fulfilled all things and continues to do so. In her (the Church's) plenitude, all is enclosed and so this all becomes itself that plenitude which is the Church" (*ibid.,* p. 170).

[15] The thought of this article will be taken up again in [subsequent volumes of] *Concilium* and applied to the problem of membership in the Churches, in connection with the pluralism of the Christian Church communities. [*Editor's note:* These issues are also taken up in subsequent articles of this volume.]

[16] I have attempted to develop this in detail in "Die Heiligung des Namen

Gottes durch die Menschenliebe Jesu des Christus," in *Gott in Welt* (Festgabe für K. Rahner, Freiburg, 1964), esp. pp. 73–90.

[17] K. Rahner, "Die Gliedschaft in der Kirche nach der Lehre de Enzyklika Pius XII, *Mystici Corporis*," in *Schr. z. Theol.*, Vol. II (Einsiedeln, 1955), pp. 7–94.

[18] E. Schillebeeckx, *Personale Begegnung mit Gott: Eine Antwort an John A. T. Robinson* (Mainz, 1964), pp. 78f.

[19] Be it noted that I do not claim that *all* those who do not belong to a church are *per se* anonymous Christians, just as we do not maintain that all church members are authentic Christians. I only say that such an anonymous Christianity is a genuine possibility, and, considering the abounding power of grace, a reality in the case of many. We do not wish, nor are we able, to affirm their number. We know well the essential ambiguity of human freedom: it is a potentiality for good and for evil. But our confidence in God is greater than that ambiguity!

[20] See A. Auer, "Kirche und Welt," in *Mysterium Kirche*, Vol. II (Salzburg, 1962), pp. 492f.

BERNARD BRO, O.P.

Man and the Sacraments: The Anthropological Substructure of the Christian Sacraments

This article continues the exploration, begun in the previous article, of an answer to the question: What is the relation between Christianity and authentic human existence? In order to understand this essay we must first ascertain the meaning of the term "integration." Are the "limits" of human existence adequately treated? How do we relate such terms as alienation, loneliness, and anxiety to the so-called limits of human existence? How do we discover our self? What is the relation between selfhood and other persons, the material world, God? What role does cultic activity have in self-integration? On the basis of this article, how could we define sacrament?

Bernard Bro, O.P., was a Professor of Dogmatic Theology at La Saulchoir and since 1964 he has been director-general of Éditions du Cerf.

I
The Integration of Human Life

Whatever approach we take to man, or to the present-day images he draws of himself, we always come up against the problem of

Reprinted from Bernard Bro, O.P., "Man and the Sacraments," in *Concilium,* Vol. XXXI, *Dogma, The Sacraments in General, A New Perspective,* ed. Edward Schillebeeckx, O.P. (Glen Rock, N.J.: Paulist Press, 1968), pp. 33–50; *Concilium,* January 1968, Vol. 1, no. 4, *Dogma* (Burns and Oates Ltd., London), pp. 18–26, with the permission of *Concilium.*

integration. It is the major problem for any living being. Of himself, he is never all that he can be; he depends on something else, which he possesses to a greater or lesser extent and which is indispensable for his full completion. "As those things which he *has* multiply and become more differentiated, so much the stronger must *be* the animating principle in him which underlies all these diversified possessions. It is a matter of life and death. Failure in this matter may only result in an unhappy life; but it may also mean total death." [1]

So we may well ask: What in man's life could be strong enough to serve as the unifying pole for all these diverse elements that make up his existence? What could provide dynamic unity and the opportunity for further development, while at the same time respecting the diversity and the dialectic tension of these elements?

To put it another way, man cannot help but see that his life is frighteningly fragmented, that he is only partly himself at all times. "At all times we are only a fraction of our being. In the depth of our nature there is a wound that prevents us from being one. This obstacle, the origins of which we do not know, undoubtedly because it is our origin, is brought home to us by such images as 'the time for death' and 'paradise lost.' " [2] Yet man cannot escape the need to unify his existence.

How is this unity to be achieved? The response to this question is the unfolding drama played out by every man, the drama of integration.

The fact is that unity exists for man only on the level of the unconscious; only there, are all the events of his existence embraced. But in that case we are talking about a unity that is effected below the threshold of his free being, a unity of which he may well become the victim. That is why each individual tries to provide his own unity by means of words, language, and all the other self-schematizations that provide a more or less integrated picture of his existence. At some point, however, this unification may well appear to be more or less artificial; it may well appear to be the arbitrary result of influences that are external to a greater or lesser degree. The individual has recovered himself; but it is not really himself at all, it is a mask, a "persona." He has played around with the dissociated fragments of his existence as best he could, and a certain amount of repression has come into play.

"A man is the sum total of his own misfortunes. He thinks that one day misfortune will finally wear itself out; instead, time itself becomes his misfortune" (Faulkner).

"Uncertain of everything from the start, we are still free to ponder the future with all our strength. Are we in our death-throes, or is something wonderful being born? We are ever on the verge of migration to some new world, any world, so long as it does not resemble our own." [3]

And so the dilemma is posed: to achieve self-unity, must we become the victims of our own unconscious, or be condemned to the unreality of our own speech?

This notion of integration can be formulated negatively or positively. If we consider the things we have to unify, the things we have, then we tend to look for some positive element that will allow us to maintain possession of these things. If, on the other hand, we consider possible unifying principles, we legitimately tend to work by a process of exclusion, eliminating one after the other. In the latter case, integration is formulated negatively. In both instances it would seem that the truth is bound up with a questioning process, for a man can never assume that he possesses his integrating principle as he does other things. Were he to make this assumption, the process of integration would come to a halt. Since we are spirit, unity must be a progressive process, continually moving forward through our "yes" and our "no." It is a continuing dialectic, always open to the future.

Let me pose this critical question again, using one negative and one positive example; this is the only way we can ascertain the anthropological status of the sacraments. Putting it negatively, we might ask this question: "What is it that I cannot resign myself to without feeling my self slip away between my fingers? What would cause my disintegration if I were to subscribe to it?" [4]

Putting it positively, we can cite the example of the huge *Diplodocus* dinosaur:

> These animals produced a huge quantity of flesh, and had to construct a gigantic bone system to support their weight. This, in turn, called for a long chain of tail so that equilibrium might be established. Their huge bodies covered a large area, so a heavy armored plate of protective material was also required. In other words, they had to assemble a huge ensemble of dead matter, to which was added other

> inert structure such as teeth and claws. The beast was a quasi-mechanical machine that multiplied its parts. The living organism became merely the support of various non-living mechanisms, and the interminable contradictions eventually led to its annihilation.[5]

It is clear from this example that "having" is not enough. It is not enough to establish equilibrium among the parts. In the last analysis, the total ensemble cannot just be an inert mass. All the elements and factors that enter into man's daily life must be informed by some vital principle; they must contribute to the efficiency of the whole organism. If they do not, a terrible revenge will be exacted. If a man does not really integrate his existence, he will never escape from fear and unrest; and one day he will cease to exist as a human being.

In this article I shall isolate three major sectors where the problem of integration exists. I shall try to show that this problem must be faced, and that the sacraments can help us to achieve integration in these areas, in a real and meaningful way. What are these three sectors? (1) In relation to himself, man is led to integrate his own individual limits, up to and including the final limit, death. (2) In relation to the world, man encounters others and discovers that his relationship to them is a decisive factor in his existence. (3) Finally, man discovers the weight of other intermediaries, of other things; in particular, he discovers the weight of symbols—things that are both themselves and something else at the same time.

II
Individual Limits

The problem of limits crops up continuously as we experience a disproportion between the range of our desire and the object that presents itself as the fuel and the response to this desire. The young Claudel expressed it well in *Tête d'Or:* "God promises through his creatures, but fulfills on his own." Or, as the young Malraux commented on his prison experiences: "What was human freedom but the awareness and the systematization of one's fatalities?"[6]

Whatever category of thought we adopt to explain the structure and the course of human destiny, we always run into certain constants, no matter how differently we may formulate them:

1. *We recognize a dynamism and a desire* that govern the whole history of the human person. In terms of ontology, we may try to account for this desire with a philosophy of liberty: the will is viewed as made for some good which is related to it in terms of finality and which always goes beyond the individual goods presented to the will; the will governs the process of obtaining these goods. This, in brief, is the outlook of Aristotelian and Augustinian philosophy.[7]

Utilizing a completely different perspective, we can describe this dynamic process by analyzing the real state of the individual, his archeology and teleology, in terms of the pursuit of subjective fullness and the narcissistic need for self-congruence. This, in brief, is the outlook of various modern psychologies and psychoanalysis.[8]

2. This dynamism and this desire are recognized to be *totalitarian.*

3. Hence, the simultaneous awareness of *disproportion* and *lack of congruence* which constitute the normal condition of all integration and all liberty.[9]

4. Man's experience of these disproportions puts him in a situation where he must *make room for negativity, for limits.*

5. Several possible solutions are suggested to him:

(a) The first solution, I think, is to plunge into forgetful *oblivion.* Man distracts himself with some form of inebriation. He may, for example, indulge in esthetic creation and plunge into the world of imagination. With the help of other objects he tries to acquire a self-image that he would like to see but does not yet have; he acquires mastery over certain representations that provide him with protection and security in the face of the external world. He uncovers an unlimited power that continually renews itself; as he projects himself from work to work, he feels his existence and actually fashions it.

Physical possession and all the other means of acquisition also give existence to desire and to plans. They provide man with the possibility of something outside him and the possession of something positive. Possession enables him to forget the undeniable limitations on the things that he has; it allows him to cherish the illusion that there are no limits to the fulfillment of his desires.

(b) The second way of escaping negation and limitation is, in my opinion, *conflict and flight.* It can take two forms: domination or submissiveness. In either case, a man is unwilling to accept the fact that his unblemished self-image is challenged. He has this image of his ideal self, and he takes flight whenever he finds a gap between this ideal image and reality. Either he retreats into passive submissiveness and depression, or else he flees by accusing and condemning those around him who oppose his self-fulfillment by their otherness.

(c) The third approach open to man is *to embrace negativity and move beyond it.* Here, I think, is one of the decisive anthropological foundations of sacramental life. Like it or not, every man stands in relation to an ideal picture of self. At birth we are not totally at one with our full self; hence we must define ourselves as beings who are involved in a continuing process of development and fulfillment, who are in a state of potentiality. In other words, we are "subjects," who cannot help but stand in a relation of dependence to something else. We discover this dependence and we master it by means of this image of an ideal self. It is the self we would like to be, although we are not it yet, and we already possess it as an image inside us. We turn back to this image constantly through our plans, our fears, and our regrets. It is here that the fate of each man is played out, as he runs into the inevitable obstacles posed by existence.

This all-embracing image, which each man has of himself, cannot be regarded as an ultimate. It must be relativized and shot through with negativity, or tragedy will ensue. This does not mean that our anguish will be suppressed; it will always be there. But this anguish itself will help us to discover gradually the illusory character of our ideal self and our possibility of achieving it by moving beyond it.

6. Now what do the sacraments offer us? Let us put it briefly. As we encounter each of the great experiences offered to man, the sacraments offer us the possibility of cooperating in this experience in all its concreteness, but in the name of Another's power. Without repudiating our most personal elements, indeed for the sake of our total integration and our total retrieval of existence,[10] the sacraments offer us a chance to cooperate concretely in our own fulfillment, while demanding that we drastically relativize our self-image.

Let me give some examples. Man is a father, he gives life. It is a fundamental experience. And then someone comes along and says that his child will find his true image only through baptism. A man loves. But even before he discovers his fundamental polygamy and the open-endedness of his desire, the danger that he may transfer this desire to others, someone offers him the help of God to insure his fidelity. In gathering up his past, man encounters his failures; then someone comes along and offers him the chance not only to be pardoned and to forget past faults, but also to use sin itself as the occasion for moving ahead and gaining control of one's life—by living in friendship with another,

Christ. Finally, man fears death; and someone offers him the chance, not of escaping it, but of making it a free act through the help of another, to whom he surrenders himself.

All these experiences are encountered progressively and lived through in hope. There is no evasion. The whole process takes account of the reality of time, and it gives meaning to our history. It teaches us to love our own history because someone other than us has taken command of it.

III
Others

In the various aspects of his life—reasoning, affectivity, and action—man encounters limits on the totality of his desire. He also discovers that "others" are a perpetual menace to the full fruition of his desire. To his discouragement he finds that they are and remain external to him.

Man experiences a permanent need for the presence and the protection of others; but at the same time he fears these others. Self-realization is caught between a "father complex" (we are destined to be children forever) and the concomitant revolt on the one hand, and the permanent need for protection and security sought from another.[11]

Our relationship to another, to others, poses some serious problems of integration. These conflicts exist on every level, in the life of families and the life of nations. Relationships between ourselves and others are infinitely difficult, whether it be a question of obeying authority or of sharing responsibility for some wrong. We may gain a greater awareness of the role of mass media. We may penetrate more deeply into the laws and structures of societal life, but this will not solve the problems of integration vis-à-vis others, because such analysis may remain quite abstract. Inevitably, there remains a twofold conflict.

1. We cannot form an adequate or exhaustive image of another. The freedom and subjectivity of my companion represent a point of departure from which there is no escape. I do not really grasp him as he is. In attempting to identify with him, I must use intermediaries that

are necessarily inadequate. I fashion an idea of him which never ceases to betray both him and me.

Furthermore, if this other person has responsibility over my group, I am constantly tempted to regard his representation of the group as inadequate. By what right does he represent the over-all group, the community?

2. At the same time, it is impossible for the other person to respect me when he intervenes in my life. By the very fact of his existence, he comes ahead of me. I count for nothing in his existence, and this fact is irreversible. Sartre describes this problem forcefully: over against me there stands someone who never leaves me in peace; by the very fact that he is another, he challenges me. In every sphere of activity (thinking or doing) I am asked to make the ideas and decisions of another my own, while still remaining the free, creative source of my own activity.

A. de Peretti, using the concepts of Carl Rogers, summarizes the dialectic very well:

> The need for growth is incoercible. It takes place within the bosom of an individual being, through the elaboration of a *self-image*. This image dynamically organizes the actualization of potentialities and the control of behavior. It develops as a dynamic form, as a *gestalt*, which *enriches* and *preserves* the experience acquired directly by the individual in the expression of his organic totality.
>
> Now this image is found to have a relationship to others. This relationship involves constant revision and modification of the image that one has of oneself. In the course of these revisions and modifications, certain anxieties crop up. (They are the result of displacement or dissipation of energy, a Joule's effect, as it were, involving resistance to interpersonal relationships.) To avoid these anxieties, the individual may react defensively and adopt an attitude of *dependence* or *imitation*. In this case, his inertia or his insecurity leads him "to evaluate his experience in terms of criteria borrowed from others, rather than evaluating them on the basis of the satisfaction (or lack of satisfaction) he himself experiences." In other words, "*he adopts the scale of values of other individuals* to determine the positive or negative value of things which he has experienced" (cf. Kinget and Rogers, *Psychothérapie et relations humaines*, p. 186).
>
> Thus the individual creates an internal discord that is more or less pronounced; his *authenticity* is injured, he is alienated. A portion of his immediate or past experience is subtracted

> from his consciousness on the basis of considerations that are external to himself. The thrust toward actualization is diverted from its proper course. The individual becomes vulnerable. Now his personality functions in an aggressive and costly manner. His perceptions become rigid, so that he may preclude certain feelings that are now partially incompatible with the self-image which he is forming and which he dares not allow to develop on its own. The individual, with all his internal complexity, now boxes himself within the simplistic support of a conformist group and closed models of behavior.
>
> On the other hand, the individual can preserve his freedom and his authenticity. In certain relationships he can be "congruent" with his experience as it develops with others. In this case, he finds within himself the basis and the justification for the feelings he experiences. He affirms his own experience, and acknowledges the *limits* implied in it. In this case we can say that the individual, being in a state of authenticity or congruence, *accepts himself* actively: that is, *he takes account of the total picture that is emerging in him.* This self-acceptance is an acceptance of evolution, under the thrust of growth. Self-acceptance means being mobile. It means using "negation" to undo established defense mechanisms. It means being truly *present* to oneself.[12]

What do the sacraments offer us here? It seems to me that current pastoral efforts have contented themselves with vague general ideas and have not followed through with their efforts. Too often they have misconstrued the real substructures of sacramental life and have focused on facile, seductive abstractions.[13] To be sure, we have discovered that the notions of individual piety and individual salvation were not Christian, that the Church is essentially a communion, and that any sacramental scheme must therefore involve "another." [14]

But while we may rejoice over the rediscovery of the communitarian nature of the sacramental system, we must realize that current work in the social sciences obliges us to do more than administer collective rites. There is always the temptation that Christian communitarianism will degenerate into sociological collectivity.[15] We can only hope that the Holy Spirit and the psychic health of the laity will join forces, forcing those responsible for the sacraments to gradually discover the fundamental laws of group life and of authentic community living.

Here I should merely like to delineate the essential elements involved in the integration of otherness as it is offered to us by the sacraments. I hesitate to use the word "dialogue" in this connection, because it is an ambiguous term and because it must be qualified constantly when the "other" is God.[16] Here we must always remind ourselves that we are dealing with a relationship that is dialectic by its very nature. The "other" is alien to me; yet he is the only instance of absolute and wholly integrative unity, because his existence includes mine. That is why we must constantly qualify what we say about man's relationship to God.

This "other" is wholly one, but his Word reaches me in the varied situations of an incarnate human existence—that of Christ. He sparks my development, but he does so by offering me a salvation plan that goes beyond me. He appeals to a unifying point of reference, but he integrates all the members of the human race, all the "others."

1. The sacraments are communion with God, first of all. They are communion with the One who, by his very nature, is beyond every fragmented grasp and every limiting word. Only insofar as his presence transcends my human condition does it reveal its unifying value. Only insofar as we surmise that he is the only "one" does his otherness reveal its ultimate efficaciousness: its ability to unify my life. It is only because he is "other" that he can save me; and I finally come to the point where I love this "difference," because it makes dialogue a real possibility. It is a blessed distinction, because it enables us to escape multiplicity.

However, this vertical identification is offered to us through communion with someone who has lived a history that is similar to my own. It is possible for me to identify with his history, from start to finish. We are not dealing with an idea or an idol; we are dealing with an incarnation, the incarnation of Christ. We are dealing with an existence that is totally in keeping with our desire and our capacity to identify with something that is one, while retaining our own diversity. And this recourse to Another, this recourse which promises to effect our own integration, is offered to us in conjunction with the most profound and most varied experiences of our life. (This, in fact, seems to be the distinctive characteristic of the sacramental economy.) For fatherhood, there is baptism; for failure and death, there is penance and the last anointing; for social responsibility, there is confirmation and holy orders; for love, there is marriage; for our existence in time and our life with others, there is the eucharist.

2. This communion, this identification, is offered to us in a dialogue, where we come to discover that the Other is the one *who takes the initiative*. (It may well be the only real dialogue where the Other does

not join ranks with us.) Yet, at the same time we come to realize that his initiative is aimed at making us the source and the master of our own creation. This is the remarkable reversal which the sacraments offer to us. In relating us to God, they turn the tables upside down. *The ties of dependence are switched around.* God does much more than show respect for our freedom. Here the Other, who is by nature father, creator, and source (with all that implies), puts himself in our hands; we become the fountainhead and wellspring of our own salvation, the creators of our own destiny.

It is an astonishing reversal. When we decide not to dispose of God or ourselves, when we freely choose to surrender to his grace in the sacraments, at that moment we actually do make what use we will of God.

3. However, we discover that we are the masters of our destiny only by accepting *a dialogue which cuts right through our own words and our own self-image.* We are not asked to live a contemplative life; but we are asked to commune with the life of Another, of someone else in the Eucharist. We are not asked to repair our failures on our own; but we are asked to confess to someone. We are not simply asked to guarantee fidelity to one love; we are asked to discover that every love involves an infinite, divine presence.

This whole process of cooperation is so real that it seems that God really wants to be conquered by our intervention. On the one hand, his sacramental presence is so real that it precludes our own words from being the ultimate thing; on the other hand, it is we who are the masters of this process, who decide whether it shall come to fruition or not.

Moreover, this salvific Word presents itself as participation in a body, in a real physical communion, in Christ. The only way psychologists have been able to describe the integrating plenitude of the sacramental relationship is in terms of death or sexual intercourse. Only unconditional self-surrender enables the Other to restore us to ourselves.

With regard to the full richness of our existence, to our freedom and autonomy, sacramental identification with Another seems to have two additional qualities. It is offered to us through the intermediary of the only existence that has ever been "psychoanalytically pure." Considering all the cancers and obstacles of which men are aware "in the face of their Father," it was only fitting that sometime, somewhere, mankind should have lived a pure and authentic filial relationship, in the full radiance of truth. This point was the consciousness of Christ and, by the wondrous designs of divine love, this Christ was truly the Son of God.

He showed us not only the full perfection of natural religion but also the secret of supernatural sonship. And the human soul of Christ, for the first time, lived the father–son relationship in all its fullness and perfection. In the human soul of Christ we discovered how man could say "Abba, Father" without introducing unconscious conflicts into this cry. And so, "taught by our divine Savior, we dare to say: Our Father. . . ."

This person, who becomes our unifying reference point in the sacraments, establishes us in full congruence with ourselves; thus he can restore us to complete communion with our brothers. The other is no longer "an" other. The sacraments enable us to enter into communion with that secret point where he, too, can say, "Our Father." The Eucharist is not just the food that gives force and unity to my existence; it is the repast of communion at the same time. Penance is not simply the absolution of my sins; it is reintegration into the reciprocal relations that form the communion of believers. When Christ says: "What you do to the least of my brethren, you do to me," or "As you measure out, so shall it be measured to you," when he invites us to love as he loves, to love as the Father loves him, we are touching on the essential characteristic of the innovation wrought by Christianity. It is no longer: "Do unto others as you would have others do unto you," but "Do unto others as you would have God do unto you." It is "Forgive us our trespasses, as we forgive those who trespass against us."

To go to confession is to do more than re-enter fraternal communion; it is to ask that we might see our brothers as God sees them. If it only involved the re-establishment of peace between ourselves and others, then the psychiatrist or the lawyer could probably do a better job. The communitarian aspect of penance obviously involves much more. In penance we accept Christ's intervention; we share his energy in the battle against the evil within us; we allow God to unleash the potential for pardon and love that lies within us; we agree to conform to his image. Confession is much easier than a psychoanalytic session, and much more ambitious in scope. To confess our sins is to encounter, in very concrete fashion, the unity of the two commandments; it is asking God to forgive us *as we forgive others.*

The upward directed search for a unifying Word and a unifying presence bears fruit in a downward-directed communion. This communion is inalienable because it comes from Another in whom "there is no change."

IV
Symbols

So far we have discussed the individual's struggle with his self-image and his relationship with others. Now we must examine the difficult process of integrating the world of external objects into the picture. In our internal dialogue, they can create conflict and difficulty as we try to formulate a total picture.

We have discussed this topic at length, and we have talked about the "revenge of symbols." Here we find the same process that we have already described in connection with individual limits and the problem posed by others. Here again the sacraments offer us an alternative in which everything that "is" preserves its proper meaning, while at the same time cooperating in the unification of our own existence. Reflection on Christian symbols as they are presented in the sacraments seems to be the major issue in the fine works of G. Durand and P. Ricoeur.[17]

The sacraments force us to analyze how the integrative power of a symbol is both safeguarded and surpassed. Art, for example, utilizes the sensible to bring us to something beyond without ever leaving the sensible realm. By contrast, the sacraments utilize the sensible to integrate us with a life and a Person that is no longer of the sensible order alone.

If we refuse to accept this chance to move beyond the sensible, we lose the opportunity to integrate the multiplicity we experience in the universe, and, at the same time, we distort and mutilate the symbols themselves. This refusal of integration leads to all sorts of surrealist nightmares, as we well know. To live in fidelity to the incarnate presence of Christ, as it is presented to us in the sacraments, provides no little help in giving us composure as we confront the sensible itself.

Man cannot help but encounter his limits. Man cannot evade the

Oedipus complex. Man cannot escape the invasion of the sensible. The anthropological course, which alone can reveal the real substructures of sacramental life, is composed of successive fears that every individual must conquer. And the fear of fragmentation is the most costly to recognize.

Contemporary theology and pastoral practice should pay close attention to all the social sciences, the sciences of man. They will keep us from spouting purely *a priori* principles, from organizing projects that do not take account of what man has learned about himself. Theology and pastoral practice have an incredible opportunity to learn that our contemporaries have shown greater insight into our human condition: our wounded state, our quest for a state of wholeness.

To be sure, modern views of man are often dominated by atheism or the rejection of religious solutions to these questions. Undoubtedly they often cast aside the yoke of faith for a freedom that could be the most seductive Trojan horse of all for a created spirit. It is for us to show that sacramental truth is liberative, so long as we respect the dialectic between man's tainted self and this Other. Only this Other can insure our unity, because in him there is no blemish or obstacle or limit.

Footnotes

[1] Cf. P. R. Regamey, *Pauvrété chrétienne et construction du monde* (Paris: Éditions du Cerf, Foi Vivante, 1967), where the drama of integration with regard to being and having is delineated well; see also the relevant pages in *Portrait spirituel du chrétien* (Paris: Éditions du Cerf, 1963).

[2] P. Emmanuel, *Le goût de l'un* (Paris: Éditions du Seuil, 1962), p. 103.

[3] G. Picon, *Panorama des idées contemporaines* (Paris: Éditions Gallimard, 1957), pp. 16–19.

[4] F. Giroud, *L'express* (June 11, 1967), p. 95.

[5] Cited by Regamey, in *Pauvrété chrétienne,* p. 79.

[6] A. Malraux, *Le temps du mépris* (Paris: Éditions Gallimard), p. 144. Then there are the classic analyses of J.-P. Sartre in *L'être et le néant* (Paris: Éditions Gallimard, 1943), Part 4 and *passim:* e.g., p. 514, pp. 653–54—Eng. trans., *Being and Nothingness.*

[7] This is the classic definition of freedom by St. Thomas. There is a disproportion between two things in man: his infinite and irrevocable open-endedness to the good as a totality, which underlies his irreversible desire for total fulfillment, and his encounter with limited objects, none of which can fulfill

this program. At one and the same time we are condemned to totality and to limitation. See, for example, Ia, q. 83, a. 3; 2 *Contra Gent.*, Chap. 47· where liberty is defined as "dominium et potestas sui actus *ad opposita*."

[8] See, among others, J. M. Pohier, *Psychologie et théologie* (Paris: Éditions du Cerf, 1967), *passim:*

> At his start and throughout his life, man is characterized by his pursuit of narcissistic completeness. In this state, he would be in perfect congruence with himself and his world. This state is envisioned as a reality in some world that exists before history or after it. The impossible attainment of omnipotence is pursued in history itself by what Freud calls the infantile megalomania of desire.
>
> From birth onward, a human being finds himself hurled into a world where he, more than any other living thing, is radically dependent on beings or on objects (it is not just a difference of degree). It is in a system of relations to these objects that he, throughout his life, will be able to find the only possible self-realization and the only possible integration with the world; the operation of these relations to objects is insured by his drives. Throughout its course, personality development will be characterized by a fluctuation between two poles: (1) narcissistic pursuit of omnipotence; (2) a drive-directed relationship to objects, which prove to be distinct from the person and thus contradicts his narcissistic outlook (*op. cit.*, p. 349).

Note also the comments and analysis of J. Y. Jolif, *Comprendre l'homme* (Paris: Éditions du Cerf, 1967):

Man cannot be regarded as a thing closed in and on himself, as an absolute end. A humanism that would make man not only a central value, but an ultimate and positively consummate value, ends up being over-human. The human is human only if it is put forward as mediation, negativity, and, in our sense of the word, transcendence. To use the terms of Nietzsche, it must be regarded as a bridge not a goal, as a transition point not an end point. Humanism survives only insofar as it escapes from itself. Although it is the ground on which man can take a firm stand, it shifts constantly beneath our feet (p. 89).

[9] In *Totem and Tabu* Freud says that religion somehow represents "the victory of the reality principle over the pleasure principle, but on the mythical level; that is why it is the supreme form of the surrender of desire and, at the same time, the supreme form of the fulfillment of desire" (p. 272).

In his reflections on the life instinct and the death instinct, Freud notes that "culture" gives man a power that was once conferred on the gods, and that man struggles with this power because it is marked with a finiteness that cannot be easily reconciled with the omnipotence of desire. This is the theme of *Civilization and Its Discontents.* Man has no more difficult or urgent task than to "convert his desire toward the finite." Man must learn the harsh law of reality: "Infantilism is meant to be surmounted; men cannot be children forever; they must eventually venture forth into the hostile world" (*The Future of an Illusion,* p. 135).

[10] I have developed these ideas at greater length in another work, in which the reader can find extensive bibliographical references to contemporary theories on man: B. Bro. *L'homme et les sacrements: Faut-il encore pratiquer?*

(Paris: Éditions du Cerf, Foi Vivante, 1967). In particular, see the bibliographies related to the following topics: "Signes et symboles," p. 419; "L'homme dans le temps," p. 428; "L'assemblée chrétienne," p. 416; "La révolution du dialogue," pp. 39–54; also these topics in the index—Anthropologie, Historicité, Langage, Symbole, Temps, Analyse structurale.

[11] Cf. J. M. Pohier, "Au nom du Père," *Esprit* (March–April, 1966); P. Ricoeur, *De l'interprétation* (Paris: Éditions du Seuil, 1965), pp. 242ff., and *passim:* they go back over the analyses made by Freud, particularly in *The Future of an Illusion.*

[12] A. de Peretti, "Carl Rogers ou les paradoxes de la présence," in *Les Études* (February, 1967), pp. 155–56. [*Editor's note:* Carl Rogers is an American and his many articles and books appear in English.]

[13] That liturgical reform could be carried out without any reference to the work being done in psychology and the other social sciences is highly unfortunate. It is, I feel, a sad indication of our failure to look at *reality.* Happily, things seem to be changing. However, for the past twenty years liturgical reform, and of a rather good quality, has taken place without any attention to psychology; it is a clear sign of the backwardness of ecclesiastical thinking. When a congress on "liturgy and the spiritual life," such as that at Angers in 1962, does not hear anything from a social scientist, one must question the realism of the liturgy and the spiritual life such a congress proposes.

[14] Cf. B. Bro, *op. cit:* "La révolution du dialogue," pp. 39–55; "Aimer ou Subir la Liturgie," pp. 247–70; "L'Assemblée chrétienne," bibliography pp. 416–19.

[15] *Ibid.,* pp. 327–29: "*Le collectif n'est pas le communautaire.*" We must firmly reject the foolish tendency to equate the common (hence, superior) good with collective activity, and individual (hence, inferior) good with private action. If a private act is truly an act of the spirit, it is an act of communion by its very nature; if it is spiritual, it is necessarily an opening out. Hence, it is useless to invoke the primacy of the common good over individual good in order to prove the superiority of a collective action over an individual or interior act. A truly "interior" act is never confined with the limits of the individual; as the high point of individual activity, it opens out to the whole community of spirits. We have every right to say that the more personal and personalized an action is, the more it expresses a spiritual nature, the more universal it is.

[16] St. Thomas quite rightly dwelled on the virtues of otherness at great length. It is in this connection that he discusses cultic worship, prayer, and all the acts associated with religion.

[17] G. Durand, *Les structures anthropologiques de l'imaginaire* (Paris: Presses Universitaires de France, 1963); P. Ricoeur, *De l'interprétation: Essai sur Freud, op. cit.;* see also, in B. Bro, *op. cit.,* "Les symboles et leur revanche," "Pouvons-nous passer des symboles?" "Des symboles religieux," "Le Christ et les symboles," "Foi et sacrements," pp. 167–246, and detailed bibliography on pp. 420–28.

GREGORY BAUM, O.S.A.

The Ecclesial Reality of the Other Churches

In exploring the relations among the different Christian Churches with Gregory Baum we can ask the following questions. Can we call all Christian communities Churches? What was the import of the encyclical *The Mystical Body of Christ* of Pope Pius XII? How does the teaching of Vatican II compare with this encyclical? How does Baum use the terms "Catholic Church" and "Church of Christ"? What is the importance of seeing the Church as the local community? Does the Catholic Church consider itself as the perfect Church and make itself the norm to measure other Christian Churches?

Gregory Baum, O.S.A., a Professor of Theology at St. Michael's College in the University of Toronto, is director of its Center for Ecumenical Studies and editor of *The Ecumenist.*

Since Jesus Christ created his Church to be one and undivided, the division of the Christian people is the work of man and in some sense involves the mystery of iniquity. Christian disunity is, at least partially, the fruit of sin. There is, and always will be, therefore, an element of unintelligibility in our divisions, and no theological reflection on the existence of many Churches can ever be presented in

Reprinted from Gregory Baum, O.S.A., "The Ecclesial Reality of the Other Churches," in *Concilium,* Vol. IV, *The Church and Ecumenism,* ed. Hans Küng (Glen Rock, N.J.: Paulist Press, 1965), pp. 62–86; *Concilium,* April 1965, Vol. 4, no. 1, *Ecumenism* (Burns and Oates Ltd., London), pp. 34–46, with the permission of *Concilium.*

a perfect system. The multiplication of Churches measured by the will and deed of Christ remains a riddle and even a contradiction.

Vatican Council II did not face the question of many Churches directly. The Constitution on the Church elaborated its theological understanding of the Catholic Church and then tried to fit the reality of the other Churches into the thin margin left to them. This shows, as we shall see, great progress over the position taken in the past by ecclesiastical documents and Catholic theology in general. A more satisfactory theology of the Church and the Churches, also from a Catholic point of view, could be worked out when we look at the Christian people as a whole and seek the self-understanding of the Catholic Church simultaneously with the understanding of the other Churches. We shall see that a first attempt at this approach, tentative and cursory, is made in the Decree on Ecumenism.

In this essay I shall study the ecclesial reality of the separated Churches on the basis of the teaching of Vatican Council II. In regard to the Orthodox Churches of the East there has never been any hesitation on the part of the Roman Church, at least in the area of practice and policy, to acknowledge them as Churches. Their doctrinal, sacramental, and hierarchical similarity to the Catholic Church has always been recognized, even if theologians have refused to let this qualify their understanding of the Catholic Church. Yet in this essay, I shall reflect on the ecclesial reality of the separated Churches *in general*, Orthodox, Anglican, and Protestant, even though a special study of the ecclesial status of the Orthodox Churches would be rewarding.

In the following pages I shall repeatedly refer to the drafts (or schemata) *De Ecclesia* [the Dogmatic Constitution on the Church] and *De Oecumenismo* [the Decree on Ecumenism]. These are the documents presented to, and discussed at, the second session of the Council. The amended documents approved by the Council during the third session are published as the Constitution on the Church and the Decree on Ecumenism.

I

Vatican Council II on Other Churches

During the second session of the Council, the ecclesial reality of the separated Churches was repeatedly the subject of episcopal speeches. Several speakers criticized the section of the draft *De*

Ecclesia dealing with non-Catholic Christians for not establishing an adequate foundation for the ecumenical dialogue. Maurice Baudoux, Archbishop of St. Boniface, Manitoba, Canada, declared:

> The document considers separated Christians only as baptized and believing individuals; it says nothing about the Christian communions that are separated from the Church. We acknowledge that the Catholic Church is the one true Church; at the same time we all know there are many communities of Christians in the world that proclaim the Gospel of Christ, announce the kingdom of God and celebrate baptism and the other sacraments. Even if it is difficult for us to determine the relationship between the Catholic Church and these Christian communions, we know that through them God saves and sanctifies men. And if it pleases the merciful God to give grace to men through these separated Churches and to accept divine worship from them, then the Catholic Church ought openly and joyfully to acknowledge this.[1]

When the draft *De Oecumenismo* was discussed toward the end of the second session, several speakers again insisted that the ecclesial reality of the Churches of the Reformation was not sufficiently acknowledged. These are the words of Bishop Gabriel Manek spoken in the name of 30 bishops of Indonesia:

> The title "Church" should not only be attributed to the Oriental Churches separated from us, but also to the communities that arose from the Reformation. As communities of baptized Christians they are united among themselves and to us by the bond of faith, hope and charity, through the proclamation and confession of the divine Word and through the worship of God. These communities are in all truth "Churches," even if in an analogous sense and less perfectly than the Orthodox Churches. They possess visible elements of ecclesial unity. Through holy rites they represent, produce and foster the life of grace, so that we must acknowledge the Holy Spirit present in their midst, making use of them as means of salvation. They also receive from that fullness of grace and truth that has been entrusted to the Church.[2]

These speeches did not remain without some effect. In the section of the Constitution on the Church dealing with non-Catholic Christians we now find a reference, a rather cursory one, to other Christian Churches. The text simply states that separated Christians "are consecrated by baptism, in which they are united with Christ. They also recognize and receive other sacraments within their own Churches or ecclesiastical communities" (n. 15). In the Decree on Ecumenism, the section (Chap. 3, Pt. 2), entitled "The Communities Established since the 16th Century," was given the new heading: "The Separated Churches and Ecclesial Communities in the West." This title and the use of the same formula in the text do not attempt to decide which Christian denominations in the West are regarded as Churches and which as ecclesial communities. This question is left open, and for good reason. Some Catholic theologians would hesitate to apply the name of Church to any Christian community in the West save the Old Catholics, because only there do we find, according to Catholic understanding, the Eucharist celebrated by episcopally ordained priests. Other Catholic theologians go much further. But whatever their precise usage of the term "Church," all Catholics today, following the lead of Vatican Council II, acknowledge the *ecclesial character* of these Christian communities not in communion with Rome.

In this connection it must also be mentioned that certain Protestant bodies refuse to regard themselves as Churches. Especially in North America, and in other continents apart from Europe, we find many Protestants who do not think of Christ's redemption offered to them in terms of Church. This may be because of a certain anti-ecclesiastical tendency that belongs to the heritage of the independent evangelicals (who have sometimes suffered under established Churches in the past); it may be because of a religious individualism that permits Protestants to change freely from one denomination to another as they move to another urban community; or it may be due to a theological liberalism that does not take seriously the total evidence of the New Testament. For this reason American Catholics are often not aware that many Protestant communities do regard themselves as Churches, and it often requires reading and ecumenical experience before they encounter those Protestant traditions in which the consciousness of being Church is strongly alive.

II
Constitution on the Church and "Mystici Corporis Christi"

In the last decades the Catholic Church has willingly and sometimes joyfully acknowledged the existence of individual Christians outside of her own borders. According to traditional teaching, whenever a man believes in Christ as Lord and Savior and is baptized into his death and resurrection, he is truly reborn, truly joined to Christ, truly a Christian. Even Pope Pius XII's encyclical *Mystici Corporis Christi* [*The Mystical Body of Christ*] acknowledges the existence of Christians outside of the Catholic Church even if, according to this encyclical, they cannot be regarded in any real way as members of Christ's Church. According to this encyclical, *reapse*, that is, "really and truly" members of this Church are only Roman Catholics.[3] In such a context very little could be said about the ecclesial reality of other Christian Churches. It was customary in the theological literature of those days to say that Protestants were Christians not because of, but despite, the "churches" to which they belonged. The gifts of Gospel and baptism that these Christians received really belonged to the Catholic Church; what they received from their own "churches" was only the set of errors that constitute the principle of division. Under these presuppositions it was possible to concede that the Holy Spirit vivified Christians in other communities. We read in *Mystici Corporis Christi:* "Those who are divided [from us] in faith or government cannot be living in the unity of Christ's Body nor can they be living the life of its own divine Spirit." [4]

Three Significant Points of Comparison

The Constitution on the Church transcends the encyclical *Mystici Corporis Christi* in many ways. In connection with our subject, however, there are three especially significant points in which the Constitution differs from the encyclical of Pius XII:

1. The encyclical *Mystici Corporis Christi* represented a great advance in Catholic ecclesiology. Before that time the theology manuals used in seminaries and theological faculties dealt with the Church, for the most part, as a subject of apologetics. With *Mystici Corporis Christi* a shift began, noticeable at once in Catholic institutions, moving the study of the Church into the realm of theology properly so called. Thanks to the encyclical the Church came to be regarded in theological teaching as the summit and summation of

Christ's saving work offered to men, and to study this mystery one had to reflect on the whole of revelation as contained in Scripture and its traditional understanding in the Church.

The particular approach of Pius XII to the doctrine of the Mystical Body was somewhat canonical. The encyclical opens with the consideration of the Church as a social body, as a Body hierarchically constituted and canonically defined, and then proceeds to show that this Body has Christ as Founder, Head, and Redeemer constantly present to it in the power of the Spirit, and hence truly deserves the name of Mystical Body of Christ.

This approach did not satisfy all theologians. St. Paul, from whom the doctrine of the Mystical Body is derived, did not approach the mystery in this way, at least not in the epistles that present the doctrine in its mature form and propose it not simply as a parable or metaphor, but as a true account of how Jesus acts in his own People. In St. Paul the Body of Christ refers first of all to the relationship or union into which Jesus draws those who believe in him and are baptized into his death and resurrection. They become one Body with Christ: there exists a community of life among them. Christians become Body of Christ when they take part in the eucharistic banquet, share in the Body of the Lord, and thus enter into a communion of life with him. These Christians, joined to the Lord as his Body and nourished by his Body, undoubtedly constitute a society, a body social, but to refer to this society as the Body of Christ was certainly not in the foreground of Paul's thought. To call this society Body of Christ is legitimate in a derived sense, after having reflected on the visible nature of the community of those whom the Lord has joined to himself.

Since Pius XII began his encyclical by equating Mystical Body and body social, he was led to an understanding of the matter which was no longer precisely that of St. Paul and which obliged him to identify in the strictest terms the earthly Body of Jesus and the Roman Catholic Church. This approach is amplified in the Constitution on the Church. The pertinent text in Chapter 1 (n. 7), tells us that communicating his own life to those he redeems, Jesus, through the Holy Spirit, joins his brothers called out of all peoples to himself as his own body. Only later in the text, reflecting on the various gifts that Jesus makes to his brothers, including sacramental and ministerial gifts, are we slowly led to the consideration of the body social that is built up through the diversity of members and their respective offices. But even when the Constitution on the Church considers the Mystical Body in its social dimension, the accent falls on the *koinonía* or communion of the brothers with Jesus, in which all are conformed to the dying and rising of their Lord and share in a common life.

2. Consistent with this fundamentally different approach, the Constitution on the Church explains the relationship of the Mystical Body and the Catholic Church in terms different from those of Pius XII. The encyclical *Mystici Corporis Christi* taught a strict identity between the Body of the Lord and the Church of Rome. Since this created serious theological difficulties and Catholic scholars were unwilling to accept this identity without the appropriate distinctions, Pius XII emphasized the doctrine again in his encyclical *Humani Generis* [*False Trends in Modern Teaching*]: "Some say they are not bound by the doctrine, explained in our encyclical letter of a few years ago and based on the sources of revelation, that teaches that the Mystical Body of Christ and the Roman Catholic Church are one and the same thing." [5]

At the Council, several bishops expressed their disapproval of asserting this doctrine without qualifications. Among the many Fathers who criticized the draft proposal *De Ecclesia* for teaching this simple identity, Cardinal Lercaro, Archbishop of Bologna, said:

> While it is true to affirm (with the draft) that "the Church as visible society and as Mystical Body of Christ comprises not two realities, but one only," they are one not according to one and the same formality but according to two distinct aspects. The Church as society and the Mystical Body of Christ express two distinct aspects that fully and perfectly coincide as far as the essential order and constitutive norm given by Christ, the Founder, are concerned. But these two aspects can never be the same in the existential and historical order. In that order, these two aspects do not always enjoy the same fullness of extension; in fact, conflicts arise between them, and will continue to arise until the very end of

> human history. Then and only then will the identity and equality of the Church and the Mystical Body be consummated and made manifest.[6]

How does the Constitution on the Church solve this problem? It asserts and defends the fundamental article of Catholic faith that the earthly body of the Lord and the Catholic Church refer basically to the same reality, yet the wording of this declaration indicates, especially when comparing it with the preceding text of the draft proposal, that the Body of Christ and the Catholic Church are not simply identical but diverse aspects of the same complex reality. In the draft we read: "The visible society and the Mystical Body of Christ are not two realities but one only," while the final version reads: "But the society structured with hierarchical organs and the Mystical Body of Christ are not *to be considered as* two realities . . . rather they *form* one *complex* reality." [7] The new wording suggests that the transcendent community of grace and the social body of the Church may have historically distinct dimensions and do not simply coincide, but that the man of faith believes them to be one single ecclesial reality which cannot be grasped or expressed in a single concept. The Body of Christ is present in the Catholic Church so that they can never be called two realities, but the Body of Christ nevertheless transcends the Catholic Church.

Another significant change of words was introduced into the same chapter of the Constitution. In the draft proposed we read that the Church of Christ here on earth "is" the Catholic Church, an identity without any qualifications. The final text of the Constitution says that the Church of Christ "subsists in" the Catholic Church. The Church of Christ, then, is realized and embodied in the Catholic Church; conversely, the Catholic Church is the realization of the Church of Christ on earth, according to Catholic faith the only institutionally perfect realization of this Church, but there is no simple and unqualified identity. The explanation for the change of words given to the Council by the Theological Commission says: "Instead of 'is' we now say 'subsists in,' so that the expression corresponds better with what is affirmed about the ecclesial elements which are present elsewhere."

3. This same understanding is carried through the entire Constitution on the Church. When the chapter on the People of God (Chap.

2) comes to the question of who is incorporated in the Church of Christ, it modifies the teaching of *Mystici Corporis Christi.* This encyclical had insisted that *reapse* (really) members of the Church are only men joined by the bonds of faith, sacraments, and hierarchical communion, i.e., only Roman Catholics. The draft proposal on the Church still repeated that *reapse et simpliciter loquendo* (really and simply speaking) only the Catholic faithful are incorporated in the Church. However, in the final text of the Constitution we read that the Catholic faithful are *plene* (fully) incorporated in the Church. This implies that apart from the full participation in the mystery of the Church there are other, less perfect, ways. This remarkable change from *reapse* to *plene*, introduced because of the demands of the Council Fathers, makes the doctrine consistent with what is taught in other parts of the Constitution. In fact, the report given by the Theological Commission to the Council reminds us that all the baptized are in some way incorporated in the Church.

We note that the word "member" and the notion of "membership" have been avoided in the Constitution. It was believed that this theological concept, variously understood in different theological systems, does not really help us in giving an account of the ways in which Christians participate in the mystery of the Church.

Since the word *reapse* was replaced by *plene*, another change had to be made in the same sentence. How is the Catholic, who has lost the friendship of the Spirit by sin, incorporated in the Church? If the adverb qualifying incorporation is *reapse*, we concede that despite the harm which this man does to himself and to others, he still remains really and truly incorporated in the Church. If, however, the adverb qualifying incorporation is *plene*, then this excludes the Christian who has lost the Spirit. A few words were bound to be added to the amended passage to limit the full incorporation in the Church to the Catholic faithful who open their hearts to the grace of Christ. The words added are *Spiritum Christi habentes* (having the Spirit of God). We shall have occasion to return to this highly significant change of the text.

Church of Christ Transcends the Catholic Church

We conclude that on these three points the Constitution on the Church has gone far beyond the teaching of *Mystici Corporis*

Christi. According to the Constitution the Catholic Church is the institutionally perfect realization of the Church of Christ on earth. We can point with our finger to the Catholic Church and say, "This is the Church of Christ," and according to Catholic faith we can do this to no other Christian body. At the same time the Church of Christ, without ceasing to be incarnate and historical in its social existence, transcends the Catholic Church so that we may not only speak of non-Catholic Christians as in some way belonging to it, but are also justified in regarding non-Catholic Christian communities as being imperfect or defective realizations of it. The teaching of the Constitution on the Church, therefore, leaves theological space for other Churches. The Church of Christ that constitutes one single complex reality with the Catholic Church is present in other Christian Churches, even though according to Catholic faith these are only institutionally imperfect or inadequate realizations of Christ's Church.

I do not wish to be misunderstood on this point. I do not assert that the Church of Christ geographically or sociologically transcends the Catholic Church, as if Christ's Church were made up of the sum of several Christian Churches here on earth. According to Catholic faith there is only one true Church visibly present in history. What I do assert is that while Christ's Church has its institutionally perfect and unique realization in the Catholic Church and with it makes up one single complex reality, it is also present, according to various degrees of institutional imperfections, in other Christian Churches. With this understanding we leave untouched the Catholic teaching that Christ's Church is undivided and that the Catholic Church is identical with Christ's Church on earth. At the same time, because of the ontological transcendence of the Church of Christ, we can speak of imperfect realizations of this one Church in other Christian communities. We have here the first theological basis for the ecclesial reality of other Churches—Orthodox, Anglican, and Protestant.

It will have been noted that I have always spoken of the "institutional" perfection of the Catholic Church. The reason for this will be more apparent further on. It is, of course, obvious that on her pilgrimage the Catholic Church is not and never will be, simply speaking, the perfect realization of Christ's Church. The unfailing perfection of the Catholic Church lies in the authentic heritage of the doctrinal, sacramental, and hierarchical gifts that the Holy Spirit preserves in her; in the dynamic possession or assimilation of these gifts, however, the Catholic Church is, according to the Constitution on the Church, in constant need of reform and purification.

III
The Decree on Ecumenism

When we come to the Decree on Ecumenism, we find that the theological notions we have just analyzed are taken for granted. The approach of the Decree, however, is different: it presents historically and concretely the division of the Christian world (Chap. 1, nn. 2–3). At first we find a description of the Church of God as called forth by Father, Son, and Spirit and built on the foundations of the apostles. Then we are told that from the beginning there were factions in the Church that the Apostle Paul condemned. Greater dissensions occurred in later centuries, and large Christian communities were separated from full communion with the Catholic Church, "for which, often enough, men of both sides were to blame." Christians born into these separated communities cannot possibly be held guilty of the sin of division; on the contrary through baptism and the other gifts received in faith they enjoy, despite the differences which are sometimes considerable, a certain, even if imperfect, communion with the Catholic Church and must be acknowledged by Catholics as brothers in the Lord.

The Separated Churches

Then follows a theological description of these other Churches. The gift or elements that together, in their totality, make up and vivify the Church exist in these Churches with greater or lesser density. As examples of these gifts present in the separated Churches are cited the Scriptures as the Word of God, the life of grace, faith, hope, and charity, the interior gifts of the Spirit and finally the visible elements, i.e., the sacramental and hierarchical gifts. Because of these gifts and elements and their celebration in the Churches separated from Rome, we must acknowledge that through them God regenerates men to the life of grace and leads them into the community of salvation.

> It follows that the separated Churches and communities as such, though we believe they suffer from defects already mentioned, have been by no means deprived of significance and importance in the mystery of salvation. For the spirit of Christ has not refrained from using them as means of salvation which derive their efficacy from the very fullness of grace and truth entrusted to the Catholic Church.[8]

What has been said in these paragraphs of the Decree? The Catholic Church, regarding herself as the authentic heir of the apostolic Church and the unique embodiment of Christ's Church on earth, finds herself surrounded by other Churches in whom she acknowledges a truly ecclesial reality. In different degrees, they are instruments in the hands of Christ to save and sanctify men, to announce the kingdom, to render worship and obedience to the Father and, hence, are part of the ecclesial mystery of salvation as it works itself out in the history of men. The teaching of the Constitution on the Church permits this inclusion of the separated Churches into the history of salvation. It may be difficult to determine theologically what the relationship of these Churches is to the Catholic Church, and since the separation is against the will of God, there is an enigma of sin involved here, but on the basis of the teaching of Vatican Council II we do not have the slightest hesitation in acknowledging the ecclesial reality of the other Christian communities. They are in a real sense, though not in a perfect and adequate sense, Churches. This is our first conclusion.

From what we have said so far the impression is created that the Catholic Church regards herself as the perfect Church and makes herself the measure of all the other Christian communities. The closer they resemble the Catholic Church, the more truly they deserve the name of Church. This impression is made stronger when we read the third chapter of the Decree on Ecumenism, where a radical distinction is made between the Churches of the East, which have preserved the apostolic episcopate and the fullness of sacramental life, and the Churches and ecclesial communities of the West, which have not preserved these visible gifts of the Church. (We do not consider in this context the special case of the Old Catholics.) The introduction to Chapter 3 refers to the Anglican Church as being worthy of special mention because it has preserved so much of the Catholic structure and tradition. The impression is indeed created that we regard the Catholic Church as made up of the totality of the gifts of Christ and that we evaluate the ecclesial reality of other Churches by counting the gifts which they share with us. We thus get the picture of the Catholic Church at the center, the perfect Church with the pope as its head, and then at varying distances from it other Churches classified according to their structural similarity to us. Is this a true presentation of the Catholic understanding of our divided Christian people or is this a caricature?

In the second session Andrea Pangrazio, Archbishop of Gorizia, Italy, complained that the draft on ecumenism could be misunderstood in this fashion. This is what he said:

> It is a good thing to list all those elements of the Church which by God's grace have been preserved in these communities and continue to produce saving effects. But to express my honest opinion, it seems to me that such a catalogue is too "quantitative," if I may use the expression. It seems to me that these elements have simply been piled together. I believe that a bond is needed to unite these separate elements. We should therefore point to the center, to which all these elements are related, and without which they cannot be explained. This bond and center is Christ himself, whom all Christians acknowledge as Lord of the Church, whom the Christians of all communities unquestionably want to serve faithfully and who graciously accomplishes wonderful things even in separated communities by his active presence through the Holy Spirit, not by any merit of men but by his gracious mercy alone.[9]

To consider the presence of the Church among men in institutional terms is undoubtedly a major aspect of Catholic ecclesiology. The gifts of Gospel and sacrament accompanied by the respective ministerial or hierarchical gifts are of eminent importance when we reflect on the questions: What is the Church? Where do we find the Church? However, this institutional aspect is not the only one, and not even the principal one. All that is visible and institutional in the Church is, after all, only a means to unite men to their Lord and Savior. Though we have no right to neglect or underrate the structural elements of the Church in the plan of God, no theologian will want to speak of them as if they were values in themselves apart from the grace which they mediate.

Concrete Fellowship of Believers

Until now, it is true, we have spoken of the separated Churches in structural terms and measured their perfection by their structural proximity to the Catholic Church. What is the complementary consideration, proper to ecclesiology, that will put this institutional evaluation in its proper light? It is the understanding of Church as the concrete fellowship of believers, created by the preaching of the Gospel and the celebration of the Eucharist, in other words, as local congregation.

In the theological tradition of the West, by Church is usually meant the Church universal, the Church founded by Christ upon the Twelve with Peter as their head and spread by him over the whole world. This theological approach is undoubtedly legitimate. In the Scriptures the Church is sometimes regarded primarily under its universal aspect, especially when the biblical authors reflect on the Church as the People of God in which Jews and Gentiles are reconciled or when they present the Church as the summing up of God's redemptive plan for mankind.

IV
The Local Congregation

In addition to this approach, however, there are others in Scripture, and they are just as important, where the Church is understood primarily as the fellowship of believers in one place, created by the sharing of the mystery of Christ, i.e., as local congregation.

The Acts of the Apostles describes, and St. Paul teaches, that the believers who have been baptized into Christ and are fed by the preaching of the Word and the sharing in the one bread become the family of Christ in the Spirit, a spiritual fellowship with Christ as the first-born brother, an assembly of the chosen people (*ekklesia*) on pilgrimage; in other words they become the Church. The local congregation reveals its true nature when gathered about the one table it shares in the Body of the Lord and becomes his Body, the Church. In the letters of St. Paul, words such as *ekklesia, People of God, koinonía,* and *Body of Christ* often refer in the first place to the local community of Christians.

If we begin our ecclesiology by looking upon the Church universal, we tend to regard the local congregation simply as a part of the Church, an administrative area. We then tend to speak of it in terms of its institutional boundaries rather than in terms of faith, hope, and charity effected by the liturgy transforming a concrete group of men into a Christian fellowship. The local congregation is not simply a part of the Church universal; it is its adequate manifestation in a particular place. If, therefore, we begin our ecclesiology with a consideration of the local congregation, an approach that is both scriptural and traditional (at least in the East), then Church signifies the actual family of men created by Word and sacrament at one place and Church universal, the family or communion of all the Churches of God. This approach throws new light on what Church and ecclesial reality are and for this reason it is highly significant for our subject.

The Local Church, a True Representation of the Universal Church

Do we find this understanding of the local congregation in the teaching of Vatican Council II? It is certainly not central in the doctrinal exposition of the Constitution on the Church. At the second session several bishops asked in their speeches that this aspect be given greater consideration. The most emphatic and systematic speech on this subject was given by Bishop Edward Schick, Auxiliary Bishop of Fulda, Germany. He concluded his statement with these words:

> What is needed, then, can be easily summed up as follows: This Church of God and of Christ truly exists in the local Church. . . . In such Churches God gathers together the faithful through the Gospel of Christ. In each of them the mystery of the Lord's supper is celebrated, something so great that the whole universal Church can perform nothing greater. It is a mystery by which the complete Christ, present everywhere among his own in each community, manifests himself as the symbol of that unity and love in which he wanted all to be joined together among themselves. In these communities, even though they be small and poor, the whole Christ is present through the one Spirit by whom all are filled with life and united among themselves. He is the Spirit of love, of consolation, and of hope, who gives his charisms to each individual, so that they make one Body with those varied gifts and bear witness before the world to the hope they have by their calling. . . . Each local Church is a true representation of the total and universal Church, which itself carries on its own life in these local Churches.[10]

The Constitution on the Church, however, does not give great prominence to the Church as local congregation. One of the reasons for this is perhaps that "local Church" in Catholic terminology usually refers not to the local congregation but to the diocese, i.e., to the community created through the ministerial office of a bishop, member of the apostolic college. Such a community, by virtue of the episcopal ministry, is one, holy, catholic, and apostolic, in other words, a Church. The renewed appreciation of "local Churches" and their groupings as "particular Churches" in the Constitution represents a considerable ecclesiological advance made by Vatican Council II. It provides a pattern for a comparative decentralization, a manifestation of catholicity, and a guarantee of greater freedom within the Church universal. But since in the Church of today the bishop is no longer the local pastor in the strict sense, this theology of the local Church continues to be expressed in institutional terms.

There is, however, one explicit text in the Constitution on the Church, introduced after the discussion during the second session, that brings out the true understanding of the local congregation. In Chapter 3 we read:

> This Church of Christ is truly present in all legitimate local congregations of the faithful which, united with their pastors, are themselves called Churches in the New Testament. For

> in their locality these are the new People called by God, in the Holy Spirit and in much fullness. . . . In them the faithful are gathered together by the preaching of the Gospel of Christ, and the mystery of the Lord's supper is celebrated, "that by the food of the Lord's body and blood the whole brotherhood may be joined together." . . . In any community of the altar, under the sacred ministry of the bishop, there is exhibited a symbol of that charity and "unity of the Mystical Body, without which there can be no salvation." In these communities, though frequently small and poor, or living in the diaspora, Christ is present, and in virtue of his presence there is brought together one, holy, catholic, and apostolic Church.[11]

This teaching is supported by other passages of the same Constitution. In a brief text, introduced after the conciliar discussion of the second session, we read that the celebration of the Eucharist renders present and active the work of redemption and that therefore through this eucharistic meal "the unity of all believers who form one Body in Christ . . . is both expressed and brought about." [12] Another text asserts the same position: "Strengthened at the holy table by the Body of Christ, they then manifest in a concrete way that unity of the People of God which is suitably symbolized and wondrously achieved by this most holy sacrament." [13] The local congregation, then, gathered for worship, becomes in a true theological sense the People of God or the Church.

This is explained in detail and applied in its concrete meaning in the Constitution on the Liturgy. There we read at the very outset: "The liturgy . . . is the outstanding means whereby the faithful may express in their lives, and manifest to others, the mystery of Christ and the real nature of the true Church." [14] A little further on we read: "While the liturgy daily builds up those who are within into a holy temple of the Lord, into a dwelling place for God in the Spirit, to the mature measure of the fullness of Christ, at the same time it marvelously strengthens their power to preach Christ, and thus shows forth the Church to those who are outside as a sign lifted up among the nations." At liturgical worship, including Word and sacrament, the local congregation becomes truly Church.

The subsequent chapters of the Constitution show that this teaching is understood in a concrete and practical way. In the liturgy God speaks to the gathered faithful, he tells them again in his Word that he is their Father and they his People, and as the power of the Word produces the faith in their hearts, they become more truly his People, they become more truly Church (cf. n. 33). Or, according to another passage of the Constitution,[15] Christ himself is present to the faithful through the proclamation of his Word, and listening to him they become more truly the community of believers whose sins are forgiven; they become more truly Church. And what Christ has wrought through his Word he repeats, intensifies, and seals through the eucharistic part of the liturgy when his death and resurrection are celebrated and the faithful, by sharing in his self-surrender to the Father, die anew to the unredeemed world and rise to a new life of love and service. Sharing the banquet with Jesus and participating in his broken and risen Body, they become more truly his Body, enter more deeply into communion with him and one another; in other words, they become more truly Church.

Approaching the mystery of the Church in this concrete way, i.e., reflecting on what Christ does within the local congregation, the Constitution on the Liturgy concludes that "the liturgy is the summit towards which the activity of the Church is directed, and at the same time it is the fount from which all her power flows." [16] The Church is here understood dynamically as a community in motion. The local congregation gathered to hear the Word of God and to share in the eucharistic sacrifice becomes more truly Church, and thanks to this healing action of Christ in their midst, the People of God are able to live a life of faith and service in their environment and fulfill their mission as Christians. But since their existence as Church is always threatened by sin, pride, divisiveness, and all the vices against unity, it is again at the next worship that the congregation receives forgiveness, is strengthened in faith by the Word of God, and dies and rises to a new life in the Eucharist; in short, the congregation becomes more authentically Church again.

V
The Ecclesial Reality of a Christian Community

These considerations are of great significance for our subject. To regard the Church as institution, focuses on one aspect of the mystery; another aspect is the Church understood as the communion or fellowship (*koinonía*) of the faithful produced by Christ. This second aspect is never static, canonically fixed, and structurally solidified. It is always vulnerable to deformation by sin, and always subject to the saving and healing action of God in Christ as he shares his life with others in Word and sacrament.

To evaluate the ecclesial reality of a Christian community, therefore, it is not enough to consider it from the institutional point of view. We can well imagine a parish or diocese of the Catholic Church which is institutionally perfect—orthodox doctrine, seven sacraments, apostolic hierarchy—but in which the concrete fellowship of believers is limited to a few. Some of the Observers at the Second Vatican Council, seeing the parish life in the city of Rome, marveled at the ease with which we call Church an ecclesiastical institution, even when it produces fellowship only among a few, and how reluctant we are to call Church a community that, though from our viewpoint institutionally incomplete, produces brotherhood of faith and charity among its members. While it is of course difficult to judge the degree in which a community is transformed into the People of God, we cannot assert that this is an altogether hidden fact. Actual and concrete fellowship enter as much into the realm of experience as faith, hope, and charity. If therefore a local congregation belonging to a non-Catholic Church listens faithfully to the Gospel, shares in the breaking of the bread of unity, and behaves as a living fellowship, then we must say, on the basis of the theology we have just explained, that it is Church, even if we regret the institutional imperfections from which it suffers.

It will be remembered that toward the beginning of this essay, I stated that the Catholic Church is the *institutionally* perfect realization of the Church of Christ, while other Churches, not in communion with Rome, are *institutionally* imperfect realizations of the same Church. Expressing myself in this careful way, I left room for the complementary aspect that permits me to say that *concretely* and *actually* the Church of Christ may be realized less, equally, or even more in a Church separated from Rome than in a Church in communion with Rome. This conclusion is inescapable on the basis of the understanding of Church that emerges from the teaching of Vatican Council II. Seen from the viewpoint of the divine institution, the Catholic Church is the one Church of Christ on earth and the other Churches are, in varying degrees, imperfect or defective realizations of this; but seen from the viewpoint of God's merciful and sovereign action, which uses institutional elements but is never dependent on or limited by them, a Christian community is more truly Church when it is more transformed into the People of God, into his family, into a spiritual brotherhood of faith and charity.

Conditions of Incorporation into the Church

This interpretation is confirmed by the passage in the Constitution on the Church that defines the conditions of incorporation into the Church.[17] We have noticed how this passage has amplified the doctrine of *Mystici Corporis Christi.* Instead of saying that only Roman Catholics are *reapse* members of the Church, the Constitution asserts that Roman Catholics are *plene* incorporated into the Church, adding however a new condition, namely, that "they possess the Spirit of Christ." In the past, the majority of Catholic theologians following the lead of the ecclesiastical documents, regarded the Church first of all in institutional terms so that Catholics were simply regarded as members without necessarily distinguishing their relation to Jesus in faith. The present definition is the victory of a more charismatic understanding of the Church: full incorporation into it depends also on the Spirit. The conversion of heart that the Spirit produces through Word and sacrament is therefore a factor that makes a Christian community more truly and more fully Church. In the same sense we must understand the passage of the Constitution on the Church (n. 8), added after the discussion at the second session, that declares the Church "at the same time holy and always in need of being purified, continually follows the way of penance and renewal."

Church of Christ Is a Mystery

We conclude that looking upon the Catholic Church and the other Christian Churches we stand before a mystery of divine judgment and mercy. On the one hand we profess that the Catholic Church, understood in its doctrinal, sacramental, and ministerial perfection, is the one and only Church of Christ on earth, and on the other hand we humbly acknowledge that the Churches are all under the judgment of the merciful God who may choose to create an equal or even greater ecclesial reality in Churches which, as institutions, we regard as an imperfect or defective realization of the Church of Christ. We do not forget, of course, that institution and communion are two aspects of one and the same divine mystery, and that it is precisely through the institutional elements that communion among men is brought about by Christ. Reflecting on the unity of these two aspects, would we have to say that the institutional defects of the Churches separated from Rome make them poorer in terms of grace? No; since God uses his gifts freely and sovereignly our conclusion still stands.

These remarks hold for the Orthodox, Anglican, and Protestant Churches. It is true that the Decree on Ecumenism makes a radical distinction between the Churches of the East that have preserved the apostolic heritage in sacrament and ministry, that have ancient and rich spiritual traditions, and that from the Catholic point of view are institutionally (doctrine, liturgy, hierarchy) so complete that, at least abstractly speaking, a reconciliation with them would not be difficult. We note moreover that the theology of the Church as local congregation is particularly acknowledged for the Orthodox Churches. The Decree states: "Through the celebration of the eucharist of the Lord in each of these Churches, the Church of God is built up and grows in stature, and through concelebration, their communion with one another is made manifest." [18]

The Anglican and Protestant Churches do not have a eucharistic liturgy nor a pastoral ministry that is regarded by the Catholic Church as being in apostolic succession. At the same time, when the Decree on Ecumenism describes the gifts of Christ celebrated in these Churches of the West, it mentions not only the Gospel, baptism, and, more generally, the presence of Christ in the community, but also refers to the eucharistic action of Christ among the faithful. Even though we do not acknowledge the full eucharistic reality in these Churches, especially because of what we regard as a defect in ministerial ordination, the Decree acknowledges that in the eucharist celebrated by these Churches the faithful "commemorate the Lord's death and resurrection . . . profess that it signifies life in communion with Christ and await his coming in glory." [19] We conclude therefore that the theology of the local congregation which we have presented above may not only be applied to the Orthodox Churches in whom we acknowledge full eucharistic reality, but also in proper proportion to the separated Churches of the West. In these Churches and ecclesial communities Christ is at work transforming the faithful into the People of God. Even if we believe that doctrinal errors and sacramental loss threaten the life of grace in these Christian Churches, we must say with the Decree: "We rejoice that our separated brethren look to Christ as the source and center of ecclesiastical communion." [20]

Challenge to Renewal

The consideration of the many Churches would be incomplete if we did not make it quite clear that as Christians we have no right to resign ourselves to the existence of Churches separated from one another. The reconciliation of men into a single family of God is the very purpose of our redemption. The disunity of the Churches accuses us. It manifests the judgment of God over our personal and corporate infidelity. But since the God of mercy permits evil to gain entry in the world only for the sake of a greater good, we must search for the positive meaning in the sad picture of our divisions. We must learn to see these Churches (and I include here the Roman Catholic Church) as caught up in a movement produced by the Spirit, a movement, which, though threatened by our infidelity and lack of repentance, seeks to reconcile them into a single visible family here on earth. This one Church, Catholics believe, will be in essential continuity with the Roman Catholic Church and, according to the deep conviction of other Christians, it will also be in essential continuity with what they regard as their divine heritage. What counts for the present is that the Churches do not work for the kingdom in isolation from one another, but that having before their eyes the whole of the Christian family, they reform their ecclesiastical life and renew the forms of their apostolate and worship, growing and developing in such a way that the common ground, the basis for which was given once and for all in the Gospel, will increase in depth and extent.

George Flahiff, Archbishop of Winnipeg, Canada, said in a speech delivered at the second session of the Council:

> I am fully convinced that the ecumenical movement is the work of the Holy Spirit through which out of schisms, or better, out of the effort to overcome them, all the Churches profit

> immensely, are challenged to renewal, find new ways of acting in love and come to a deeper understanding of the Gospel. In this ecumenical movement, for the first time in history all the Churches and ecclesial communities witness together to Jesus the Savior, thus giving new vigor to the proclamation of the Gospel in the world." [21]

Since the renewal of the Churches is an essential part of the movement for Christian unity, the Churches engaged in ecumenism do not strive after an ideal in history but strain after a fulfillment that even a single visible Church on earth embracing all Christians could not supply. They reach out toward the heavenly Jerusalem. By engaging herself, therefore, in the ecumenical movement a Church, any Church, becomes more conscious of her pilgrim state and yearns more ardently for the day of Christ's return, and anticipating God's judgment in repentance and God's mercy in eschatological hope, she becomes more truly Church.

Footnotes

[1] *The Ecumenist,* II (July/August 1964), p. 91.
[2] J. C. Hampe, *Ende der Gegenreformation?* (Stuttgart, 1964), p. 330.
[3] Cf. Denz. 2286. [*Editor's note:* Denz. refers to H. Denzinger, *Enchiridion Symbolorum* (Freiburg-Barcelona, 30th ed., 1955). Many of these citations can be found in *The Church Teaches: Documents of the Church in English Translation,* John F. Clarkson, *et al.,* eds. and trans. (St. Louis: B. Herder Book Co., 1955).]
[4] Denz. 2286.
[5] Denz. 2319.
[6] *The Ecumenist,* II (July/August 1964), p. 90.
[7] Constitution on the Church, n. 8.
[8] Decree on Ecumenism, n. 3.
[9] *Council Speeches of Vatican II* (Glen Rock, N.J.: Paulist Press, 1964), pp. 190–91.
[10] Ibid., pp. 37–38.
[11] Constitution on the Church, n. 26.
[12] *Ibid.,* n. 3.
[13] *Ibid.,* n. 11.
[14] Constitution on the Liturgy, n. 2.
[15] *Ibid.,* n. 8.
[16] *Ibid.,* n. 10.
[17] Constitution on the Church, n. 14.
[18] Decree on Ecumenism, n. 15.
[19] *Ibid.,* n. 22.
[20] *Ibid.,* n. 20.
[21] *Council Speeches of Vatican II,* pp. 186–87.

SARA BUTLER, M.S.B.T.

Intercommunion: The State of the Question

This article affords insight not only into the Eucharist as that which unifies and keeps the community in existence but also into the interconfessional discussions that have taken place in recent years in the search for Christian unity. The conclusion of the article contains many important questions, which the author feels need further exploration; the reader should examine them all carefully. What does the author mean by "intercommunion"? What is the distinction between inter- and intraconfessional discussions? What are the forces causing Christian communities to examine their policies of intercommunion? Must individual Christians wait for their particular Church to take the lead in common worship, or can they participate before official assent is given? What does the author see as one of the chief obstacles to intercommunion that is "receding into the background"? What do we mean when we say that the Eucharist is the sacrament of unity? What are the rules governing intercommunion for Catholics?

Sister Sara Butler is at present writing a doctoral dissertation in theology at Fordham University.

The divided state of Christ's Church is nowhere more painfully obvious than in the inability of Christians to celebrate together the

Prepared for the Department of Faith and Order, National Council of the Churches of Christ in the United States of America, as the initial paper of a major study project on intercommunion. Reprinted with the permission of the author and the National Council of the Churches of Christ of the United States of America.

great Sacrament of unity. The pain of this division is compounded by the fact that while some experience this inability as profoundly rooted in a coherent set of beliefs concerning the Church, its ministry and structure, and the Eucharist, others—on the basis of a different conception of these same realities—do not themselves experience any inability but are obliged to suffer the consequences nevertheless. From the outset of the ecumenical movement, few questions have provoked such passionate outbursts of confessional loyalty, holy impatience, and deep anguish as that of intercommunion. Division at the Lord's Table is the concrete translation of as yet unresolved differences in faith and order. Such visible testimony demands attention in a way that keeps the intercommunion question very much alive.

The whole question of whether eucharistic fellowship between separated Christians and their respective Churches is imperative, appropriate, permissible, or simply dishonest is raised within the admittedly abnormal situation of a divided Church.[1] It would not be raised at all except that earnest Christians, removed by generations and even centuries from the circumstances of their division, are actively seeking reconciliation and ultimately some manner of visible unity. Intercommunion, then, has the character of an interim problem posed by an irregular situation; it belongs to the period of transition from separation to full communion.

Interest in intercommunion provides a kind of barometer of progress in the ecumenical movement as a whole, even though there is no general agreement on the degree of correlation between eucharistic sharing and ecclesial union. Because so many of the crucial issues which continue to divide Christians are recapitulated in this question (the role of confessional statements of belief, the nature of the sacrament, the nature and proper ordering of the Church), continued attention to it helps advance mutual understanding on several interrelated fronts simultaneously.

The terms of the intercommunion debate are generally familiar. Clarified quite thoroughly at the Third World Conference on Faith and Order (Lund, Sweden, 1952), they have been restated repeatedly since then. The two basic positions were admirably summarized in a report of the Montreal Faith and Order Conference (1963) as follows:

> Some Christians believe that the degree of ecclesial communion which we have in the body of Christ, through baptism and through our fundamental faith, although we are still divided on some points, urges us to celebrate Holy Communion together and to promote intercommunion between the Churches. It is Christ, present in the Eucharist, who invites all Christians to his table; this direct invitation of Christ cannot be thwarted by ecclesiastical discipline. In the communion of the same holy table, divided Christians are committed in a decisive way to make manifest their total, visible and organic unity.
>
> Some Christians believe that eucharistic communion, being an expression of acceptance of the whole Christ, implies full unity in the wholeness of his truth; that there cannot be any "intercommunion" between otherwise separated Christians; that communion in the sacraments therefore implies a pattern of doctrine and ministry, which is indivisible; and that "intercommunion" cannot presume upon the union in faith that we still seek.
>
> Between these two views of Holy Communion there are others, some approximating to one side, some to the other.[2]

Today, more and more Churches which formerly maintained closed communion have modified their stand and agreed to allow intercommunion under certain limited and controlled conditions. This gradual shifting from closed to limited open communion on the part of certain major Christian Churches is an important indication that the gap is being closed and that the intercommunion impasse is not absolute.

That the several Churches would situate intercommunion differently on the road to organic union is, as J. C. Hoekendijk remarks, well known, "even if it is brought up in each conversation as the latest and most exciting news." [3] Interest in reviewing and comparing the old and newly modified positions of the Churches as they inch forward toward a meeting at the Lord's Table, necessary as this process may be, does not account for the attention being given to intercommunion today. The breakthrough that really characterizes the present moment is located not in the cautious alteration of either communion discipline or theological conviction on the part of ecclesiastical authorities, but in *acts* of intercommunion contrary to existing regulations on the part of persons moved by an experience of their given unity in Christ. The rising incidence of unauthorized intercommunion services is beginning to demand from those responsible theological reflection and ecclesiastical action.

There is, then, a two-pronged effort to force a way through the impasse on intercommunion: on the one hand, theologians and churchmen are soberly, painstakingly working toward what many feel to be the necessary preliminary agreements on matters of faith and order, and consolidating hard won gains in disciplinary changes; on the other, more and more Christians—whether through insight, exuberance, impatience, theological naïveté, or theological sophistication—are taking matters into their own hands in disobedience to Church rules and celebrating the Eucharist together. With deliberations and deeds exerting a reciprocal influence, the pace of the intercommunion discussion has been increased appreciably. Hopes that the old stalemate can be broken are high.

It will be necessary, in stating the question, to consider both the process whereby consensus on faith and order is being advanced (and in some cases achieved and ratified in mergers and covenants for union) and the developments or circumstances productive of the new climate in which intercommunion is fast becoming a fact. Following this, an identification of the major topics needing further exploration will be attempted.

Faith and Order Studies on Intercommunion[4]

The question of intercommunion was forcefully raised from the outset of the ecumenical movement by the simple fact that Christians gathered from the ends of the earth to discuss reunion could not in conscience gather around a single Table to celebrate the sacrament of that unity they hungered for. Although it was proposed at the First World Conference on Faith and Order (Lausanne, 1927) and discussed at the Second (Edinburgh, 1937), not until the Third World Conference (Lund, 1952) was the problem of intercommunion presented and thoroughly studied. The contributions of Lund were many: terms were defined, confessional positions stated, points of agreement and disagreement acknowledged, central problems identified, and guidelines for communion services at ecumenical gatherings proposed.[5]

Faith and Order studies in the post-Lund period are marked by a change in methodology. Once the Churches had become acquainted with one another's positions on the key issues, the shortcomings of the comparative method which had been in use became apparent and it was exchanged for a more strictly theological method founded on an unprejudiced return to the sources. With the exception of the Bossey Consultation on Communion at Ecumenical Gatherings (1961), subsequent studies directed toward resolving the intercommunion problem have taken as their starting point the construction of a common theology of the Holy Eucharist and of worship.[6]

Section IV of the Fourth World Conference on Faith and Order (Montreal, 1963) dealt with intercommunion within the context of the larger concern, "Worship and the Oneness of Christ's Church." This report produced a statement on the Lord's Supper which represents a significant advance over the attempt of Lund some ten years earlier.[7] The Commission on Faith and Order, meeting at Aarhus, Denmark, in August, 1964, proposed a study entitled "Eucharist—Sacrament of Unity" in hopes of following up the growing consensus on the nature of the sacrament and exploring its relation to the unity of the Church.

A Consultation on the Holy Eucharist met at Grandchamp, Switzerland, in July, 1965 to begin this project.[8] Its members proposed that the proper approach to this study required, in terms of method, appreciation of the correlation between Eucharist and Church, fidelity to the biblical evidence, attention to the historical character of the Eucharist (adaptations and developments over the years), and a willingness to distinguish eucharistic reality from eucharistic theology. The topics considered by this consultation were: Baptism and the Eucharist, Ministry and Congregation, aspects of the Eucharist (*anamnesis*, *epiclesis*,[9] consecration, communion, proclamation of the Word), the Eucharist as Reconciliation, the Eucharist as the Act of the Local Church and as Act of the Catholic Church, Sacrifice and Eucharist, the Eucharist as Eschatological Event, and the Eucharist and Prayer. This careful and thorough examination of the Eucharist identified as continuing problems the question of ministry (What authorization is needed? What about apostolic succession?) and of the sacrificial character of the sacrament (Does the Church "offer Christ" to the Father?).

A theological Commission met at Crêt-Bérard, Switzerland, in

April, 1967 to continue work on this study and submitted its report to the Faith and Order Commission of the World Council of Churches meeting at Bristol, England in 1967.[10] In view of the response to the Grandchamp report it concentrated on three points: *Anamnesis* and *Epiclesis*, Catholicity of the Eucharist, Eucharist and *Agape*. Each consideration was seen to have some bearing on intercommunion: a recovery of the *anamnesis* and *epiclesis* as moments in the whole prayer action might resolve difficulties over a special moment of consecration; an appreciation of the relation of every Eucharist to the whole Church might promote recognition of the contribution made by each particular tradition and the extension of mutual recognition; a fuller understanding of the *agape* might encourage this form of interconfessional celebration at ecumenical gatherings.

An Appendix on Intercommunion—the goal of these reflections—enumerated changes which have occurred since the Montreal Conference (widening of ecumenical contacts, impact of liturgical renewal, decisions to permit intercommunion between Churches committed to union, growing sociological pressures toward unity) but recorded that the impasse had not yet been broken. It was pointed out that "as the churches in their eucharistic experience move toward the fullness which is in Christ, the problem of intercommunion will move toward its solution." [11] Further study of the following topics was encouraged: (1) the theology and sociology of disunity, (2) the nature and necessity of the ministry in general and the episcopacy in particular, and (3) the implications of mutual recognition of Baptism for eucharistic sharing. The Commission recommended that a résumé of the emerging ecumenical consensus on the Eucharist be drawn up.

This résumé[12] was prepared for the use of participants at the Fourth Assembly of the World Council of Churches, Uppsala, 1968. Based on statements from Lund, Montreal, and Bristol, this report contributes nothing new, but it successfully synthesizes the gains made in common understanding of the sacrament under the following headings: (1) The Eucharist, the Lord's Supper, (2) Thanksgiving to the Father, (3) Memorial (*anamnesis*) of Christ, (4) Gift of the Spirit, (5) Communion of the body of Christ, (6) Mission to the world, (7) End of divisions. The final section deals with intercommunion and draws chiefly on the Bristol Report.

A report of the Assembly Committee on Faith and Order, Uppsala, 1968,[13] calls attention to some new reasons for continuing to pursue the study of intercommunion, namely, Roman Catholic participation through full membership in the Faith and Order Commission, the significant consensus exhibited in the résumé document, the recent acknowledgment of the ecclesial reality of one Church by another (which recognition would seem to challenge separation at the Eucharist and raise again the Baptism–Eucharist relationship), and the increase in acts of intercommunion beyond ecclesiastical regulations. In addition to the recommendations received, the Assembly Committee suggested: (1) a reclassification of the terms agreed upon at Lund, (2) a re-examination of obstacles in light of the emerging consensus on doctrine, (3) further inquiry into the questions of ordination and conditions for admission to communion, and (4) consideration of issues raised by growing incidence of unauthorized intercommunion.

Section IV of the Uppsala Assembly considered "The Worship of God in a Secular Age." [14] In its final report, "Worship," [15] the centrality of the Eucharist in the life of the Church is reaffirmed, and the following conclusions urged: (1) that all Churches consider celebrating the Eucharist every Sunday, (2) that the desirability of new styles of celebration be considered, (3) that normally all Christians present at eucharistic services should take part in Holy Communion, and (4) that every Church examine again its discipline regarding participation in this sacrament.

It appears that Faith and Order studies of intercommunion have succeeded in drawing the Churches much closer to reconciliation at the Lord's Table than might have been thought possible a few years ago.[16] The need to press forward with the work of reducing and finally eliminating the barriers to this reunion is evident.

Renewal in Eucharistic Theology and Liturgy

The ecumenical experience of division at the Lord's Table has been an important stimulus to a thorough-going re-examination of eucharistic belief and practice. Such re-examination was, however, by no means confined to Faith and Order studies as such. Independently of these, theologians have made great strides toward a *rapprochement* on the most divisive issues—the sacrificial character of the Eucharist and the manner (and duration) of Christ's sacramental presence. In large measure the advances made were rooted in biblical research. It would be premature indeed to claim that all doctrinal differences had been resolved, but it can be said at least that caricatures of earlier days have given way to sympathetic appreciation of the truth of each tradition and a concern to preserve in harmony the complementary aspects of the total mystery.

There has been, for example, a new willingness to consider the sacrificial aspect of the sacrament now that "Catholics" have made it clear they do not intend a separate and autonomous sacrifice independent of the cross, but a mysterious, cultic re-presentation of the one, all-sufficient, unrepeatable self-offering of Christ. Attention to the biblical notion of sacrifice, to the Paschal context of the Last Supper, and to the relationship of the Last Supper to the death and resurrection of Christ has borne fruit. More thoughtful consideration of the way in which the sacramental action of the Church makes present the historically unique events of our redemption brought to light the essential continuity between the cross and the Lord's Supper, while reflection on the unity between Christ and his members resulted in the rediscovery of the reality of the Church's sacrifice as something more than the offering of praise and thanks from the community of believers, but rather a true sharing in the one offering of the Head.

Again, the Roman Catholic re-examination of the classic Tridentine formulation of eucharistic transubstantiation has opened the way to fruitful dialogue. By insisting upon the independence of dogmatic statements from any particular system of philosophy (without denying their reliance on these categories at that moment in history when it was deemed necessary to formulate a position), contemporary theologians have pushed the discussion beyond the impasse of former days. Although the new categories (e.g., transfinalization, transignification) proposed may have difficulties of their own, the common search for an understanding that will both maintain continuity with the past and provide meaning in the present has proved remarkably successful. Generally speaking, one can say that all of eucharistic theology is undergoing a profound transformation through its recent exposure to more biblical, personal, and dynamic thought patterns.

The harvest of all this may be seen not only in the statements of the World Council of Churches and the Faith and Order Commission, but also in the joint statements announcing some measure of doctrinal consensus on the Eucharist issued recently by the following bilateral consultations in this country: Lutheran/Roman Catholic, Disciples of Christ/Roman Catholic,[17] Anglican/Roman Catholic,[18] Lutheran/Reformed,[19] and the statement on "The Lord's Supper" in *Principles of Church Union* adopted by the Consultation on Church Union.[20]

What used to comprise one of the chief obstacles to intercommunion, namely, conflicting interpretations of the meaning of the Lord's Supper, is little by little receding into the background. As one theologian observed recently:

> As time goes on one needs more and more theological expertise to explain how these differences are still relevant, for they hardly play any real part in everyday church life. If this is the case, then theology must no longer be allowed to lag behind the concrete, less reflexive life of faith.[21]

This renewal has both stimulated fresh interest in liturgical theology and been supported by it in Anglican, Protestant, and Roman Catholic circles. There is a well-defined trend to restore the Eucharist to the heart of the Church's life not only in theory but in practice. A searching critique of present practice has prompted more frequent celebration of the sacrament for some and the purification of overgrown eucharistic liturgies for others. A better understanding of the ecclesial significance of Holy Communion appears to have been reached, as the growing demand for intercommunion seems to indicate.

Numerous ecumenical centers, associations, and conferences are devoted primarily to the revitalization of worship. Efforts to provide common translations of the central Christian prayers, to prepare hymnals with an ecumenical scope, and to propose a common ritual for the celebration of the sacraments are being made in the interests of facilitating joint worship.

The recommendations passed at Uppsala that the Lord's Supper be celebrated weekly and that new styles of celebration be considered may indicate a trend in member Churches of the World Council. The advent of new styles is, perhaps, most visible today in the Roman Catholic Church, but it is certainly not restricted to that communion. The success of the liturgical movement is seen even in those *ad hoc* groups which have separated themselves from the parish community in order to experience Christian fellowship more fully in a less structured expression of worship.

It must be admitted that just when this commonly experienced liturgical renewal seemed to be reaching its height, the Churches were brought up short in a new confrontation with the secular, and the "unworldly" activity of formal worship was sharply challenged as irrelevant—an escape from the true responsibility of mission. This challenge is serious, but of itself does not render liturgy irrelevant. It cannot be denied that the Churches have been growing together in a realization of the centrality of the Eucharist, and that this attention to eucharistic doctrine, celebration, and life has proved a significant factor in uniting the divided Church.

Modification in the Positions of the Churches

A glance through any recent bibliography on intercommunion will reveal that the impetus given to the discussion of this old ecumenical problem has come largely from relative newcomers, Roman Catholics. During the course of the Second Vatican Council a significant evolution of the official Catholic attitude toward *communicatio in sacris* [common worship] took place. From the adamant position against any communication in the official worship of dissident Christians expressed in canon law,[22] and reiterated in the first preparatory schema on ecumenism, the bishops moved to the acceptance of a statement of principles which allows the possibility that such *communicatio* (which includes eucharistic sharing) might, when engaged in prudently, be a means for the restoration of unity among Christians. The two principles governing common worship are: "It should signify the unity of the Church; it should provide a sharing in the means of grace. The fact that it should signify unity generally rules out common worship. Yet the gaining of a needed grace sometimes commends it."[23] The application of these principles belongs to the ecclesiastical hierarchy. This application was made with respect to *communicatio in sacris* with the separated Eastern Church;[24] a more lenient policy was adopted, not simply allowing but encouraging some reciprocal sharing in liturgical worship under certain circumstances and with the approval of Church authority. No application was made with respect to other separated brethren during the Council. The authoritative *Directory for the Application of the Decisions of the Second Ecumenical Council of the Vatican Concerning Ecumenical Matters*[25] of May, 1967 confirms and spells out further the decisions relative to Eastern Churches but gives very little help toward applying the same principles in other cases. In the pertinent paragraph (no. 55) it is noted that in light of the first principle—the sign of unity—*communicatio in sacris* is forbidden where oneness in faith, worship, and life is lacking; however, in light of the second principle—sharing in the means of grace—Roman Catholics may for "adequate reasons" admit to their sacraments those separated brothers who spontaneously ask for them and who possess both right faith in these sacraments and the proper dispositions. Roman Catholics in similar circumstances may request the sacraments only from a minister who has been validly ordained (by Roman Catholic standards). The diocesan bishop or episcopal conference is to judge which reasons are "adequate."

Many have noted that the instruction in this paragraph is ambiguous.[26] The examples given to illustrate instances in which exceptions might be made are cases of urgent necessity (danger of death, persecution, imprisonment), even though the phrase "adequate reasons" used above ordinarily connotes less extreme need and might be thought to include reasons of friendship, ecumenical concern, mixed marriage, etc. Another problem is raised with respect to the exercise of authority in admitting non-Catholic Christians to the sacraments. Whereas the Decree on Ecumenism authorizes the local bishop to determine what course should be taken in particular circumstances (giving due regard to "all the circumstances of time, place, personage"), unless the episcopal conference or the Holy See has ruled otherwise, the 1967 *Directory* seems to restrict the grounds for exercising this to the discernment of situations qualifying as "urgent need." Again, the recent "Note on the Application of the Ecumenical Directory"[27] gives a more strict interpretation, requiring as a further condition for sharing the circumstance that the separated brother be unable to approach a minister of his own confession. In the last analysis, this interpretation seems to exclude any "discriminate" use of the sacraments "for the restoration of unity among Christians" when the separated brothers involved are Anglicans or Protestants. Some have asked whether the Secretariat for Promoting Christian Unity has not rendered void a decision of the Ecumenical Council in thus restricting the application of the principle.

In any case, it is clear at least in principle that while common worship (including eucharistic sharing) is forbidden as a general rule, it may be permitted on occasion, under certain conditions. In practice, the sharing allowed and even encouraged with Orthodox Christians will not take place because of reservations on the part of the Orthodox.[28] Anglican and Protestant Christians are to be admitted to the Roman Catholic Eucharist only in cases of urgent necessity. Several Roman Catholic theologians have suggested that a limited and controlled sharing with the latter would be a responsible though "imperfect" expression of our present state of "imperfect" ecclesial unity. Others insist that such sharing must be delayed until satisfactory agreement has been reached on the nature of the Eucharist and on the ministry.[29]

Only a few years ago (when Yves Congar wrote an essay in the Lund volume, *Intercommunion*), the entrance of Roman Catholics into the ecumenical movement would have meant a heavy tipping of the balance in the direction of closed communion, since at that time their ecclesiological position was nearly identical to that of Eastern Orthodoxy. This classic position was revised significantly, however, during the Council. Many theologians believe that when the full implications of the Constitution on the Church and the Decree on Ecumenism have been worked out, especially in respect to the ecclesial reality of other Christian Churches, there will be room for intercommunion.

There has been an equally dramatic shift in the official position of the Anglican Communion. From the early days of the ecumenical movement, an abundance of Anglican ink has been spilled on the question of intercommunion, much of it in an intra-Church debate between Catholics and Evangelicals. Recently the question was reopened, roundly discussed, and eventually summarized by the Archbishops' Commission on Intercommunion for presentation to the 1968 Lambeth Conference. The report, *Intercommunion Today*, contains an excellent survey of the question, a fine delineation of different positions and the reasons behind them, and an improved set of terms for carrying on the discussion.[30] Modification of regulations for admitting individuals to Holy Communion and for reception of Holy Communion in other than Anglican Churches was expected and had, in fact, been anticipated in some of the younger Churches. Members of the Commission were unable, however, to reach agreement on the vexed question of reciprocal intercommunion between episcopal and nonepiscopal Churches, a question of more than theoretical importance in view of the pending union of the Church of England with the (English) Methodist Church. The bishops at Lambeth decided in favor of the more lenient policy advised by the majority of the Commission members. The following resolutions on intercommunion were adopted:

1. That Baptized non-Anglicans, under the direction of the bishop, be admitted to Holy Communion in Anglican Churches "in order to meet special pastoral needs."
2. That Anglicans be free to receive Holy Communion in other Churches "holding the Apostolic Faith as contained in the Apostles' and Nicene Creeds," again, "under the general direction of the bishop, to meet special pastoral needs."
3. That when Churches have agreed on Faith and Order and have committed themselves to seek unity, reciprocal acts of communion be allowed.[31]

There is no single policy-making body in world Lutheranism to effect a similar change, but the achievement of consensus and altar fellowship in three specific instances since 1955 strongly indicates that a wedge has been driven in the strict Lutheran policy of closed communion. It has been suggested that these three agreements—The Agreed Statement on the Lord's Supper (Lutherans and the Church of South India), Consensus on the Holy Communion (Lutheran Church in Holland and the Dutch Reformed Church), and the Arnoldshain Lord's Supper Theses (Lutherans and the Evangelical Church of Germany)—provide models for further negotiations.[32] Among Lutheran bodies in the United States, the Lutheran Church in America now encourages eucharistic sharing and intercelebration within Lutheranism (at the invitation of the host Church) and permits reception of the sacrament with non-Lutherans under certain circumstances; the American Lutheran Church admits confirmed members of Lutheran congregations, provided they give evidence of sincere repentance and right faith, although pastors may with discretion admit nonmembers who fulfill the other requirements.[33] At the conclusion of the American conversations between members of the Lutheran and Reformed traditions in 1966, pulpit and altar fellowship appeared to be a distinct possibility in the future.[34]

Of the major Churches which in the past had a policy of closed communion, only the Eastern Orthodox Churches have maintained this stand unequivocally. The Roman Catholic invitation to some limited degree of intercommunion prompted a reaffirmation of the traditional position in the form of a Patriarchal Encyclical on Intercommunion from Athenagoras I of Constantinople, March, 1967.[35] While the majority of Orthodox theologians are opposed to intercommunion, some few adopt a more lenient position, and Greek Orthodox Archbishop Athenagoras of Great Britain recently issued a call *for* intercommunion as a means toward unity.[36]

Progress in Interconfessional Conversations

Daily one reads of new contacts made, new alliances formed, new lines of communication set up among the Churches. In numerous cases since the onset of the ecumenical movement, increased contact has led to formal mergers, both intra- and interconfessional. In many parts of the world active Church union negotiations are under way. In the United States alone there have been some ten mergers in the past twelve years. Of special importance today in our country is the Consultation on Church Union, which numbers nine Churches among its active participants and nineteen as observer–consultants.

It was suggested at the Bossey Consultation that the context of an active and mutually pledged search for organic union provides a clearly responsible basis for eucharistic sharing. The "covenant for union" firmly declares each party's intention of achieving this goal, and reciprocal intercommunion is understood to be a necessary, joint appeal for this grace as well as a tangible expression of mutual acceptance.

Bilateral conversations, meetings between representatives of two confessional families desiring to become better acquainted, have multiplied rapidly in the past few years. Even when such meetings do not represent a step toward formal union negotiations, they stand to contribute greatly to advancing the growing consensus on the critical issues which continue to divide the Church. These conversations provide excellent forums for theological reflection and exploration; they have stimulated not only some very important papers but also some significant statements of consensus on various thorny topics. While these groups have no authority to speak for their respective Churches, they promise to do much toward clearing the ground of obstacles to eventual union. It is noteworthy that intercommunion has been the formal topic for discussion in numerous bilateral conversations.[37]

In this country, intercommunion has been considered by the Lutheran/Reformed, Anglican/Roman Catholic, Orthodox/Roman Catholic, Lutheran/Roman Catholic, and Disciples of Christ/Roman Catholic consultation groups. Briefly, the outcomes of these considerations are as follows:

Lutheran/Reformed: After an initial statement to the effect that intercommunion could not be considered due to different views of the relation of doctrine to the unity of the Church, members of the conversation revised their position and concluded that intercommunion is "not only permissible but demanded wherever there is agreement in the gospel," but prohibited where this gospel is denied. The revision is evidently based on consideration (1) of the obligation to manifest existing unity publicly, (2) of the modern context (mobile population, anonymity of urban life) (February 1966).

Anglican/Roman Catholic: Since their second meeting (February 1966) on the Eucharist as sign and cause of unity, ARC members have concerned themselves with barriers to intercommunion. At their fourth meeting (May 1967), they announced substantial agreement on the doctrine of eucharistic sacrifice. At the conclusion of their fifth meeting (January 1968) on the role of the priesthood, it was announced that minor differences on this question "do not in themselves constitute a barrier to the two churches celebrating and receiving Communion together."

Orthodox/Roman Catholic: A joint statement released by members of this consultation (May 1967) announced that the possibility of intercommunion is excluded because the Eucharist cannot be isolated from the total life of the community in which it is celebrated; intercommunion does not respect the necessary link between the bishop and the communicant.

Lutheran/Roman Catholic: A fourteen-page statement outlining beliefs on the Eucharist as sacrifice and the presence of Christ in the Lord's Supper was issued by this consultation after its fifth meeting (September 1967). The statement records substantial agreement on the former topic and some disagreement on the latter (concerning the manner of Christ's presence). Their sixth consultation (March 1968) had intercommunion as its topic. It was concluded that consensus on this issue awaited study of "the entire problem of the ministry." A joint statement issued at the conclusion of the study on ministry indicated that further exploration of this and related topics was required (September 1968).

Disciples of Christ/Roman Catholic: This consultation discussed "A Responsible Theology for Eucharistic Intercommunion in Our Divided Church" at its third meeting (May 1968) and issued a statement recording certain points of agreement about the Eucharist and the concluding: "We have found sufficient theological justification *in principle* for some eucharistic sharing." The members strongly urged the promotion of this for "theological, ecumenical, and especially pastoral reasons." [38]

An overview of contemporary discussions of intercommunion, taking these conversations as representative, reveals that the resolution of this question rests upon the achievement of consensus on certain controlling issues: the Eucharist, the Church, the nature of the Church's unity, the ministry. Because of the integral interrelationship of these doctrines, it is profitable to reassess frequently the gains made in any one area and set it in the context of the whole. Intercommunion serves as an excellent focal point for doing this.

Pastoral Considerations and New Directions

The Bristol Report has pointed to the "unprecedented widening of ecumenical contacts" and the power of "sociological pressures" as factors promoting the desire for intercommunion. Real hope that Christians are serious about doing together all that they can is offered by the growing number of federated parishes, the opening of experimental parishes with shared facilities and team ministries, the collaboration of seminaries, theology and religion departments in the academic world, the success of ecumenical institutes, workshops, retreats, "living-room dialogues," joint educational programs, youth organizations, and interfaith service groups. As individuals and congregations grow together through these means in understanding and appreciation of one another, the division at the Lord's Table becomes more of a scandal to them. The impossibility of sealing an experienced Christian unity with eucharistic fellowship becomes painful in a concrete way and invites action to remove the barriers. This spontaneous desire to join in Holy Communion has begun to generate more and more pressure on Church officials to permit it.[39]

Many are not seeking or waiting for permission. They believe the fellowship experience of an ecumenical gathering or of a rather stable natural community (e.g., students living at a university or seminary, mixed marriage) warrants eucharistic expression. Among the groups most likely to take Holy Communion together are those joined in pursuit of a Gospel ideal embodied in some common social or political cause. Christians engaged in a joint inner-city mission, a civil rights demonstration, and anti-Vietnam war protest, for example, seem most ready to mark their brotherhood in Christ by a Communion service. Their experience of oneness in these settings matches and probably far surpasses the sense of community they feel with certain members of their own parish, their own clergy, and hierarchy. They may be worlds apart from "their own" on all the questions which matter most in the business of living and witnessing here and now, while they are "of one heart and one mind" with their "separated" brethren. Regulations proposed on the basis of institutional criteria of membership are not found very compelling when serious ideological cleavages exist within that institution.

The "underground" or "free" Church is often the result of new alignments founded on a common understanding of the Christian ethic in the modern world. The drawing power of an established body is diminished in proportion to the enthusiasm awakened by "Church" experienced as event in a gathering alive with Christian purpose and a sense of common mission. Intercommunion in the contemporary group-church speaks a message that churchmen will ignore at their peril.

In still another category fall those modern Christians for whom reform from within is not enough. These revolutionaries are totally disenchanted with the forms and structures, the symbols and liturgies of a now defunct Christendom. The question of intercommunion, not to mention the entire dream of an organically united Church, is simply no concern of theirs; its problems of doctrinal orthodoxy and ministerial validity could not worry them less. As the Introduction of the Report of the Archbishop of Canterbury's Commission on Intercommunion candidly acknowledges:

> When the credibility of speaking at all about God is at stake, and men doubt whether the Christian religion has a relevant word to speak on nuclear annihilation or race conflict or mass starvation, the domestic differences among Christians as to how far they can worship God together may seem almost blasphemously trivial.[40]

It must be admitted, then, that the ecclesistical frame of reference within which the whole problem occurs is found scandalously provincial by many who have lately revealed their sentiments by voting with their feet. This does not mean that theologians may dismiss the intercommunion problem—for it matters a great deal to much larger numbers—but it is important that they situate the whole issue as realistically as possible. This means recognizing the limits of the ecclesiastical viewpoint and trying to keep the Church's mission to the world within the horizon of their considerations.

Topics Needing Further Exploration

It has been noted that the discussion of intercommunion forces to the surface one's presuppositions about the nature of the Eucharist, the Church, the ministry; it also reveals one's view of doctrinal statements and one's general frame of reference. As agreement is approached or reached on any of these topics, the possibility of resolving the intercommunion question grows. On this understanding, the following points are suggested for further investigation.

1. Doctrinal Consensus: Its Possibilities and Its Limitations

What is the worth of consensus statements?

Which are the remaining problem areas? Are the differing views antithetical or merely complementary?

What are the possibilities and limitations of any doctrinal formulation? How great is the need for an authentic, normative teaching? What purpose does it serve?

What is the relationship of doctrine to faith? How is the faith of the faithful tested or determined? What do the debates of theologians mean to the simple faithful? May eucharistic doctrine be distinguished from eucharistic theology?

How are doctrinal views influenced by liturgical practice? What is the role of liturgical renewal in effort to arrive at consensus in doctrine?

2. Communion, Intracommunion, Intercommunion: Ecclesiological Presuppositions

What correlation is there between one's policy on intercommunion and one's ecclesiology?

How far have the Churches come towards a common ecclesiology? To what extent is this a "eucharistic ecclesiology"? What is the relation of eucharistic communion to ecclesial communion? Is it appropriate to subordinate one to the other as means to end?

Does the present imperfection of ecclesial unity allow us to tolerate a certain "imperfect" eucharistic unity? Can the Church *in via* hope for perfect communion?

What is our vision, our expectation for the future union of the Church? Would mutual recognition manifested in eucharistic sharing itself constitute the union of the Church?

How is it that the unity acknowledged as the effect of our Baptism cannot be manifested in a common Eucharist?

3. The Bishop, the Eucharist, and the Unity of the Church

How has the episcopal office functioned as a sign or "sacrament" of unity in the history of the Church? Is this office essential to the Church?

How is the celebration of the Eucharist in the local Church linked to the Catholic Church except through the bishop? Is not the bishop's role as high priest and guardian of the Eucharist related to ecclesial communion?

Can the Eucharist be a true expression of the nature of the Church when the ecclesial communion between bishops is broken?

What must the relationship between the bishop and the communicant be for the sacrament to be a true sign of unity? What measure of allegiance or recognition must the communicant give? Must it extend to the bishop's authority as teacher? His juridical authority? Is eucharistic communion possible where this allegiance is not given? What commitment does the communicant make by sharing in the Eucharist authorized by the bishop?

4. The Celebrant of the Eucharist: Problems in Church Order

What does it mean to say that the whole Church celebrates the Eucharist? What is the relationship between the universal priesthood and the ministerial priesthood?

Who may celebrate the Eucharist? Is episcopal ordination essential for a valid ministry? Does the irregular situation of ecclesial division constitute an emergency in the life of the Church? Are there other ways of ascertaining a valid ministry than in terms of episcopal ordination? Does the line of apostolic tradition in some way incorporate apostolic succession? Does a man's function as celebrant of the Eucharist with the authorization of his local Church constitute him a "valid" minister?

What is the relationship of valid ministry to valid Eucharist? What is the precise meaning of validity? Does the recognition of the ecclesial reality of another Church imply recognition of its ministry and sacraments?

5. *Communion Discipline in an Ecumenical Age*

Has the communion discipline of apostolic and patristic times any pertinence today, or does the present situation of division make the application of those norms impossible?

Are there any limits on the Church's role as guardian of the Eucharist? What might be the ill effects of exercising an excessively rigid control? of failing to exercise any control? Does failure to exercise control indicate failure to appreciate the place of the Eucharist in the life of the Church, or does it rather indicate a sensitivity to the communicant's need to be responsible for this decision (and the Church's corresponding inability to determine his dispositions)?

What should the conditions for admission to communion be: on the part of the communicant? in relation to the minister? the bishop? Can Church law adequately take into account any except the external factors in a given case? What is the place of "economy" and dispensation? Could a given context (e.g., an ecumenical gathering) change the conditions for admission? Should nonbelievers ever be admitted?

If a Church makes exceptions for individuals on the basis of pastoral need, can it not extend these exceptions to cover the need of a divided Church? Are we not presently in a state of emergency? Where does admission of individuals stop and open communion begin?

6. *Divisions in the Church, Old and New*

To what extent are doctrinal differences interrelated with and reinforced by such factors as geographical, national, and social divisions?

What is the effect of divisions *within* the Churches on unity efforts? Will the fact that the lines of theological and ideological controversy today cross denominational lines contribute to or retard dialogue? What is the influence of nontheological factors on these new alignments and new divisions?

What is the role of the Eucharist as agent of reconciliation and source of unity?

7. *The Sacrament for the World*

How can the Church contribute to the growing pressure toward unity felt in the human family today if it is racked by internal division, if it cannot manifest its unity at the Lord's Table? How can the Church serve this unity if the Churches are unwilling to die to their own ways?

What has the contemporary theological effort to heal the split between the sacred and the secular to say concerning the Eucharist? Does the nature of a sacrament admit different degrees of realization? Is there not a continuity between nonsacrament and sacrament which can be explained in terms of the relative explicitness of the sign? At what point does the secular (meal) become an earthly point of articulation for the sacred (eucharistic meal)? What can be said of stages in between: the *agape*, the shalom meal?

Why is the Church's stewardship of the Eucharist so strict whereas it eagerly shares with all its other forms of worship (formal and free prayer, Sacred Scripture)? What is the truth of J.-J. von Allmen's insight that "the Lord's Supper [is] a crucible which brings together all that makes the Gospel specific. . . . [It] is the one element of the Church's life which the world cannot reduce to that which is characteristic of itself." [41]

Appendix I

Terminology on Intercommunion as Defined in the Report of Lund 1952

1. *Full Communion* (though the adjective need rarely be used): where Churches in doctrinal agreement, or of the same confessional family, allow communicant members freely to communicate at the altars of each, and where there is freedom of ministers to officiate sacramentally in either Church (i.e., Intercelebration). . . .

2. *Intercommunion and Intercelebration:* where two Churches not of

the same confessional family, by agreement allow communicant members freely to communicate at the altars of each, and where there is freedom of ministers to officiate sacramentally in either Church. . . .

3. *Intercommunion:* where two Churches, not of the same confessional family, by agreement allow communicant members freely to communicate at the altars of each. . . .

4. *Open Communion:* where a Church on principle invites members of other Churches to receive communion when they are present at its communion services. . . .

5. *Mutual Open Communion:* where two or more Churches on principle invite each other's members and the members are free to accept the invitation. This does not necessarily involve intercelebration.

6. *Limited Open Communion* (Communion by Economy or Dispensation): the admission of members of other Churches not in full communion or intercommunion to the Sacrament in cases of emergency or in other special circumstances.

7. *Closed Communion:* where a Church limits participation in the Lord's Supper to its own members.

Appendix II

Definition of Terms Accepted by Report of the Section on the Renewal of the Church in Unity of the 1968 Lambeth Conference.

Full Communion involves mutual recognition of ministers and members (e.g., the relationship between Churches of the Anglican Communion).

Reciprocal Intercommunion is the occasional and reciprocal sharing in the Eucharist by members of Churches which are seeking, but have not yet achieved, full communion or organic union. This reciprocal intercommunion arises from a relationship between Churches and necessarily involves the mutual consent of the Churches concerned.

Admission to Communion is the practice of controlled admission to communion where a particular Church defines not only its own domestic discipline but also the condition under which the communicants of other Churches may be welcomed to receive Holy Communion.

Open Communion is the practice whereby one particular Church welcomes all baptized communicant members of other Churches to receive communion on occasion within its fellowship.

Free Communion is the practice of inviting to the Lord's Table "all who love the Lord Jesus" irrespective of whether they have a Church affiliation or are in good standing with their own communion, or even whether they are baptized.

Footnotes

[1] Not all Christians, of course, would care to employ the expression "divided Church." The Orthodox have repeatedly stated their conviction that the unity of the Church is preserved in their communion. Likewise, some Roman Catholics are still reluctant to use a phrase which tends to obscure the unique status and role they believe their Church to have with respect to unity.

[2] *The Fourth World Conference on Faith and Order, Montreal, 1963,* Patrick C. Rodger and Lukas Vischer, eds. (New York: Association Press, 1964), p. 78.

[3] *The Church Inside Out,* eds. L. A. Hoedemaker and Pieter Tijmes, tr. Isaac C. Rottenberg (Philadelphia: The Westminster Press, 1966), p. 154. Chap. 9, "Safety Last," is a very provocative contribution to the intercommunion discussion.

[4] Cf. three recent dissertations: Herman Docx, "Le problème de l'intercommunion dans le mouvement 'Foi et Constitution' pendant la période Lund-Montréal–Bristol, 1952–1963–1967" (Doctoral dissertation, Louvanium, Kinshasa, 1968); Thomas Foley, "Intercommunion in the World Council of Churches" (Doctoral dissertation, Gregorian University, Rome, 1964); Leo J. Steady, "Intercommunion in the Faith and Order Movement" (Doctoral dissertation, University of Ottawa, 1964).

[5] Cf. *Intercommunion*: Report of the Theological Commission Appointed by the Continuation Committee of the World Conference on Faith and Order, eds. Donald Marsh and John Marsh (London: SCM Press, 1952). For the Lund definitions, consult Appendix I, p. 99.

[6] The influence of the development of a number of topics closely related to intercommunion cannot be underestimated, viz., "The Church's Unity" (New Delhi, 1961), "The Church in the Purpose of God," "The Redemptive Work of Christ and the Ministry of His Church," "'All in Each Place': The Process of Growing Together" (Montreal, 1963).

[7] *The Fourth World Conference,* pp. 69–76. Cf. also the section "Communion Services at Ecumenical Gatherings," pp. 76–80.

[8] Cf. "The Holy Eucharist" [an interim report from the WCC Faith and Order Commission Consultation at Grandchamp, Switzerland, July 19–25, 1965], *Study Encounter,* XI (1966), pp. 57–61. Members of the consultation discussed papers by L. Vischer and J.-J. von Allmen, later published. Cf. Lukas Vischer, "Questions on the Eucharist, Its Past and Future Celebration," *Studia Liturgica,* V (1966), pp. 65–86; J.-J. von Allmen, "Some Notes on the Lord's Supper," *Study Encounter,* XI (1966), pp. 54–57, later revised and published as *Essai sur le repas du Seigneur* (Neuchâtel: Delachaux et Niestlé, 1966).

[9] By *anamnesis* is understood the effective calling to mind of God's mighty deeds in Christ through proclamation and cultic re-presentation; by *epiclesis,* the invocation of the Holy Spirit upon the people of God and the whole eucharistic action.

[10] *New Directions in Faith and Order. Bristol, 1967. Reports–Minutes–Documents.* Faith and Order Paper No. 50 (Geneva: World Council of Churches, 1968), pp. 60–68.

[11] *Ibid.*, p. 68.

[12] This résumé has been published under the title "The Eucharist in Ecumenical Thought," in *Study Encounter,* IV (1968), pp. 153–58.

[13] *Ibid.*

[14] *Drafts for Sections* prepared for the Fourth Assembly of the World Council of Churches, Uppsala, Sweden, 1968 (Geneva: World Council of Churches, 1968), pp. 96–102.

[15] *Uppsala Speaks:* Section Reports of the Fourth Assembly of the World Council of Churches, Uppsala, 1968, ed. Norman Goodall (Geneva: World Council of Churches, 1968), pp. 74–85.

[16] "The Eucharist in Ecumenical Thought," p. 154.

[17] Cf. *Unity Trends,* I (February 15, 1968), pp. 6–10; *idem,* I (June 1, 1968), pp. 12–13.

[18] Cf. *The Ecumenist,* VI (November–December, 1967), p. 112.

[19] Cf. *Marburg Revisited,* eds. Paul C. Empie and James I. McCord (Minneapolis, Minn.: Augsburg Publishing House, 1966), pp. 103–4.

[20] *Principles of Church Union,* adopted by the Consultation on Church Union at its meeting (Cincinnati: Forward Movement Publications, 1968), pp. 40–43.

[21] B. A. Willems, "Room for Intercommunion," *One in Christ,* IV (1968), pp. 250–60.

[22] *Codex Iuris Canonici,* canons 731 (and 2364), 1258 (and 2316), 882, 2261, 2252.

[23] Decree on Ecumenism (*Unitatis Redintegratio*), article 8 (Abbott ed., *The Documents of Vatican II,* p. 352).

[24] *Ibid.,* article 15; Decree on the Eastern Catholic Churches, articles 26–29 (Abbott ed., pp. 358f., 282–85).

[25] Secretariat for Promoting Christian Unity, *Directory for the Application of the Decisions of the Second Ecumenical Council of the Vatican Concerning Ecumenical Matters,* May 14, 1967 (Washington, D.C.: United States Catholic Conference, 1967).

[26] E.g., Gregory Baum, "'Communicatio in Sacris' in the Decree on Ecumenism," *One in Christ,* III (1967), pp. 417–28; *idem,* "Liturgy and Unity," *The Ecumenist,* VI (November–December, 1967), pp. 97–100; Jean Corbon, "La *communicatio in sacris* dans les Églises d'Orient: Comment se pose la question aujourd'hui?" *Proche Orient Chrétien,* II–III–IV (1967), pp. 126–40; Godfrey Diekmann, "Inter-Communion: Its Ecumenical Dimensions and Problems," *IDO-C* [*Information Documentation on the Conciliar Church*] No. 68–38 (September 22, 1968), pp. 2–11; Robert E. Hunt, "Eucharistic Sharing: Roman Catholic Church Today," *Mid Stream,* VII, No. 2 (Winter 1968), pp. 65–84.

[27] Augustin Cardinal Bea, The Secretariat for the Union of Christians, *L'Osservatore Romano,* No. 29 (October 17, 1968). This "Note" is generally believed to be a response to the intercommunion at the Second Conference of Latin American Bishops (CELAM), Medellin, Colombia. Five non-Roman Catholic observers who requested to receive the Eucharist were permitted to

do so by the ranking Catholic bishops. Cf. "Ecumenical Notes," *The Ecumenist,* VI (September–October, 1968), p. 189.

[28] Cf. Athenagoras I, *Patriarchal Encyclical on Intercommunion, Diakonia,* II (1967), pp. 179–80, and *Guidelines for the Orthodox in Ecumenical Relations,* published by the Standing Conference of Canonical Orthodox Bishops in America and commended to the clergy for guidance, written by the Reverend Leonidas Contos [1966]. Cf. also *Diakonia,* I, No. 4 (1966) for several articles on the question of Roman Catholic–Orthodox intercommunion.

[29] Those in favor: G. Baum, J. Corbon, R. E. Hunt (*supra,* n. 26); Thomas E. Ambrogi, "Roman Catholics and Intercommunion: Changing Perspectives," *Experiments in Community*: Twenty-eighth North American Liturgical Week, XXVIII (1967), pp. 152–58; Eugene C. Bianchi, "A Case for Intercommunion," *America,* CXIX (August 31, 1968), pp. 125–27; Bernard Cooke, "Eucharist: Source or Expression of Community?" *Worship,* XL (June–July, 1966), pp. 339–48; Hans Küng, "Intercommunion," *Journal of Ecumenical Studies,* V (Summer 1968), pp. 576–78; Daniel J. O'Hanlon, "Limited Open Communion," *The American Church News,* XXXI (May 1964), p. 9; Martin Redfern, "Freedom of Worship: Intercommunion," in *Christians and World Freedom,* ed. L. Bright (London: Sheed and Ward Stagbook, 1966), pp. 48–97; Franz Jozef vanBeeck, "Towards an Ecumenical Understanding of the Sacraments," *Journal of Ecumenical Studies,* III (Winter 1966), pp. 57–112. Those opposed: Diekmann (*supra,* n. 26); Jerome Hamer, "Stages on the Road to Unity: The Problem of Intercommunion," *One in Christ,* IV (1968), pp. 235–49; *idem,* "Why Not Intercommunion?" *America,* CXVIII (June 1, 1968), pp. 734–37; Bernard Leeming, "Again Intercommunion," *The Heythrop Journal,* IX (January 1968), pp. 17–28. Those "in favor" advocate limited and controlled intercommunion, or more precisely, admission to communion; those "opposed" would restrict any *communicatio* in the Eucharist to cases of urgent individual need.

[30] *Intercommunion Today:* The Report of the Archbishop of Canterbury's Commission on Intercommunion (London: The Church Information Office, 1968). Abbreviated definition of terms from Chap. 3 is given in Appendix II, p. 100.

[31] "Ecumenical Aspects of the Lambeth Conference," unpublished release from the office of Dr. Peter Day, Ecumenical Officer of the Episcopal Church.

[32] Cf. Eugene M. Skibbe, *Protestant Agreement on the Lord's Supper* (Minneapolis, Minn.: Augsburg Publishing House, 1968).

[33] Cf. "Positions of the Churches on Intercommunion," *Unity Trends,* II (November 15, 1968), pp. 4–5.

[34] *Marburg Revisited,* p. 183.

[35] *Supra,* n. 28.

[36] N. Afanassieff, "L'Eucharistie, principale lien entre les Catholiques et les Orthodoxes," *Irénikon,* XXXVIII (1965), pp. 337–39; H. Symeon, "The Eucharist as the Sacrament of Unity," *Sobornost,* IV (1964), pp. 637–50; L. Zander, "Réflexions sur les problèmes oecuméniques du jour," *Le Messager Orthodoxe,* XXIV–XXXV (1963–1964), pp. 33–39; *Unity Trends,* II (January 1, 1969), p. 11.

[37] The most recent and complete resume of these may be found in "Ecumenical Notes and Documentation: The Eucharist, Intercommunion, Ministry," *One in Christ,* IV (1968), pp. 288–302. This entire issue of *One in Christ* is worth consulting.

[38] For Lutheran/Reformed, cf. *Marburg Revisited,* pp. 103–4, 183. For Anglican/Roman Catholic, cf. *One in Christ,* II (1966), pp. 302–5, and IV (1968), pp. 298–300. For Orthodox/Roman Catholic, *Diakonia,* II (1967), pp. 183–86. For Lutheran/Roman Catholic, *The Eucharist as Sacrifice,* "Lutherans and Catholics in Dialogue III," published jointly by Representatives of the U.S.A. National Committee of the Lutheran World Federation and the Bishops' Committee for Ecumenical and Interreligious Affairs, 1967, and *One in Christ,* IV (1968), pp. 300–301. For Disciples of Christ/Roman Catholic, *Mid-Stream,* VII, No. 2 (Winter, 1968).

[39] Cf. *One in Christ,* IV (1968), pp. 283ff. Mention is made here of the resolution passed by the first Ecumenical Conference on Christian Worship, petitioning common eucharistic celebrations during the Week of Prayer for Christian Unity. A similar resolution was passed at the Fifth National Workshop on Christian Unity at Detroit in June, 1968.

[40] *Intercommunion Today,* p. xiv.

[41] von Allmen, *Study Encounter,* XI, p. 54.

CHARLES DAVIS and
JOHN L. McKENZIE, S.J.

Is the Catholic Church Relevant Today?

The main body of this selection is a statement by Charles Davis, a highly respected theologian and until recently a Catholic priest. What is the importance of pointing out that statements about the Church are sociological as well as theological? What does Mr. Davis mean when he says that the Church is corrupt? Why does he make such an issue of the statements of Vatican I? Why didn't he feel that he could remain within the Catholic Church and try to reform it? Is he correct in his use of the concept of doctrinal development? Would his concept of the Church as movement lead to anarchy in the Church? What are Mr. Davis' views on the sacramental life? How are we to understand Father McKenzie's feeling that the statements of Vatican I need correction?

Charles Davis is Visiting Professor of Religious Studies at the University of Alberta, Edmonton. He taught theology at Heythrop College and St. Edmund's College in England.

John L. McKenzie, S.J. is an American biblical scholar; at present he is a Professor of Theology at the University of Notre Dame.

Mr. Davis on the Question: Is the Catholic Church Relevant Today? [1]

A decision to leave the Church can be explained only in relation to what the Church is. Now, in one sense I have left the Church.

This article first appeared as a tape recording by Argus Communications. It is transcribed and printed here with the permission of the copyright holders, Argus Communications.

I have severed my formal allegiance to the Roman Catholic body. In another sense I have not left the Church. I'm still a Christian adhering to the community of Christ and, indeed, acknowledging that I do so with the Roman Catholic tradition as my particular inheritance. There are then two possible meanings of the word Church. I need to explain my decision in relation to each of these.

For the first meaning of the Church I will quote these words of Pope Paul VI in a general audience of the twenty-fifth of May, 1966.

> The Church is like a city, a *civitas*. And what is a city? More than a place to live in, a number of houses. It is a gathering of individuals, families, tribes, human groupings, gathered to form a society to which, by an authority and by its own laws, homogeneity and autonomy are granted. It is a society unified and administered by a distinctive social *ius*, or law. If we consider its ethnic, historical, and linguistic elements we can speak of a nation. If we consider it from a juridical point of view it is a state. Thus the Church is precisely a juridical, organized, visible, perfect society or community. Let us remember that classical definition of St. Robert Bellarmine: "The Church, the gathering of the people who confess the same Christian faith, unified by participation in the same sacrament, under the direction of lawful shepherds and especially the Pope of Rome."

I consider it important, in discussing the papal statement, to notice that it is not simply a theological statement but, of its nature, also a sociological statement. Much talk about the Church is intellectually useless because of a failure to recognize the sociological implications of statements about the Church in the concrete. Such talk is equivalent to biblical interpretation that ignores the critical historical method. Just as biblical interpretation must now be wedded to the method of historical criticism, so too with the advance of the social sciences, ecclesiology must make use of sociological method when it discusses the Church in the concrete. Otherwise one finds the result deplored by the sociologist Peter Berger, himself a Christian, in *The Noise of Solemn Assemblies*.

> What can happen here with frightening ease is that ecclesiology becomes an escape from social reality, the reality of the world as much as the reality of the religious institution.

> One then constructs an ecclesiological structure, perhaps one that is theologically impeccable. And then one lives in the illusion that this structure can be found in the empirical Churches in which one worships, and not to be forgotten, which often pay one's salary.

To return to the Pope's statement. Considered as theology, namely, as an account of the nature of the Church drawn from the sources of faith, it is poor and inadequate theology. Most theologians today would want severely to criticize it, they would want to supplement it and correct its one-sidedness, and some would question it even more radically. However, I think it should be stressed that the elements from which the Pope constructs his concepts of the Church are vigorously reaffirmed in the latest Church documents, those of the Second Vatican Council. If they are there counterbalanced by other elements, they are still retained. For example, the papal primacy of jurisdiction solemnly defined at First Vatican is emphatically reiterated by Second Vatican together with the duty of submitting to it. All the same I freely admit that the Pope's statement does not represent the best Roman Catholic theology today. Nevertheless, if one considers it from a sociological viewpoint the Pope's statement is verifiably true. Sociological statements refer to the Churches insofar as they are social institutions subject to empirical investigation according to the principles and methods of sociology. Any statement about a Church in the concrete, because it deals with facts, has an aspect that is open to sociological inquiry.

Now, I think it is fair to say that any sociologist would recognize the existence of a social collectivity called the Catholic Church, which organizes itself juridically as a visible society, makes its own laws, imposes conditions of belief and discipline upon its members, independently administers its life and activity as a social body, and in particular is distinguished by the required adherence of its members to the Roman Pontiff as the vicegerent of Christ. This social collectivity is not limited to members of the ecclesiastical hierarchy. Within its visible boundaries as a society it embraces a multitude of ordinary members. Admittedly, sociologically speaking, this religious body is marked by sharp distinction between a clerical and lay class with a tendency, disputed in theory but rampant in practice, to reduce the laity to an inferior associate membership. Nonetheless, the juridical structure of the society includes both clergy and laity within itself, though with a varying hold and impact upon each group.

It remains true, however, to speak of the whole society as hierarchically structured in the sense that down to its least member it is hierarchically governed and administered. And further that membership is available only in relation to the hierarchy understood as mediating the saving gifts promised to Christ's followers in the Church. Now, whether the theology of the Church as a juridical, organized, visible, perfect society came after the social reality as a subsequent doctrinal legitimation or that theology preceded and gave birth to the social reality may here be left an open question.

The point is that the Church described by the Pope is a social reality. The Pope may have given his description in the form of a theological statement but whatever its theological value it undoubtedly has reference to a verifiable social fact. I should add that a sociologist would observe that the powerful social collectivity called the Catholic Church is now in a state of unusual turmoil, the outcome of which is still uncertain. There has been a rapid spread of insubordination among both laity and clergy due to the inrush of ideas long resisted and kept at bay, and this is seriously threatening the structure of authority. But the revolutionary forces have not yet been successful, and the juridical and administrative structure of this organized religious society remains intact and, despite much disaffection, keeps a tenacious hold upon most of its members.

The religious body I have described in its social reality is the Church I have left. Why? Not because it is a Church of sinners marred by human sin and failure. Only the Church at the end of time will be free from such defects. Nor is it my concern to measure present corruption against past corruption, though some writers seem to suppose that the absence of sexual immorality among the episcopate proves that the Catholic Church is healthier than ever. No, I was not concerned with what Gregory Baum has called "the random manifestations of human sin." The conviction I reached was that the present corruption of the Roman Church in regard to truth, love, and hope was due to the obstinate imposition of an obsolete structure which, contradicting the consciousness of contemporary Christians, was seriously impeding and distorting the Christian life and activity of Church members. My conviction, therefore, was that the Roman Catholic Church as an organized, visible society was a corrupt and un-Christian structure. Consequently I wanted to oppose it as such.

But here a further factor determined my decision to do so by leaving that Church. In a process going back over centuries, but reaching a point regarded as irrevocable only in the First Vatican Council, the Roman Church formulated the theology implicit in its existing social reality in doctrinal statements. The social structure I regard as obsolete and corrupt therefore now rests upon a doctrinal legitimation that declares as a dogma its key features—papal primacy in episcopal jurisdiction and papal infallibility—declares these features to be permanently normative of the institution of Christ. I wanted to maintain as a conviction of conscience that the dogmatic statements of the First Vatican Council, together with much that they imply about the nature of the Church, were wrong. I am convinced they are erroneous statements. I could not with intellectual integrity, content myself with speaking of development or reinterpretation. The appeal to development in this instance seems to me to be an ideological evasion. No one, so far, has given me even an inkling how the development many desire can prove compatible with the retention of the First Vatican declaration as true. Since the price of remaining a formal member of the Roman Church by keeping a judicious silence or speaking ambiguously about development seemed to me to be too high, I left it in order to give plain witness to my convictions.

But there is a Church I have not left. To describe that Church I will refer to the last chapter of the book Gregory Baum recently wrote in reply to mine.[2] In that chapter he says that the Catholic Church is ceasing to be a society with a clearly defined membership and becoming a movement without visible boundaries. According to his analysis, movement, not society, should be the sociological model for the Church. I find this analysis excellent provided one insists (while Baum does not) that the Christian movement which in its revival is breaking up the existing Church institutions, is found in all the present denominations, not just the Roman Church, and is issuing forth from all of them to find new forms. Needless to say, I consider myself as belonging to the Christian movement.

Whatever may be said about the theological merits of such an understanding of the Church, it undoubtedly describes a verifiable social reality. Indeed, the present combination of transconfessional

Christian revival with an increasing disaffection from the existing Churches is making manifest the fundamental social form of the Church of Christ. As a social reality the Church of Christ is not primarily a society or group of societies. It is primarily a movement within the human community, uniting men by adherence to a common set of meanings and values. Its fundamental social form is not that of a clearly defined social group with a determinate membership, but that of a movement of thought and action where no clear boundaries can be drawn between those who do and those who do not belong to the community of meaning and action. There are many varieties of participation.

The Christian Church as a movement within the human community does form more precisely defined social groups such as the present denominations. But, in relation to the Church of Christ these are secondary social formations derived from, and dependent upon, its fundamental communal existence as a movement. They never succeed in embracing or institutionalizing the total social reality of the Christian Church. They are transitory and take their structural forms from the surrounding culture. They should come and go. But, unfortunately, with the inertia of social ideology, they remain well beyond their useful span of life. When in doing so they become obstacles to Christian faith and life they should be opposed.

I have not therefore left the Church of Christ, if this is understood as a movement based upon commitment to Christ or in other words a community of meaning and action, a community of conscience. I acknowledge, too, that by the laws of man's social existence such a community can arise and be sustained only through institutional forms. But like all social institutions, Christian institutions change. The Roman Church is clinging to obsolete institutions and justifying this by an official ideology imposed in the name of faith. The Christian movement is meanwhile struggling toward new forms. At the same time the understanding of the Church I have outlined is making its way among an increasing number of Roman Catholics. On that level I recognize my continuing unity with them. Especially since there is much in the distinctive Roman tradition I am convinced should be preserved. If my unity with them does not find eucharistic expression it is because of the restrictions they impose, not I.

Mr. Davis, in the Following, Gives Us the Central Reasons for the Position He Has Outlined Above

Let me try to get to what I think [is] the heart of the matter here. . . . I've not been asking for a compelling credibility. My difficulty was not of the pagan seeking a credibility for the Church, but a convinced Christian who found, in fact, a conflict between the credibility of Christ and the credibility of the Roman Catholic Church. This is the conflict which has to be considered. It is not as if one were outside the Christian faith and asking for some compelling argument to come in. I'm taking faith as a basis. This is faith seeking understanding and seeing a contradiction, a conflict, between the adherence I owe to Christ and what is demanded of me in the Roman Catholic Church. This conflict of credibility, then, has to be considered here and this is not met by saying that, "Well, it has always been difficult to believe in Christ." Yes it has; I don't find it easy to be committed to Christ. Faith is something that requires a decision that involves risk. But having committed myself to Christ fundamentally, I don't want to contradict this by my membership of a particular Christian denomination.

It's no use here being vague and saying that the Church was always corrupt and the Church is going to develop from its present corruption even though there will still be further corruption. One has to analyze why it is corrupt and endeavor to meet that corruption, not in the sense of supposing that the Church is going to be free from corruption until the last day, but at least not to be a participant in a corruption that can be avoided.

Now if one looks at history, of course the Church has seen corruption. But I like to look at the historical data and take a stand accordingly. The Church was corrupted in the Middle Ages, but a great deal of its corruption arose from the exorbitant claims the Church made vis-à-vis the secular power. And now we see that it is, in fact, a source of corruption if the Church claims the power to depose political rulers and kings, and so we resist that doctrine and reject it. Likewise, one of the most ghastly corruptions in the Church has been the burning of heretics, the use of physical force in matters of faith. But we see that that was a source of corruption and so we reject that. Now this is the same in regard to the present corruption and in regard to future development.

You have to look at the present Church and say, "Well, it's corrupt"; but it's no use saying the Church is always corrupt. We have to deal with our own present situation. And we have to ask, "Well, what is the source of corruption?" and if we find the source then we have to move for development in a given direction. Now what I've put forward as an analysis is that, in fact, the source of the present corruption of the Church is *not* in fact the evilness of the people in charge. No indeed, a very great part of my problem intellectually was to try and fathom why so many good people, and such idealism, were so constantly distorted in the Church—that there was this disregard of truth and disregard of persons by people who, considered merely individually, were not wicked men. And my conclusion was that they were the victims of the system and that this operation of the system can be seen from top to bottom in the Church. The operation can be seen by the action and the authority exercised by the Pope and bishops. It can be seen by the position given to the priest. It can be seen by, in fact, the prissility [sic] accepted by so many laity. It can be seen, in fact, in the subjection of the religious to wrong systems, systems that were wrong from a Christian, not merely a psychological, point of view. And therefore it's a question of analyzing this corruption and saying, "Well if this is the source of corruption, we must do something about it."

I think if the Church is to develop, then along what lines is it going to develop. We have to use here a critical intelligence, an intelligence enlightened by faith, but intelligence nonetheless. Now, I'm quite prepared to see that the Church is developing. In fact my whole thesis is that there is a movement developing within the Christian world. But what is going to happen if that development takes its logical course? And my point is that if the development continues, then its logic is the abolition of the present institutional structure, which is formulated in a series of doctrinal statements and imposed as permanently normative. I want to say that this is a corruption and that these statements are wrong. . . .

Now this seems to me to be the danger. Are we being asked to commit ourselves to a religious mythology without faith? Is that what is being put forward in terms of loyalty, or have we to have faith that is an entry into the truth of God? If it's faith that is an entry into the truth of God, then we can't ignore the requirements of our intelligence in working out our commitment.

The Following Question Is Put to Mr. Davis at the Conclusion of His Statement

Mr. Davis, many of us who question the relevancy of the Church today, while feeling that we could easily, perhaps, leave the so-called institutional Church, question our ability to ever alienate ourselves from the sacramental Church. Could you comment on this?

Answer Given by Mr. Davis

I think that this particular question arises from a wrong understanding of the sacraments. And as I said in the book,[3] I found myself able to undergo what was for me personally the deprivation of a sacramental life such as I had known it because of the work that I had done on the theology of the sacraments.

You see, if one approaches the sacraments as it is done in modern theology—I give as an example Schillebeeckx's book on the sacraments[4]—then the fundamental Sacrament is Christ. This fundamental Sacrament is found made permanent in the world, made visible in the world, the reality in action of Christ, in the community of Christians, in the Church. And the sacraments, the seven sacraments we call sacraments, are sacraments insofar as they are the actions of the Christian community. And this is in fact what gives them their status as sacraments. If you take them as things or actions and separate them from the Church then, in fact, they are distorted in their meaning and it's very difficult to avoid a superstitious approach to the sacraments.

Now if that is the case, then clearly the fundamental question must be the Church and not the sacraments. It's to put the thing the wrong way around to start with the seven sacraments and go from them to the Church. The process has to be the other way. You have to decide what is the reality of the Church of Christ in the world today. When you have determined what *is* the reality of the

Church in the world today, then you are in a position to ask how that community gives itself symbolic expression. And consequently, if in fact one's belief in a particular Church structure breaks down, he cannot forsake it by appealing to the seven sacraments as means of grace. This, I think, would betoken a superstitious approach to the sacraments themselves. They are the actions of the Christian community and can only be understood as functions of the reality of that community as the Church of Christ.

At This Point Mr. Davis Asks John L. McKenzie, S.J., the Following Question About Vatican I

I couldn't help noticing that when John answered his question he chose, as so many Catholic theologians choose, a harmless word to describe the First Vatican Council decrees, "They were unfortunate." I want to ask, can I say they are wrong? You see it's always easy to say they were inopportune, they were unfortunate, they can perhaps be developed. But as statements go they are pretty clear, they are hammered out into pretty precise formulations. Now can I ask John, will you say that they are not merely unfortunate, but will you say that they are wrong?

Answer Given by John L. McKenzie, S.J.

Charles, as a theologian you ought to know that that is really not a fair question to ask me. There was a time when you would have said they were unfortunate and you would have known exactly what you meant and you know exactly what I mean. I say as statements they will not endure because they are not final. They need correction. This is a question of technical theological language and it still exists. Even the members of the Second Vatican Council said that, so I'm not being very daring. But, as it has been studied, it's almost a hundred years now. You have to admit that they are no longer understood in the Church, except by a very few people in an official caste, in the sense in which they were intended in 1870 when they were voted in. And this is what I mean by development. We live with our unfortunate past. We have a strange way of living with it of course. After all somebody suggested in Vatican II that they rehabilitate Galileo. The bishops as a body thought that would be unfortunate. We never make mistakes; therefore we don't correct them. This is not one of the charismatic features of the Roman Church. It's one of its more human features and one of its less amiable, no question about it.

Footnotes

[1] [*Editor's note:* All of the headings in this selection are supplied by the editor.]

[2] [*Editor's note:* This refers to Charles Davis, *A Question of Conscience* (New York: Harper & Row, Publishers, 1967) and to Gregory Baum, O.S.A., *The Credibility of the Church Today* (New York: Herder and Herder, Inc., 1968). A portion of Father Baum's last chapter is included in this volume, pp. 239–57.]

[3] [*Editor's note:* This refers to Charles Davis, *A Question of Conscience* (n. 2).]

[4] [*Editor's note:* This refers to Edward Schillebeeckx, O.P., *Christ the Sacrament of the Encounter with God* (New York: Sheed & Ward, 1963).]

FREDERICK SONTAG

Are You a Catholic?

What does Dr. Sontag describe as the "classic Protestant attitude"? What is the role of the Bible in interpreting Christianity? Is there a difference between accepting the Bible as the definitive norm and accepting it as the sole norm? What is tradition? Must we accept the need for historical continuity in the institutional form of the Church? Dr. Sontag differentiates between community and institution; what is his differentiation?

Frederick Sontag is a Professor of Philosophy at the Claremont Colleges in California. He was a visiting professor at the Collegio di S. Anselmo, Rome during 1966–1967.

As a Protestant—and as a philosopher—teaching this year at a Benedictine seminary in Rome, I confess that I was sad and disappointed when I heard the news of Fr. Charles Davis' "defection." Being in Rome among young seminarians, the overwhelming impression one gets is of great ferment, of radical rethinking, and of perhaps the greatest opportunity ever for achieving renewal and reform. In such a situation, every alert and critical Catholic is needed inside the Church. For I also sense that, if these ambitions and prayers for new life are not translated into practice, if the hopes of the present generation of young Catholics are politically frustrated, then the situation could quickly become as dangerous as it is presently hopeful.

Because of the crisis of the hour, because the fruits of Vatican II are not secured but must still be won by explicit definition and practice, this is a time when every generous Protestant wants to see every progressive force stay within Roman Catholicism and work there to make present hopes into an available reality. Thus, Davis' desertion appeared at first as a loss, since he seemed more needed and more likely to be valuable inside Catholicism than outside it. In the present ecumenical spirit, we no longer cheer the proselyte and keep score on how many can be seduced from the other side.

Furthermore, it seems a recognized fact that those who leave a rightful heritage are never as vigorous and as creative in an adopted setting, even if it is a more congenial place for them personally. Cardinal Newman may appear to deny this point, but that fact only illustrates the important difference between a positive conversion to a new position, toward which one has been moving, and a radical outbreak against a situation, one that drives you away because it is no longer tolerable.

Fr. Davis seemed more to represent the latter situation than to be a "Newman in reverse." The reasons he has given for his decision all amount to why he can no longer tolerate Roman Catholicism, not why some specific and unique form of Protestantism attracts him. In this situation, there is some reason to doubt that he can be as helpful as a Protestant as he might have been as a Roman Catholic, and thus some justification for a Protestant to lament the personal necessity for his move. Or at least that is a logical first reaction.

But a reading of Charles Davis' own statement, as reprinted from the London *Observer*, together with the reply of Fr. Gregory Baum in the *National Catholic Reporter* for January 25, provides good reason to reverse this first judgment on Davis' move. For as a Protestant reads Davis' statement, it emerges as a classic example of a basic Protestant attitude. And if he really has come to hold those fundamental assumptions, then his presence within Roman Catholicism would be a living falsehood, and we might as well be clear about it.

As I talk to the younger Catholic generation today, I wonder just how many have come to accept basic views about Christianity that are really more Protestant than Roman Catholic, so that, if their views remain that way, their continued allegiance to Catholicism is more a matter of circumstance than of principle. I suspect that this is a crucial question today, perhaps *the* crucial issue, and thus we ought to thank Fr. Davis for posing the question so dramatically for us. Not that it is somehow "wrong" for an individual to come to hold "Protestant views" and still to remain in communion with his historic Church, but Davis' situation points out that, when a crisis comes, it may then become clear that one actually has become a Protestant in principle.

Even in such a situation, as I have already suggested, it may still be most beneficial for us all if such individuals remain within Catholicism and work for its renewal and reform. That may be their most effective Protestant service. But Davis' case points out the dangers of living on in ignorance of the fact that one is Protestant in his basic views; for when the hard tests of loyalty come (e.g., birth control), then one may discover that he has unknowingly lost his ground for continued loyalty.

Perhaps even more important than what Davis' statement itself reveals is the impression that strikes a Protestant very forcefully on reading Fr. Baum's reply. Gregory Baum seems to miss the basic point of Charles Davis' essential Protestanism, and, even more appalling, there is no basic argument that Fr. Baum advances that a loyal Protestant could not also endorse in good conscience. This being the case, Fr. Baum does not seem to realize that his arguments do not *force* one who accepts them to move only toward Roman Catholicism. They fit Protestantism as well, and it is then a pragmatic choice in which direction one moves.

But first let me point out what it is about Fr. Davis' statement that so tellingly reflects a Protestant attitude and thus makes his leaving the Church a necessity of honesty, not a loss but the highlighting of a crucial test that many Catholics today ought to face clearly for themselves. Next, let me consider Fr. Baum's reply and indicate why its assumptions too are Protestant, and why it argues no more to Catholicism than to Protestantism, but rather makes choice an individual affair.

Our concern here is not with the specifics of Fr. Davis' "complaints." That is a personal and a Catholic family-matter. What is important is the principles to which he appeals, those that clearly have come to be the "first principles" of Davis' thought. As a metaphysician—and a Protestant—I am more interested in the fundamental principles involved than in the details of the rightness or accuracy of the issues and the charges. In this light, the first thing a Protestant notes is Davis' continued appeal to the Bible as his basic norm. If it becomes his only norm, then surely this is the essence of Protestantism, and he is no longer Catholic. In that case, if tradition and authority in one form become cumbersome (as they did for Davis), then you shed them for another form, as Protestants have always felt free to do. If tradition is itself a norm independent of the Bible, then even if it is painful and inhibiting to one's creativity to carry it along, it is a burden a Catholic cannot escape.

Fr. Davis retraces the traditional Protestant route when he reports: "The more I study the Bible, the less likely Roman claims become." For an appeal to the Bible as the definitive norm in cases of doubt is a Protestant principle, but not a sufficient Roman Catholic norm. If the sole basis for judgment of institutional Christianity is the New Testament spirit, then one is free to reject any given institution that he finds not in conformity with it and to seek one that is more in conformity with it—but surely that is not the basis of Roman Catholic claims. The issue concerns the basic norm or norms to which you appeal, and for a Protestant this can be simply biblical understanding.

Fr. Davis cannot accept the dogmas of the Assumption of Mary or of the Immaculate Conception. It really does not matter, as he suggests, whether or not he can reconcile these pronouncements with a theory of "doctrinal development." If, in the back of your mind, an appeal to the biblical presentation of Christianity is the norm, then these dogmas are not very likely to win your support, whereas an appeal to other norms could render them acceptable to a Catholic. The papal system becomes "theologically indefensible" if you insist on the individual right of conscience to judge it by the biblical norm alone. Otherwise, you might accept it as necessary to insure the validity of the sacraments.

The first three chapters of Vatican II's Constitution on the Church worry Charles Davis. He likes the first two chapters' vision of the biblical Church, but he cannot accept the remoteness of the third chapter from the New Testament view. This reaction further supports my contention that Davis' attitude is basically Protestant. Only if one has already decided on the biblical witness as his sole norm can it seem appalling and unacceptable to grant that Roman Catholicism's view of the Church may reflect a long distillation of tradition, not a biblical approach.

What bothers Fr. Davis is the compromises that are forced on the institution—e.g., in the matters of Nazi Germany and birth control. This fact only indicates that one has ceased to hold the *form* of the institution to be important and has come to feel that the institution may be rejected when it is inconvenient, or if a better form can be found. A good Catholic certainly must believe in the necessity for the mediation of the Church and its historical tradition for the validity of his religious life; a low-church Protestant does not (and Fr. Davis should feel equally restless as a high-church Anglican). If you accept the need for the mediation of the historical Church, you will stay within and work for reform in spite of its pain and difficulties. A Protestant may not feel this need, and he can therefore shift his institutional form when it becomes inconvenient.

An institution learns who its friends are, not in the blush of enthusiasm when everyone thinks he can have the reforms most dear to his heart, but when it is necessary to compromise with the institutional inheritance. A Protestant feels free to consider the institution as being purely secondary and as not essential to his religious life, if a choice is forced upon him. How many Roman Catholics are really Protestant—as Fr. Davis discovered he was—in their attitude toward the institutional Church? Even such Catholics can still remain Catholics so long as they do not feel the burden of the institution to be excessive. But when they do feel it to be so, how many Protestants might a crisis of disappointed hopes reveal within Roman Catholicism today?

The issue is not the rightness or wrongness of any particular papal action, but the necessity of the historical institution as such. Whatever the Pope may or may not be enmeshed in, he is not to be abandoned, unless one rejects the validity of the sacraments as resting on that particular line of succession. The fault, in the case we are discussing, is not with anything the Pope did or did not do, but with Fr. Davis' Protestant feeling that he can find a purer Christianity by himself and that he can abandon the historical institution and its authority in order to do so. In such a situation, a Catholic will yield, because he accepts that institution's mediation; a Protestant will not.

If one accepts the need for historical continuity in institutional form, then he will simply have to move a "mountain of the ecclesiastical rubble," and he will feel this burden to be unavoidable and as more important than his own tiny creative thoughts. A Protestant is more free in his thought here, but a Catholic must go through the whole complexity and not around it. Davis still appeals to his need for a Christian community, as most Protestants do too, but his idea of what a "community" ought to be is basically Protestant and anti-institutional. When the official Church is believed not to be a mode of Christian presence in the world, then the man who believes that it is not is unquestionably Protestant.

After the break, Davis' conscience feels relieved; but the attitude that holds personal feeling to be more important than continuing an ecclesiastical tradition is a very Protestant one. Millions might feel "spiritually cleansed" not to have to struggle any longer with the complexities and the compromises of an ancient institution, but if you feel the continuance of that institution to be crucial, as Catholics do, you continue to struggle. If you do not feel a continuity of institutional form to be essential, you turn to "informal groupings."

The basic Protestant principles in Davis' thought, and even the presence of similar principles in the minds of many Roman Catholics who have not been forced to the necessity of a choice as Davis and Luther were, any sensitive reader might easily discern. What is even more startling is that Fr. Baum's reply to Charles Davis is equally Protestant in its appeal to principles. Accepting Baum's arguments in no way commits one to Roman Catholicism. As a Protestant, I can accept his every appeal and remain unmoved.

Fr. Baum claims to differ with Charles Davis over his evaluation of the institutional Church. What is important to see here is not the cogency of Fr. Baum's replies but the principles to which he, too, ultimately appeals. Baum points to Vatican II's call for a reform of the structure, and he admits that he, too, suffers when authority is abused. He then moves on to his main point: "Institution is absolutely necessary for the promotion of social life on this earth." But Fr. Baum misses the important point.

Charles Davis has not denied the need for institutions to promote

Christianity, and no Protestant does either, except for a few very left-wing rugged individualists. Protestants form institutions too, and Davis also wants to join new groups of Christians. The issue is the importance of a particular historical institution and its teaching authority as it has developed. If your basis is biblical, then you may feel free to break from one institutional form and to join or to form another, one that seems to you more conducive to what you think a Christian community ought to be. The issue is not institution vs. no institution; rather, it is whether one is free to judge a given institution by a norm external to its historical evolution and to abandon it for new forms if he finds it wanting.

What Fr. Baum goes on to argue is that the Roman Catholic institution, in spite of its admitted inadequacies, is really the best form available, and so one should stay within it and work for reform. What Fr. Baum seems to fail to notice is that this places the decision on a basis of prudential and pragmatic tests. If this really is to be the ground for our decision, then Fr. Baum should remain a Catholic and work from within, but Fr. Davis should not. He applied Baum's test, and he is free to come to a different evaluation, all the while using the same norm of "best available."

Fr. Baum wants a person to be free to work from within for institutional reform. But amazingly enough, to support his argument that the Roman Church offers the best available means, he joins Davis in an appeal to the Gospel teaching about the institution. If the Gospel teaching is to be the norm, then Charles Davis is free, because he applied this test and found the Church wanting. Protestants accept the biblical norm, too. They just do not find its best embodiment in Roman Catholicism.

On Fr. Baum's own admission, the hierarchy is not primary, but the Christian people to whom its members minister are. If this is the basic primary, then one is—judging by this alone—free to change one hierarchy for another if he finds that that particular hierarchy is not fulfilling its pledge to the people. We Protestants consider our ministers to be our servants, in good biblical fashion, but on this appeal alone we do not feel bound to any one hierarchy. Certainly, Fr. Baum will have to go farther than that if he wants to find anything essentially Roman Catholic. So far he has not argued against Davis, but has actually supported Davis' basic principles, although perhaps himself making a different evaluation of the Catholic hierarchy in the light of them. So far, that is a difference of personal evaluation, not of principle.

Fr. Baum says that the mystery of salvation is celebrated in the Catholic Church in an adequate form. Yet if he agrees in considering the Church as first of all the people, and the hierarchy simply a ministry to them, then he has not on principle undercut Davis' evaluation that since "people are being injured," it is "change the hierarchy." Other norms than these must define a Catholic, but Fr. Baum has put forward only those to which any good Protestant—including Davis—might also appeal. If "Popes and bishops have no power" over what is really important in life, then surely one is free to support them if they do not hinder that life and also free to deny them if they do hinder what is essential, as Davis believes.

As a Protestant, I cannot think that Fr. Baum's cavalier attitude toward the essential lack of spiritual power of Popes and bishops is really an acceptable Roman Catholic criterion. If the Pope is the "vicar of Christ," then for a Catholic his spiritual importance is central and considerable—though to a Protestant this exclusive claim is not acceptable. But if Roman Catholicism has really changed as much under Vatican II as Fr. Baum believes, we Protestants have won; it is we who should turn the tables and start talking about how we can now accept back our brothers who, by temporarily accepting the essential power of bishops and Popes, had become separated from us!

Gregory Baum concludes that Fr. Davis' decision was not universal but individual. In some cases, this is always true of an individual struggle, but that conclusion is a shocking one if Fr. Baum does not realize that the principles to which Fr. Davis appeals will allow him and any other who accepts them to make that choice for himself.

The issue is not whether Jesus Christ is celebrated in the Catholic Church. Davis has not denied that. But if the biblical norm is primary, and if the historical mediation of the institution and its line of authority are not essential, and if the structure is to be judged by its success as compared with other available forms of institutional Christianity, then Fr. Davis is free to decide that the Roman Church does not serve these purposes as well as some other form, and Fr. Baum is free to decide that it does and to remain within. The issue as it is posed is not one of principle but of individual assessment, and both priests appeal to Protestant norms that do not in themselves require one to remain Roman Catholic on principle.

I have observed that there may well be many within Roman communions whose basic principles are really Protestant but upon whom no issue or necessity of choice has been forced. Even so, for the health of Christianity as it is maintained through the vitality and the existence of a variety of forms, no Protestant (believing in pluralism) should want all such Catholics to defect. But we might all wish that appeals were not made to norms as if they supported Roman Catholicism alone, when in fact those principles actually leave the choice of form open to the prudential judgment of the individual.

Even the *National Catholic Reporter*, in its editorial of January 4, misses the basic issue. It laments Fr. Davis' loss because he could have been so helpful to the cause of reform inside the Church (my own first reaction, too), and concludes by saying: "The community was willed by Christ." That is not the point. We Protestants accept the community as willed by Christ; we just do not connect it necessarily and exclusively with the Roman community. Not doing this, we do not feel it essential to stay in communion with Rome in order to be in a Christian community.

Historical circumstances may not force it upon him, but essentially every Catholic must make the same decision. The *Reporter* nowhere gives an argument as to why Davis should accept the Roman form of community over any other. Why must it be the Roman community to the exclusion of other alternatives? Nowhere in the debate has Davis' basic challenge been answered. And until it is, his application of a biblical norm may allow him—and any other Catholic—to opt for a less cumbersome form of community if he wishes. If grasped in their full significance, Fr. Davis' principles should force every Roman Catholic to ask himself: Just how Protestant am I in principle, and how Roman Catholic by circumstances or weakness? It is to be hoped that most Catholics can come up with a more definitive norm than the Protestant principles to which Fr. Baum and the *Reporter* both appeal.

HANS KÜNG

What Is the Essence of Apostolic Succession?

In this article, as in all previous articles, we should begin by trying to understand what the author means by "Church." Why does the author claim that "every individual member of the Church stands in apostolic succession"? How does the author relate "ecclesial tradition" to "apostolic tradition"? What does the author mean to say when he speaks of the plurality of structures in the early Church? When did the present institutional order become established? How rigidly must we hold to the present structure? How does pastoral succession take place? What does he mean when he states that some members of the community have a special power?

Hans Küng is the Dean of the Catholic Theological Faculty of the University of Tübingen. One of his most recent books is *The Church*.

The concept of apostolic succession suffers from undue clerical and juridical constriction. We do not breathe the free air of the Bible and this paralyzes our ecumenism. New life can only be breathed into it by a return to Scripture. How this can be done is summarized here in a few theses with which I have dealt more in detail elsewhere.[1]

Reprinted from Hans Küng, "What Is the Essence of Apostolic Succession?" in *Concilium,* XXXIV, *Apostolic Succession Rethinking a Barrier to Unity,* ed. Hans Küng (Glen Rock, N.J.: Paulist Press, 1968), pp. 28–35; *Concilium,* April 1968, Vol. 4, no. 4, *Ecumenism* (Burns and Oates Ltd., London), pp. 16–19, with the permission of *Concilium.*

1. Basic is the point that the *whole Church* and *every individual member* share in this apostolic succession: the Church as a whole is committed to obedience to the apostles as the original witnesses and the original messengers. In the *negative* sense this means that the concept suffers from a clerical narrowing down if this apostolic succession is seen exclusively as a succession of ecclesiastical functions. In the *positive* sense it means that the whole Church is involved. It is the Church as a whole that we believe in when we say: "I believe in the apostolic Church." The Church as a whole is successor to the apostles. And insofar as the Church is not an institutional apparatus but the community of the faithful, this means that every individual member of the Church stands in this apostolic succession. Every later generation remains bound to the word, the witness, and the service of the first apostolic generation. The apostles are and remain the once-for-all and irreplaceable original witnesses: their witness, the sole original witness; their mission, the sole original mission. The whole Church is founded on the foundation of the apostles (and the prophets).

2. The apostolic succession of the Church as a whole and of every individual consists in this *essential cohesion with the apostles* to be put into practice constantly; it demands the constant accord with the apostolic *witness* (Scripture) and the constant rendering of the apostolic *service* (missionary extension in the world and the building up of the community). Apostolic succession is therefore primarily a succession in apostolic faith, apostolic service, and apostolic life. This means in the *negative* sense that it is a juridical narrowing of the concept to see apostolic succession primarily in a continuous chain of impositions of hands—as if such a chain of ordinations by itself could supply the apostolic spirit! In the *positive* sense it means that the point of the succession lies in the constantly renewed daily loyalty to the apostles. This means, not fanaticism, but sober obedience. The apostles are dead. Any authority and power in the Church can only arise from obedience to the Lord of the Church and the apostles. Apostolicity is at the same time a gift and a task. Both the Church as a whole and every individual member need to be in harmony with the apostolic witness: they can only hear the Lord and his message *via* this apostolic witness. In fact, sound *ecclesiastical* tradition can only be an interpretation, explanation, and application of the original *apostolic* tradition contained in Scripture. And

the Church cannot be true to this apostolic witness otherwise than through continuing the apostolic service in its many forms of proclamation, baptism, the communion in prayer and the eucharistic meal, the building up of the community and service to the world.

3. Within the apostolic succession of the Church as a whole there is a special apostolic succession of the many *pastoral* services, through which the pastors, without being apostles themselves, continue the mission and function of the apostles, namely, the founding and guiding of the Church. In the *negative* sense this means that apostolic succession becomes a mere abstraction if we divorce it from the historical reality. We must not only see the Church as a whole but also in the concrete reality of her many services which are not all equally important. In the *positive* sense it means that the pastors are not apostles but continue the mission and function of the apostles by founding and leading the Church. They are not a governing class with a one-sided power to command. But there is a superposition and subordination determined by the kind of service.

4. Among the many charismatic gifts of leadership which continue the apostolic mission, the pastoral services of *presbyter* (pastor), *episkopos* (bishop), and *diakonos* (deacon), based on a particular function (imposition of hands), came to stand out with increasing prominence during the post-apostolic age. This means in the *negative* sense that we make an undue presupposition when we draw a simple straight line of succession from the apostles to the bishops. Apart from those charisms that appear freely and by their very nature cannot be brought under a system ("being the first," stewards, presidents, guides, etc.), it is equally impossible to systematize the services transmitted by imposition of hands (at least at that time) such as presbyters, *episkopoi*, deacons, etc., on the basis of the New Testament. The threefold order of functions mentioned by Ignatius of Antioch has, no doubt, its roots in the original period but cannot simply be identified as the whole original order and distribution of all the functions. It is the result of a very complex historical development. It is also impossible to trace the dividing line that separates these three functions among themselves, particularly in the case of the *episkopos* and the presbyter, on the basis of *dogmatic theology*. It means in the *positive* sense that the distinction between the various services is, on the one hand, a matter of factual development, and on the other, of pastoral expediency. Even if one

wholly accepts the threefold division of the Church's function into presbyters, bishops, and deacons as a meaningful and practical development, one cannot treat such a juridical definition, which at most is the practical realization of *but one* possibility, as if it were a dogmatic necessity. The rich beginnings of a Church order in the New Testament leave plenty of room for other possibilities in practice.

5. Pastoral service as a special kind of succession to the apostles is surrounded in the Church by *other gifts* and services, particularly in those that have succeeded to the New Testament *prophets* and *teachers* who, in cooperation with the pastors, have their own original authority. This means in the *negative* sense that, through an unbiblical limitation, canalization, and monopolization of the free charism in the Church, there arises a kind of pastoral hierocracy when pastors feel that they alone possess the Spirit and so try to quench the Spirit in others. There is an un-Pauline absolutization of a function when an official considers himself to be apostle, prophet, and teacher all at once and so wants to grasp everything unto himself. In the *positive* sense it means that every individual stands in the line of apostolic succession according to the particular charism that has been bestowed on him. This succession is therefore not limited to the one line of pastoral services. There is also—and second in the order of St. Paul—the succession of the prophets in whom the Spirit expresses himself directly and who, in their awareness of their calling and responsibility, show the way, present and future, in a given situation of the Church. And, third in St. Paul's list, there is the succession of the teachers, the theologians who go to endless trouble in order to transmit and interpret in a genuine way the message of the past in the present situation of Church and world.

6. The *pastoral succession with imposition of hands* is neither automatic nor mechanical. It presupposes faith and demands a faith that is active in the apostolic spirit. It does not exclude the possibility of failure and error and therefore needs to be tested by the community of the faithful. This means in the *negative* sense: any isolated mechanism of succession of an official hierarchy which makes an abstraction of the human condition and, by the same token, of the constantly necessary grace of God and the constantly new demands on faith and life, cannot appeal to the New Testament. The power of the community, of the universal priesthood, cannot be

simply derived from the pastoral service. That would be an unbiblical clericalization of the community; it would separate the pastoral service from the universal priesthood and absolutize it in its succession. On the other hand, the power of the pastoral service also cannot be derived from the power of the community and the universal priesthood. This would be an unbiblical secularization of the community and reduce the pastoral function to the level of the universal priesthood. In the *positive* sense it means that cohesion *and* distinction of pastoral service and the community with all its special gifts and services are important. The special call to the *public service of the community as such* by the imposition of hands, the ordination, must be seen against the background of the universal priesthood. We must therefore distinguish between the "empowering" of every Christian and the special power of some individuals for the public service of the community as such. All Christians are empowered to proclaim the Word; to witness to the faith in the Church and in the world, all are "sent." But only those called to be pastors (or commissioned by them) have the special power to preach in the assembly of the community. All Christians are empowered to promise forgiveness to the brother troubled by conscience. But only those called to be pastors have the special power to pronounce the words of reconciliation and absolution in the assembly of the community as such and thus apply it to the individual. All Christians are empowered to take part in the administration of baptism and the eucharistic meal. But only those called to be pastors have the special power to administer baptism publicly and to preside responsibly over the communal Eucharist.

7. The apostolic succession of the pastors must take place in the communion of mutual service to Church and world. Admission to the apostolic succession in the pastoral line should normally take place according to the mind of the New Testament through a *cooperation of pastors and community*, a cooperation of as many different elements as possible. This means in the *negative* sense that it is a false view of ecclesiastical office to see obedience and subordination as a one-way traffic. The ecclesiastical functions are there for the community and not the community for the functions. An absolutist government of the Church, at the level of the whole Church, the diocese, or the parish, is a contradiction of the Gospel. In the *positive* sense it means that, because of the specific mission of the

pastor to the community, the pastoral function already implies an authority. The pastor has his credentials from the beginning and he is officially accepted as empowered to fufill this public service for the community. Nevertheless, this in no way deprives the community of its right to examine whether the pastor acts in truth according to this mission, according to the Gospel. The specific power given to the pastor even requires that every day he obediently use this power anew. But in spite of all the legitimate relative autonomy of the pastor (bishop or priest) the appointment of pastors in the Church must come about basically through a cooperation of those who already are pastors and the community. And apart from their appointment, even when the pastors are entitled to a certain responsible autonomy in the guidance of the community because they need this in the exercise of their function, nevertheless, the community as the royal priesthood should have a voice in all the affairs of the community, and this can be done directly or through a representative body. This corresponds to the juridical principle, so often quoted in the Church's tradition: "What concerns all, must be dealt with by all."

8. If we base ourselves on the Pauline, or the Gentile Christian, Church order, we must leave room for *other ways of pastoral service and apostolic succession* of pastors. The Church order, based on the presbyter and the *episkopos*, which has as a matter of fact prevailed in the Church, must today, too, remain open in principle to all the possibilities that existed in the Church of the New Testament. This means in the *negative* sense that the institutional order, mainly determined by the Palestinian tradition must not be absolutized. The present organization of the offices in the Church developed essentially in three stages: (a) over against the prophets, teachers, and other charismatic functionaries, the episcopal line (including presbyters and *episkopoi*) prevailed as the dominant and finally exclusive leaders of the community; (b) over against the plurality of bishops (presbyters and bishops) within a community this led to a monarchical episcopacy; (c) from being the presidents of the individual communities the bishops became presidents of ecclesiastical territories.

This schematic sketch of the development cannot be ruled out *a priori* as unjustified. Nevertheless, a definite new order cannot be proved right simply by arguing from the existing situation nor from the possible misuse of charisms. It is justified rather by the decisive difference between the original phase and the time that came after, between the apostolic age of the foundation and the post-apostolic age of building up and expansion. In the *positive* sense this means: an exposé of the Pauline Church order can demonstrate that a charismatic order of the community is possible without a specific admission to a service (ordination), and that perchance Corinth knew of neither *episkopoi* nor presbyters nor any kind of ordination but only free and spontaneous charisms, apart from the apostles. And yet, according to Paul, the Church of Corinth was a community provided with all that was necessary, equipped with the proclamation of the Word, baptism, Eucharist, and all other services. On the other hand, there is at the same time enough evidence to show that these Pauline communities showed relatively soon that there were bishops and deacons, and, after Paul, ordained priests, so that the presbyteral and episcopal order became general in the Church. Nevertheless, the Church as she developed later cannot in principle exclude the Pauline Church order. However unlikely this order may be now, it can be important today for an extraordinary situation in the missions and particularly in the field of ecumenism.

And so my theses run into questions which need to be discussed, and today more urgently than ever before. Could the present Church wish or be able to prevent that somewhere—a concentration camp, distant captivity without contact with the outside, an extraordinary missionary situation (e.g., in Communist China, or in the case of those Japanese Christians who lived for centuries without ordained pastors)—the same thing should happen that happened in Corinth and other Pauline communities, namely, that guidance is simply provided by the free action of the Spirit of God through the charisms? When we assume the universal priesthood and the charismatic structure of the Church, should we still hold that the special apostolic succession via a series of impositions of hands is the *only* and exclusive way into pastoral service, and should this be the only way in which we must think of apostolic succession? Even if this chain of impositions of hands is not taken so exclusively, would it still not remain an impressive sign of the apostolic succession in the pastoral line and therefore a sign of the unity, catholicity, and apostolicity of the Church? Would we then not have every reason to judge apostolic succession and the validity of the eucharistic celebration in those Churches which are not part of this "chain" of ordinations in a different and much more positive manner? Would this not help us to see also other questions, like that of the ordination of women or that of Anglican orders, in a new light? And if we do not, is it at all possible to do justice to the full spiritual life, the fruitful activity of pastors, men and women, of other Churches? Is it then possible to mend the divisions of Christendom and to arrive at a mutual recognition? The enormous implications of these questions, both in theology and in the field of ecumenism, would seem obvious.

Footnotes

[1] Cf. H. Küng, *Die Kirche, Ökumenische Forschungen,* I, 1 (Freiburg/Basle/Vienna, 1967), esp. Chap. D IV, 2, and Chap. E II, 2. [*Editor's note:* This refers to Hans Küng, *The Church* (London–New York, 1967) a selection from which appears on pp. 142–67.]

JAMES F. McCUE

Bishops, Presbyters, and Priests in Ignatius of Antioch

This article relates to many of the issues raised in the previous article, for example, the plurality of structures in the early Church, the concept of the "power" of the official functionaries in the Church, and ordination. What is the bishop's main function? How does this relate to the eucharistic ministry? Who can preside over the eucharistic celebration? Is this necessarily a permanent function?

James F. McCue is on the faculty of the School of Religion at the University of Iowa. He has written for *The Commonweal* and *Theological Studies.*

It could well be the case that the Church in the twentieth century will not wish to or will not be able to copy every feature of the Church order of the early second century. The precise way in which the thought and order of the early Church is normative for the Church of all time is a difficult question, and one which I do not propose to deal with here. It is, however, not at all helpful to read into early Christian writers later forms and attitudes simply on the grounds that so it must have been because so it now is.

What I wish to consider here is the status of bishops and presbyters in Ignatius of Antioch, and specifically to inquire into the relationship between the Ignatian presbyter and the "priest" of

Reprinted from *Theological Studies,* XXVIII (1967), No. 4, pp. 828–34, with the permission of the publisher and author.

Roman Catholic ecclesiology. It will be my contention that the "priesthood," defined in terms of a eucharistic ministry, was not a permanent, specific ministry within the Ignatian Church order, but that in principle any member of the community could preside over the Eucharist, provided he be appointed (temporarily) for this purpose by the bishop. This was not something which the presbyter *ex officio* [by virtue of an office] could do, or which could be delegated only to a presbyter.

I realize that what Ignatius says on the subject is not detailed or precise enough to allow of complete certitude in the matter, but I would maintain that the interpretation developed here suits the materials better than do the alternatives.

I

The crucial passage occurs in the eighth chapter of Ignatius' *Epistle to the Smyrnaeans:*

> See that you all follow the bishop, as Jesus Christ follows the Father, and the presbytery as if it were the Apostles. And reverence the deacons as the command of God. Let no one do any of the things appertaining to the Church without the bishop. Let that be considered a valid Eucharist which is celebrated by the bishop, or by one whom he appoints. Wherever the bishop appears let the congregation be present; just as wherever Jesus Christ is, there is the Catholic Church. It is not lawful either to baptise or to hold an "agape" without the bishop; but whatever he approve, this is also pleasing to God, that everything which you do may be secure and valid.[1]

This is a fairly typical Ignatian exhortation to unity with and under the bishop, and can be properly understood only within the context of his entire ecclesiology. There is, however, one point here that is not paralleled in the other Ignatian letters. Usually Ignatius is content to speak as though the bishop were always himself present at the Eucharist and could actively function as the presiding minister. Here, however, Ignatius indicates that the bishop was not always present and suggests what was done (or to be done) in this eventuality. The Greek of the relevant passage is as follows: ἐκείνη βεβαία εὐχαριστία ἡγείσθω, ἡ ὑπὸ τὸν επίσκοπον οὖσα ἢ ᾧ ἂν αὐτὸς ἐπιστρέψῃ. The translation quoted here ["Let that be considered a valid Eucharist which is celebrated by the bishop."] is thus somewhat misleading. Ignatius does not speak of the bishop "celebrating" the Eucharist, but rather of the Eucharist taking place under the bishop. Before we consider the specific question of who could so preside, it will be helpful to consider more generally Ignatius' understanding of the ministry of bishops and presbyters. We can reasonably leave out of account his view of the diaconate, since this is neither problematic nor relevant.

We can best understand Ignatius' view of the episcopal ministry from a consideration of his exhortations to submission and obedience to the bishop. It is interesting to note that, whereas the somewhat earlier *I Clement* argues for obedience to the presbyters on the grounds that they have been appointed, via a continuous succession from the apostles, by Christ himself, Ignatius argues instead from the very nature of Christianity as a covenant of unity and love. Whereas *I Clement* parallels certain Pastoral motifs, Ignatius argues along what might be termed more Johannine lines. The Church is characterized by unity and love, and the bishop is both sign and instrument of this unity in charity. Characteristic is the fifth chapter of Ignatius' *Epistle to the Ephesians.*

> For if I in a short time gained such fellowship with your bishop as was not human but spiritual, how much more do I count you blessed who are so united with him as the Church is with Jesus Christ, and as Jesus Christ is with the Father, that all things may sound together in unison! Let no man be deceived: unless a man be within the sanctuary he lacks the bread of God, for if the prayer of one or two has such might, how much more has that of the bishop and of the whole Church? So then he who does not join in the common assembly, is already haughty, and has separated himself. For it is written "God resisteth the proud": let us then be careful not to oppose the bishop, that we may be subject to God.

To similar effect is *Magnesians*, the seventh chapter:

> As then the Lord was united to the Father and did nothing without Him, neither by Himself nor through the Apostles, so do you do nothing without the bishop and the presbyters.

> Do not attempt to make anything appear right for you by yourselves, but let there be in common one prayer, one supplication, one mind, one hope in love, in the joy which is without fault, that is Jesus Christ, than whom there is nothing better. Hasten all to come together as to one temple of God, as to one altar, to one Jesus Christ, who came forth from the one Father, and is with one, and departed to one.

In view of these passages, what can we say of the bishop's eucharistic function? His function at the Eucharist would seem to be precisely the same as his function in the life of the Church in general. It is through him that the Church is one and entire. Anything done with the bishop is done in union with the entire community, and is thus the work or prayer of the entire Church. The bishop presides at the Eucharist in order that it may be the united prayer of all the assembled faithful; and beyond that, that it might be the prayer of the entire community, present and absent. The bishop's primary function here is thus that of epitomizing the community.

It would seem to be foreign to Ignatius' whole approach to think of the episcopal eucharistic ministry in terms of *potestatem aliquam consecrandi et offerendi* [power of consecrating and offering] [2] (Denz. 1771 [961]). Until such time as the physical presence of the body and blood of Christ in the bread and wine would be spelled out and be deemed a matter of primary importance,[3] a *potestas consecrandi* [power of consecrating] would have to be suspended in midair; the bishop's function is described with reference to the community rather than with reference to the elements. Is it *possible* that Ignatius thought of the episcopal ministry in this latter sense as well? It is a possibility, but one suggested by the later development rather than by anything in Ignatius' own writings. The Eucharist is something that all do, and it is the function of the bishop to include all, the entire community, in this communal act. The bishop's ministry is to enable the community to act as a community.

The bishop's ministry, of course, extends beyond the celebration of the liturgy. He has both a disciplinary and a teaching responsibility. We must inquire whether these aspects of his ministry allow or force us to modify or amplify what we have said about his role in the liturgy. There is no question but that Ignatius thinks of the bishop as having real authority from God. To the Philadelphians he writes (Intr.): "I greet her [the Church in Philadelphia] in the blood of Jesus Christ, which is eternal and abiding joy, especially if men be at one with the bishop, and with the presbyters and deacons, who together with him have been appointed according to the mind of Jesus Christ, and He established them in security according to His own will by His Holy Spirit." And to the Ephesians (6): "And the more anyone sees that the bishop is silent, the more let him fear him. For everyone whom the master of the house sends to do His business ought we to receive as Him who sent him. Therefore it is clear that we must regard the bishop as the Lord Himself." The contrast which we initially made between Ignatius and *I Clement* should not obscure the fact that for Ignatius, too, the bishop wields authority in God's name. And though there is no reference to apostolic succession, Ignatius quite clearly considers the bishop to be appointed by God. No doubt this disciplinary and teaching authority would have consequences for the celebration of the Eucharist. We may suppose that the bishop would have something decisive to say about the general order of the Eucharist. We may further suppose that it would be principally in connection with the eucharistic celebration that he would teach. But it is difficult to see that either of these factors would have any relevance whatsoever to the matter of the bishop's function in the eucharistic prayer itself. There is nothing here to lead us to suppose that Ignatius' other ideas on the episcopal ministry would have forced him to go beyond the view which we have already attributed to him.

Having said this much about the bishop, let us turn briefly to the question of the presbyters. Their function, their ministry, is more difficult to define than that of the bishop, since the presbytery is not central to Ignatius' letters. The presbyters remain in the shadow of the bishops. "The bishop and the presbyters" is so frequent a conjunction that one wonders whether the presbytery had any specific function of its own. It is tempting to suppose that even at Antioch the monoepiscopacy was preceded by a ruling presbytery, and that some of Ignatius' still fairly recent predecessors had been leading or presiding presbyters rather than members of an order distinguished from that of the presbyters.[4] In this case the presbyters would now be a kind of advisory body with which the bishop would naturally and properly consult. It would not have functions in addition to those of the bishop, but rather would assist him in the proper execution of his responsibilities. They act primarily as a body—a *synedrion.*

What of the role of the presbyters in the Eucharist? I should imagine that presbyters would have had *some* role to play in the eucharistic celebration; but Ignatius' thought seems to leave room for only one really vital ministry, the episcopal-unifying one.[5]

We return, then, to the question of whether or not we should suppose that the reference in the eight chapter of the *Epistle to the Smyrnaeans* presupposes that it must be a presbyter who functions in the bishop's place. First, I should say that I imagine that ordinarily it would be a presbyter who would take the place of the absent bishop at the Eucharist. The presbytery is always spoken of second whenever mention is made of the threefold ministry, and doubtless the presbyters were second to the bishop in dignity. However, if Ignatius thought that it had to be a presbyter who performed this task, it is strange that he does not say as much. Ignatius speaks of only one qualification necessary if one is to take the bishop's place in the Eucharist: appointment by the bishop. Because, as we have seen, Ignatius does not think of the bishop's eucharistic role in terms of *potestatem consecrandi et offerendi,* it is difficult to imagine why Ignatius would have required anything more than authorization by the bishop; for the essential thing was harmony with the bishop in the one communal act of worship, and this could be achieved simply by episcopal delegation.

Nor can it be maintained that this episcopal delegation would constitute a priestly ordination, at least not in the later sense of a permanent ordination; for in the nature of the case there would be nothing permanent about such delegation. Only to the extent that the bishop here and now wants and so designates an individual to take his place could that individual fulfil *the* hierarchical function. Consequently, to speak here of a permanent ordination or of a "character . . . qui nec deleri nec auferri potest" [which can be neither blotted out nor taken away] [6] (Denz. 1767 [960]), would run counter to Ignatius' entire way of thinking. And it is not merely that this would represent a form of conceptualization that would be foreign to Ignatius. A difference of this sort would hardly be worth reporting. Rather, Ignatius' views of the nature of the episcopal eucharistic ministry would seem to preclude the possibility of a priestly character and power that would be independent of the will of the bishop. The Eucharist is the worship of the community with and under the bishop, not because the bishop has a unique power of rendering Christ present in the bread and wine, but because Christian charity requires that the community be united in its prayer.

II

Suppose this to be the case; what follows? It would seem to follow that for Ignatius a Eucharist is valid and licit (though he would not put it that way) at which the bishop or someone whom he delegates for this purpose presides; and one who presides in place of the bishop is not *ipso facto* permanently set aside as a member of the hierarchical priestly order. To speak a more anachronistic language, a layman could offer mass.

As we have already indicated, if this *is* Ignatius' position, then he seems to be rather seriously at odds with Trent. While it seems reasonable to suppose that Ignatius considered the episcopate and the presbyterate to be permanent or lifetime ministries, there seems to be no historical evidence or even likelihood that he thought that there was a permanent, subepiscopal, priestly (eucharistic) ministry.

There are three ways of dealing with this at least apparent contradiction between Ignatius and Trent: (1) We can modify our interpretation of Ignatius. (2) We can modify our interpretation of Trent. (3) We can suppose that no amount of reinterpretation of Ignatius and Trent can get rid of the contradiction, and then ask what follows.

The first alternative is the most immediately inviting. After all, the interpretation of Ignatius advanced here depends upon a single phrase in *Smyrnaeans*. One could simply assume that Ignatius understood the presbyters to be priests in the later sense of the word. My argument has been, in part, an argument *ex silentio*, and an argument of this type based on early-second-century materials cannot afford to be overly dogmatic. However, I have argued not only *ex silentio*, and for the reasons already given I think that the interpretation of Ignatius advanced here is the most plausible one.

The second alternative is inviting too, but is so complex a matter that it cannot be entered upon here. If it is the case, as is not infrequently alleged, that the doctrine of the Church and the ministry is the principal and apparently insurmountable obstacle to Church unity, then it is of the utmost importance that Catholics consider and attempt to spell out just what it is that they take to be irrevocably and irreformably asserted by the Tridentine chapters and canons *de sacramento ordinis* [on the sacrament of holy orders]. However, as already indicated, this is too complicated a matter to be developed here; and in any event it is difficult to see how any amount of interpretation of Trent could bring Trent into agreement with Ignatius.

At first sight the third alternative is also attractive. After all, why not (a) grant that Ignatius and Trent contradict each other, and (b) suppose that therefore Ignatius was in error? After all, no one has ever maintained that a bishop could not be in error, even a saintly bishop. But the difficulty is that Ignatius at least seems to suppose that the Churches in Asia Minor with which he had at least some contact were in general agreement with him. Since his views on the priesthood and the *character indelebilis* [indelible character] of priestly ordination would seem to follow from his understanding of the nature of Christianity, the Eucharist, and the episcopacy, if the Asia Minor Churches agreed with him on these more basic issues it would seem legitimate to conclude that they would agree with him on the *character indelebilis*. Thus we would have a substantial portion of the early Church in opposition to Trent.

Whether or not Roman Catholic orthodoxy can accommodate serious disagreement between a substantial portion of the early Church and Trent (or conceivably between the entire Church at a certain moment in its history and Trent) will depend upon our solution to the problems of change, development, and error in the Church. In view of the fact (or at least what I take to be the fact) that we are only at the beginning with these problems, it would seem especially important at present that in our studies of the actual course of the Church's doctrinal and institutional development we do not suppose that in every case we know in advance what must and what cannot be the case.

III

To summarize: I have advanced an interpretation of Ignatius that is either difficult or impossible to bring into agreement with Trent. I have suggested three possible subsequent lines of study. Since the first part of the paper argues against the first of these three proposals, I really suggest only two alternatives: a re-evaluation of the relevant statements of Trent and a reconsideration of the problem of change in the Church. These two are not, of course, mutually exclusive.

Footnotes

[1] Throughout I have used the translation in *The Apostolic Fathers,* Kirsopp Lake, ed. and trans. (Cambridge, 1912). [*Editor's note:* There is considerable scholarly disagreement on the main thesis of McCue's article. Cf. Myles M. Bourke, "Reflections on Church Order in the New Testament," *Catholic Biblical Quarterly,* XXX (October 1968), pp. 493–511.]

[2] [*Editor's note:* Denz. refers to H. Denzinger, *Enchiridion Symbolorum* (Freiburg-Barcelona, 30th ed., 1955). This can be found in *The Church Teaches: Documents of the Church in English Translation,* John F. Clarkson *et al.,* eds. and trans. (St. Louis: B. Herder Book Co., 1955), 844.]

[3] See J. Betz, *Die Aktualpräsenz der Person und des Heilswerkes Jesu im Abendmahl nach der vorephesinischen griechischen Patristik* (Freiburg, 1955).

[4] See J. Colson, *Les fonctions ecclésiales aux deux premiers siècles* (Paris, 1956) pp. 237–39.

[5] Again I would note that we are here not concerned with the deacons.

[6] [*Editor's note:* Cf. *The Church Teaches,* 843.]

HANS KÜNG

The Petrine Office

Here Hans Küng addresses himself to the following questions. Are there grounds for assuming the primacy of Peter? Was the primacy of Peter something that was to continue? Is the bishop of Rome the successor of the primacy of Peter? What happened historically so that men accepted the claims of the bishop of Rome? What can be done so that the papacy can once again develop a primacy of service? What are the ecumenical dimensions of this view of the Petrine Office?

Hans Küng is the Dean of the Catholic Theological Faculty of the University of Tübingen. This is the second article in this volume by Father Küng.

Since the time of Vatican I there has appeared an imposing collection of books for and against the justification of the primacy. We shall not attempt the impossible here; rather than attempting to clear up the problems, all we can do is to shed some light on the questions at issue, with a view to an improved mutual understanding; this understanding will be aided in the future less by theoretical discussions than by the historical development of the Churches which has yet to come. All the difficulties are centered on three questions;

the second and third questions depend on a positive answer being given to the preceding one. Are there grounds for assuming the primacy of Peter? Was the primacy of Peter something that was to continue? Is the bishop of Rome the successor of the primacy of Peter? All we can do here is to give a short summary of the Catholic answers to this, given at Vatican I, and of the Protestant difficulties. By doing so frankly and without beating about the bush the cause of Catholicism and the ecumenical cause may best be served. Our intention, here as elsewhere, is to go beyond criticism to a constructive position, which will, it is hoped, become clear.

1. The existence of the primacy of Peter. Vatican I (Denz. 1822 f.),[1] using the new Testament dogmatically rather than historically, bases its arguments for the Petrine primacy of jurisdiction on two points: (a) The *promise* of the primacy to Peter alone: "You shall be called Cephas" (John 1:42), and "You are Peter, and on this rock I will build my church, and the powers of death shall not prevail against it. I will give you the keys of the kingdom of heaven, and whatever you bind on earth shall be bound in heaven, and whatever you loose on earth shall be loosed in heaven" (Matt. 16:18). (b) The *giving* of the jurisdiction to Peter alone, as supreme pastor and leader of the whole Church, by the risen Christ: "Feed my lambs, feed my sheep" (John 21:15–17).

From the *historical viewpoint* we can say that at least the following points would in the main be accepted by exegetical scholars. Peter was, at all events, specially marked out from among the twelve, by being the first witness to Christ's resurrection (1 Cor. 15:5; Luke 24:34); as the first of the Easter witnesses, he may be regarded as the rock of the Church. Further, Peter was the leading figure in the community at Jerusalem. Up to the time of the "apostolic Council" he seems, in practice at least, to have governed the original Christian community and the Christian diaspora. This is confirmed by Galatians 2:7f.; which establishes that the mission to the Jews and the Gentiles was divided up between Peter and Paul. Even though Luke had already, in his gospel, tried to give a much more idealized picture than either Mark or Matthew of this very human figure, this fisherman who was born in Bethsaida and lived, as a married man, in Capernaum, and even though an idealizing bias can be discerned in Acts 1–12, we can accept with certainty that Peter was the driving force of the young Church in its first missionary activity. And even though there is no sound historical basis for the interpretation of Petrine theology in Mark's gospel (Papias' story that Mark was Peter's interpreter is probably not reliable), nor in the letters attributed to Peter, and we can only infer it cautiously from the Pauline letters and Acts, we can at least be certain that Peter was the representative of Judaeo-Christianity, who in friendly fashion was opposed to Paul's mission to the Gentiles. He alone among the twelve definitely undertook missionary work outside Jerusalem. His stay in Antioch is testified to by Galatians 2:11f. (cf. Acts 15:7), and a visit to Corinth is possible (cf. 1 Cor. 1:12). It is not possible, however, to establish a definite itinerary of his journeys, nor a precise chronology. This is about the bare minimum which must be accepted, on the evidence of the sources, with regard to Peter's position in the early Church.

The *difficulties* which arise in connection with further and more positive statements about Peter's position in the New Testament Church result from the following undeniable problem: How far are the statements about the position of Peter during Jesus' lifetime merely a reflection of the position of Peter after the resurrection? True, it cannot be denied (and the priority of Peter with regard to the postresurrection appearances is probably connected with this fact) that Peter was one of the most intimate disciples of Jesus (Mark 5:37; 9:2; 14:33), indeed the spokesman of the disciples (cf. Mark 8:29; 9:5; 10:28; 11:21), and that no doubt for that reason his name always appears at the head of the list of the twelve (Mark 3:16; Matt. 10:2; Luke 6:14; Acts 1:13). Three questions, however, remain the subject of fierce controversy: (1) Whether the title added to his original name Simon (Mark 1:16), the name Kephas (Aramaic *kepha* = rock = Peter) which become an additional name and finally his proper name, was given by the historical Jesus himself (as a promise for the future?) *or* whether it was given to him by the primitive Christian community (*vaticinium ex eventu*?) [statement (added) after the fact]; (2) whether the saying at Matthew 16:18f., which in view of its Aramaic character very probably originated in Palestine, and which strikingly enough has no parallels in the other synoptic gospels, was a saying of the historical Jesus (the historical context for which may have been different from that of Caesarea Philippi), *or* whether the saying was attributed to Jesus by the primitive Christian community, in order to authorize the position of Simon in the community by the story of the change of name or by recasting accounts of the postresurrection appearances; the answer to this question will depend on what view is taken of the relationship between the eschatological preaching of Jesus and the possible intention to found a Church; (3) whether the saying at Matthew 16:18f. gives to Peter a genuine monarchical and legal ruling authority (jurisdiction) over the whole Church *or* whether it merely gives him a prior historical position as the first confessor of Jesus and first witness of his resurrection; as the spokesman and representative, perhaps even the leader of the twelve, who nonetheless remains on the same level as the other apostles. In the second case the word "rock" can refer to Peter as believer and confessor, or as an apostle; the "keys" can refer to a teaching authority or a governing authority, or both; finally "binding and loosing" can refer to a disciplinary power, or to the power to exclude others from the community, or to full authority over the kingdom of God and over sin, or quite generally to a juridical authority. John 21:15–17 will then be judged in an analogous way to Matthew 16:18f.

2. The continuation of the Petrine primacy. Vatican I (Denz. 1824f.) deduces from the primacy of Peter the permanent continuation of this primacy. This primacy, appointed for the eternal salvation and the continuing good of the Church, must according to the appointment made by Christ necessarily continue. There are no quotations from Scripture in support of this, simply the declaration: "Whoever asserts that blessed Peter's permanent successors do not have the chief place in the whole Church, appointed by Christ the Lord, that is by divine right . . . let him be anathema."

From the *historical viewpoint* it is significant that Peter is not mentioned again after Antioch (cf. Acts 15:7; Gal. 2:11f.). By contrast with the martyrdom of James, there is no mention of the death of Peter in the New Testament. On the other hand, a knowledge of his martyrdom evidently underlies the last chapter, added subsequently, of John's gospel. Nothing is reported about the appointment of a successor to Peter. Neither Matthew 16:18f., nor John 21:15–17, nor Luke 22:32 makes any special reference to a successor of Peter. On the other hand these writings, composed after Peter's death, indicate a continuing interest in Peter's special position, which is more than episodic; an interest that does not, for example, attach to James. In this connection two points are the subject of controversy: (1) Whether James, who after Peter's departure was clearly the leader of the Jerusalem community, was quite simply the leader of the local Jerusalem community and remained subject to Peter as the leader of the whole Church, *or* whether Peter, if he ever was the leader of the whole Church, was replaced in this position by James the brother of the Lord, as can be inferred from the second half of Acts (from 12:17 onward), from Galatians 2:12, and from uncanonical sources (Ps-Clem. *Rec.* 1:17 and *Hom.* 1:20; *Ep. Pet.* 1; *Gospel of Thomas*, saying 12); (2) whether the Petrine texts imply a unique foundation *or* a continuing foundational *function;* that is, whether "rock" simply means the chronological beginning of the Christian community *or* the unique foundational element of the community *or* the continuing stabilizing fundament of the Church; and whether the "key-bearer" or representative "pastor" is a pattern for future forms of government *or* should be seen as the first incumbent of a continuing governmental authority.

3. The continuation of the Petrine primacy in the bishop of Rome. Vatican I (Denz. 1824f.) sees the permanent continuation of the Petrine primacy realized in the bishops of Rome: "Anyone following Peter in this episcopal see, receives from the institution of Christ himself Peter's primacy over the whole Church. . . . Therefore whoever maintains . . . the bishop of Rome is not the successor in this primacy . . . let him be anathema." This statement is supported by a quotation from Irenaeus of Lyons (died *circa* 200), according to which "all Churches in all places are in agreement with the Church of Rome concerning the '*potentior principalitas*' " [because of more efficient leadership].[2] Apart from that, and an allusion in Ambrose, there are only two fifth-century references, both from the Roman side; one by the Roman legate at the Council of Ephesus in 431, the other by Leo the Great.

From the *historical viewpoint* it is uncontestable that the Roman claim to primacy in the government of the Church, whatever the situation may have been with regard to its recognition in the East, was solidly established and clearly formulated in the West by the time of Leo I at the latest. The possibility that Peter may have been in Rome and been martyred there is one that has found increasing acceptance in recent times, both by Catholic and non-Catholic historians. This acceptance is not in fact founded on the archaeological evidence of a Petrine grave beneath the Vatican Basilica, which has been regarded very sceptically by leading experts even on the Catholic side. The literary evidence is, however, very impressive. On the basis of *I Clement* 5f. a tradition of the martyrdom of Peter and Paul in Rome seems established with a high degree of probability for the Neronian period (does the reference to Babylon at 1 Peter 5:13 really mean Rome?). This Roman testimony from the end of the first century is confirmed by one from Asia Minor at the beginning of the second century (Ignatius, *Rom.* 4:3). It would be very difficult to challenge the credibility of a tradition which seems established from about A.D. 95, which is straightforward and undisputed at the time, and which at that time was free from any bias of ecclesiastical politics.

The *difficulties* do not therefore center of the proof of Peter's presence in Rome; moreover, it would not be absolutely necessary to prove that Peter was martyred in Rome in order to justify the Roman primacy. The difficulties, which we must simply acknowledge without prejudice, concern the establishing of the succession of a monarchical bishopric of Rome, even assuming that there was a Petrine primacy for it to succeed to; it is difficult to establish that there was a *legitimate* succession, authorized in some way or another. The fact that Peter himself cannot possibly have been the founder of the Christian community in Rome, any more than Paul can, is irrelevant to the issue.

With regard to the early history of the Roman community there remain, despite extended discussions of the matter, certain difficulties which await solution and which can only be offered here as material for further discussion. It is not only that we have no idea what form Peter's activity in Rome took, and cannot know whether he was the leader of the Roman community at all—something we cannot simply assume for Peter any more than we can for Paul. The oldest and most important evidence for Peter's sojourn and death in Rome is a document which establishes at the same time a very strong case against the existence of a monarchical successor to Peter. In the letter of the Roman community to the community at Corinth, which according to a statement of Denis of Corinth, *circa* 170, reported by Eusebius, was composed by Clement, no single authority is obvious. At all events there is no sign of a monarchical episcopate in the first epistle of Clement, either in Corinth or in Rome. For this reason, it is difficult to see how Peter could have had a monarchical bishop as his successor. It is a peculiar fact, already referred to above, that even Ignatius, who in his letters to the communities in Asia Minor is already addressing, with some emphasis, monarchical bishops, does not address a bishop at all when he comes to write to the Romans. It is impossible to ascertain when a monarchical bishop first emerged from among the many bishops and presbyters in Rome. Details of the successors of Peter, like the oldest list of the bishops of Rome given by Irenaeus, which refers not to Peter but to Linus as the first bishop of Rome, who received his episcopal ministry from Peter *and* Paul, are second-century reconstructions, which may possibly have drawn on well-known Roman names. Our information about the Roman Church and its bishops is very fragmentary up to the middle of the third century; the first precise chronological dating of a Roman pontificate is the resignation of Pontian on September 28, 235.

It is understandable that the old-established, large, and wealthy community of the capital of the world should from the first have been aware of its importance (cf. *I Clement*) and could rightly enjoy a considerable reputation (as early as Rom. 1:8), not least because of the activity of Peter and Paul (Ignatius, *Rom.* 4:3) and because of the exemplary charity of the community (cf. the opening of Ignatius' letter). But for a long time there is no sign of a claim to primacy, neither on behalf of the community nor of an individual. With the struggle against gnosticism and the increasing importance of apostolic tradition and apostolic bishoprics, the importance of the Roman community, which could claim two apostles, the two greatest apostles, for itself, necessarily grew in stature. But even the passage in Irenaeus quoted by Vatican I (*Adv. Haer.* III, 3:1–2) does not refer to any *legal* obligation for other Churches to agree with the Roman Church. The Roman Church (there is no mention of a Roman bishop) figures not as the holder of a legal primacy, but as the most distinguished guardian of tradition, because of its double succession (Irenaeus too refers back to Peter *and* Paul); by ascertaining what *its* faith is, the faith of all the other Churches is assured.

The high repute of the Roman community is attested to in many letters and visits by bishops, theologians, and heretics; and on this basis, toward the end of the second century, Bishop Victor could assert his claims against the Churches of Asia Minor in the dispute over Easter; still more clearly Stephen I appealed to this authority against the Africans in the dispute over baptism. But both of them had to face serious opposition in the Church as a whole, from the most important churchmen of the time; Victor was opposed by Irenaeus and Polycrates of Ephesus, Stephen by Cyprian and Firmilian. But the claims of the Roman bishops were greatly strengthened in this way, even though until far into the second millennium claims and theories always preceded reality. In all this development it is a remarkable fact that Matthew 16:18f. in its complete wording is not quoted on a single occasion in all the Christian literature of the first few centuries, not even in the first epistle of Clement. The passage is first quoted by Tertullian in the second century, but not in support of Rome, merely in support of Peter. Not until the middle of the third century does a Roman bishop, Stephen I in fact, appeal to the precedence of Peter in his support of what he considers the superior tradition. And not until the fourth century is Matthew 16:18f. used in support of a claim to primacy (Optatus of Mileve, Jerome, Dasmasus, Leo I). In Eastern exegesis the situation is even more negative: right down to the eighth century and of course beyond that, Matthew 16:18f. is thought of in connection with a personal primacy of Peter, unless the passage is quite simply thought of, as it is to some extent in the Western tradition, as referring to Christ or to faith. Matthew 16:18 is unanimously associated with the forgiveness of sins, which is not of course reserved to Peter alone (cf. Matt. 18:18). There are no signs that anyone seriously thought of a connection between the Matthew passage and Rome.

The aim of this analysis is not to give the impression that all these difficulties cannot be debated and in part at least answered. All these questions are historical ones; and unless one is going to take refuge in historically unfounded dogmatic postulates, the solving of them, as the vast amount of books on the subject makes very clear, is going to be a fairly exacting task. The difficulties of the argument about primacy can, as the foregoing summary has shown, be graded: before proving "*perpetuitas*" [perpetual], it is essential to prove "*petrinitas*" [Petrine]; and before proving "*romanitas*" [Roman] it is essential to prove "*perpetuitas.*"

Despite all these difficulties Catholic exegesis and theology have decided for a primacy of Peter, even if Matthew 16:18f. is attributed not to the historical Jesus, but to the postresurrection course of events. Catholic scholars remain convinced that the Petrine texts of the New Testament are only exhaustively interpreted if we infer that while there are not continual new foundations, there is at least a continuing foundational function; if the people of God of the new covenant, like that of the old covenant, has its divinely appointed pastor. They also hold, on the basis of subsequent history, that the bishop of Rome can exclusively lay claim to this function, and has with increasing clarity in the course of time fulfilled that function; at the same time, the "*ius divinum*" [divine right or order] of the primacy can only be realized and fulfilled within the "*ius humanum*" [human law or order].

Whatever view one takes, there is one thing that Orthodox and Protestant theologians, even if they find the Catholic arguments unconvincing, cannot dispute: the ministerial primacy of a single person is not contrary to Scripture. Whatever may be the justification for it, there is nothing in Scripture which would exclude such a ministerial primacy. A primacy of this kind is not from the very start in opposition to Scripture. Indeed, Orthodox and Protestant theologians will probably even concede that a ministerial primacy of this kind could be in accordance with Scripture, and at any rate provide that it is justifiable, and is carried out and exercised, in accordance with Scripture. Most of the Reformers from the young Luther via Melanchthon to Calvin conceded this, and many Orthodox and Protestant theologians today would concede it.

What was said above about the apostolic succession of pastoral ministries in general applies equally to an apostolic succession of the Petrine ministry. The decisive thing is not the historical aspect of a proven succession, however valuable that may be. The decisive thing is succession in the Spirit: in the Petrine mission and task, in the Petrine witness and ministry. If someone could prove conclusively that his predecessor and the predecessor of his predecessor and so on backward were ultimately successors of Peter, even if he could prove that the original predecessor of all his predecessors had been "appointed" by Peter himself and invested as Peter's successor with all rights and duties, and yet on the other hand he completely fails to fulfill the Petrine mission, if he does not carry out the task it implies, if he does not give witness or perform his ministry, what use to him, what use to the Church is all the "apostolic succession"? Conversely, if there were someone whose succession, at least in its earliest years, were difficult to establish, whose "appointment" two thousand years ago was not at all documented, but who on the other hand fulfilled the Petrine mission as described in Scripture and performed this ministry for the Church, would it not be a secondary, if still important, question whether this real servant of the Church had a regular ancestral tree? He might not have a commission through the laying on of hands, but he would have the charism, the charism of governing, and that would basically be enough.

The point we are trying to make is this: it is not the claims, the "rights," the "chain of succession" as such which are decisive, but the exercise and carrying out of a ministry in practice, service in action. When John XXIII began his great ecumenical work for the Church, for Christendom, and for the world, mankind was not very interested in his place in a chain of succession and whether the legitimacy of his office was historically founded. What mankind saw with relief and joy was this: here was a man who for all his human weakness was a real rock in the modern age, able to give a new anchorage and a new sense of communion to Christianity (cf. Matt. 16:18). Here was a man who from his own deep sense of faith was able to strengthen and encourage the brethren (cf. Luke 22:32). Here was a man, who was able to tend his sheep, as his Lord once did, with unselfish love (cf. John 21:15–17). Not that the whole of mankind therefore became Catholic. But they felt spontaneously that these actions and this spirit had the Gospel of Christ behind them and were at all events justified by that Gospel. And this kind of legitimacy is more decisive for the Petrine ministry than any other.

This does not make discussion of the exegetical and historical problems superfluous. But this discussion must be seen in the proper light, in the proper perspective. One further point must be stressed here. Our discussion of the arguments has made it clear how much room to maneuver there is—not only in the historical questions (cf. Tertullian and Cyprian), but still more in the exegetical ones. There is a world of difference in interpretation between interpreting Matthew 16:18f. in the light of Matthew 18:18, or vice versa, between putting greater emphasis on the passages about Peter or on those about James, etc.

How can we explain the fact that the same handful of words and short sentences can be interpreted by scholars, who claim to be working with the same historical and critical methods, in such diametrically opposed ways? There can be no doubt that the whole personality of the theologian is involved here, something that is determined by far more than these short passages themselves. Theologians, some admittedly more than others, quite obviously approach this question above all others with quite definite preconceived ideas, which can only be corrected to a very limited extent by the texts themselves. To put it more concretely: the view a theologian takes of the papacy today is not irrelevant to his interpretation of the problems which arise from the exegetical and historical texts. After looking at the centuries of controversy which have surrounded this point, we must conclude that it is improbable that greater agreement will be reached with regard to the interpretation of the texts unless to begin with a greater agreement is reached about the role of the papacy today. And this greater agreement about the role of the papacy today depends not least, indeed perhaps depends primarily, on the papacy itself, and its need to see itself more and more as a Petrine ministry.

It is an absurd situation that the Petrine ministry, which was intended, as Catholics in particular see it, to be a rocklike and pastoral ministry, preserving and strengthening the unity of the Church, should have become a gigantic, apparently immovable, insuperable, and impassable block of stone barring the way to mutual understanding between the Christian Churches. Those of us who are convinced of the value of a Petrine ministry should be particularly taxed by this situation. How could such a situation possibly have arisen? Does it stem simply from a lack of knowledge, an undeveloped understanding or even a wicked refractoriness on the part of those who oppose the Petrine ministry? No one today would have the temerity to assert that. Even if the blame for the division between the Churches cannot be laid exclusively on one side or the other, we cannot evade the question: Did this complete reversal of the function of the Petrine ministry not come partly, even particularly, from the fact that the Petrine *ministry* appeared to men to be more and more a Petrine *dominion*? There were of course very various historical reasons for this, and it was certainly not the result of bad faith on the part of one or more individuals. We have already indicated the long process by which the papacy became a world power.

As we have shown, things could have developed differently.

Whatever view we take of the exegetical and historical basis for the Petrine ministry, and the divine or human authorization of a permanent Petrine ministry in the Church, it is clear that there might have been a different kind of development. The Roman community with its bishop, which in fact possessed quite outstanding gifts and capacities for service, could have become a truly pastoral primacy, in the sense of a spiritual responsibility, an inner leadership and an active caring for the welfare of the whole Church; this is a conception which in the pre-Constantinian age would have been totally acceptable. In this way the Roman bishopric would have become a general ecclesiastical court of appeal, capable of mediating and settling disputes, and had a primacy of selfless service, being responsible to the Lord of the Church and exercising humble charity toward all men; a primacy not in the spirit of Roman imperialism, but in the spirit of the Gospel.

No one will deny that the Roman Petrine ministry also fulfilled this role; indeed one can say that in the pre-Constantinian era this was its basic attitude. There was a genuine attempt to help the other Churches in a variety of ways, without ruling over them and without trying to stifle their individual natures and their independence in doctrine, liturgy, and Church order. A good example is the part played by Rome in establishing Catholic norms in the second century (the rule of faith, the canon, ecclesiastical office) or in the struggle against Arianism. Only two examples from all the first three centuries have come down to us which reveal a different attitude, an attitude of rigid, impatient, and aggressive authoritarianism and centralism, which was out to make the whole Church uniform and was ready to use extreme measures of force to do it, rather than working with the spiritual means of brotherly admonition and exemplary action. The first example is that of Bishop Victor, who wanted to excommunicate the whole of Asia Minor, merely in order to force on these ancient apostolic Churches the new date of Easter, which had only been introduced in Rome a generation before. The other is Bishop Stephen who, because of opposition to his view concerning the baptism of heretics, again wanted to use the powerful means of excommunication to exclude whole areas of the Church from the communion of the Church, and who accused the great Cyprian of being a pseudo-Christian and a pseudo-apostle.

This was the beginning of the road of unevangelical spiritual dominion, the course which can be illustrated from later apparently unimportant incidents. For example Damasus (died 384) was the first to call the Roman *cathedra* [seat of authority] the *sedes apostolica* [apostolic see], although in the original usage of the Church all Churches which had been founded by the apostles were called *ecclesiae apostolicae* [apostolic churches], and although in the middle of the fourth century all episcopal sees were still called apostolic sees (in this way Rome began to monopolize titles of dignity). Then Bishop Siricius (died 399) began to call his own statutes quite simply "apostolic," adopted the official imperial style in his writings, instead of the earlier pastoral style—a manner of approach which was to be so successful in the future and was also to cause so much damage—and began to claim for himself, in quite a different sense from Paul, the "*sollicitudo omnium ecclesiarum*" [anxiety for all the Churches] (2 Cor. 11:28), in order to confuse the areas of genuine responsibility, and to extend the authority of the Roman bishop so that he became the metropolitan of central and southern Italy, and then the authority of the metropolitan so that he became the patriarch of the West, and then the authority of the Western patriarch so that he became the primate of East and West.

Then Bishop Innocent (died 407) tried to insist that all important matters after they had been discussed by a synod of bishops should be presented to the Roman bishop for his decision, and brought about the centralization of the liturgy on the basis of historical fictions (namely that the Roman tradition was the Petrine tradition, thereby neglecting the Pauline tradition; that the Roman liturgy was the liturgy of Peter; that Peter had founded all the Churches of the West). Then subsequent bishops—Zosimus, Boniface, Celestine, Leo the Great, and then Felix II, Gelasius, Symmachus, and Hormisdas—continued to develop their claims to domination and their actual power, like rulers of this world, so that with time the Roman patriarchate grew more and more powerful, and the successors of the Galilean fisherman became secular princes with extensive lands, rich sources of income, and an army, a strange development which was legitimized *post hoc facto* [afterward] by the influential forgery of the Donation of Constantine in the eighth to ninth centuries. Then finally in the ninth century Nicholas I imposed the ban of anathema on anyone who failed to observe a doctrinal or disciplinary decision of the Pope, set himself up as the lord of the whole earth, and did not even shrink from declaring that the most scandalous forgeries of Church history, the pseudo-Isidorian decretals, a very recent work of Frankish forgery which had been handed over to him, had been preserved from earliest times in the Roman archives and were a binding and fundamental part of ecclesiastical law.

From this point the road necessarily led, despite the *saeculum obscurum* [dark ages], to Humbert and to Gregory VII, whose *dictatus papae* [papal statement] goes far beyond even the colossal claims of the pseudo-Isidorian forgeries, both in its claims to power within the Church and its claims to worldly power. In this way a Petrine ministry which might originally have been possible turned into a papal world domination, which celebrated the height of its triumphs at the beginning of the thirteenth century and came to a catastrophic end at the conclusion of that century.

This was all by no means necessary, but was the result of a ministry which, as has been variously stressed, on the one hand rendered great services to the Western Church, and on the other hand saw itself increasingly as a source of power and dominion. The view of the Petrine ministry as a spiritual power and dominion did not change much in subsequent times, despite all the criticisms of a Bernard of Clairvaux, despite the heretics, scholars, and saints who opposed it. It continued unabated, while the power politics of the crusades and the policy of latinization definitively alienated the entire East from the bishop of Rome, while the Western schism brought the papacy itself to the brink of collapse, while the Protestant Reformation removed from the papacy the greater part of the Germanic and Anglo-Saxon area, while modern developments caused a majority of Catholics, especially the intellectuals, to undertake a silent inner exodus. The Pope of the First Vatican Council was not far behind many of his medieval predecessors as far as a sense of spiritual domination was concerned; not only because he praised an anthology on the Roman Pontiff which reproduced the forged decretals as genuine testimonies of the papacy; not only because he described the abolition of the Papal States as sacrilege, appealing to the inalienable rights, sanctified by so many titles, of the apostolic see to its possessions; but particularly because in the Council itself he identified himself with ecclesiastical tradition, branded the representatives of the opposition as his enemies, and imposed his personal views on the Council by not precisely fastidious means. The difference between this approach and that of the Popes of Vatican II is evident.

These historical notes are of course one sided and simplified; it was not our intention to sketch out a history of the papacy. But the darker and shadowy side must be brought out, especially because it has been customary in Catholic apologetics to fail to put it into context, and to concentrate on the admittedly important service the papacy has rendered to the Church; it must not be overlooked if we are to realize the extent of the problem and hope to find a possible positive solution. When we look at the lost unity of the Church of Christ and the considerable rigidity within the Catholic Church, the question arises with great force; is there a way back, which would also be a way forward, from this primacy of dominion to the old primacy of service and ministry?

Cautiously but with conviction we can give an affirmative answer to this question. Three points, the second more important than the first and the third than the second, must be taken into account.

1. Historical experience shows that the high points of papal dominion have always been followed immediately by times of outward humiliation and restrictions of power. After Leo I and his successors came the time of the emperor Justinian (527–565), who reduced Rome to a mere Western patriarchate, on the same level as Constantinople in the East, and regarded and confirmed himself as the real ruler of the whole Church in matters both of doctrine and discipline. Again, after the spiritual imperator Nicholas I came the disgraceful "dark age" of Rome, in which the Pope, caught between the merciless struggles of the Roman nobility, was reduced to the rank of a minor country bishop. Again, after the proud universal dominion of the Popes in the Middle Ages, there came the humiliations of exile, the great schism, and the conciliar era; the splendid age of the Renaissance was followed by the enormous losses of the Reformation period; the period of baroque dominion and the Counterreformation was followed by a time of decline with the Enlightenment and the age of revolution. . . .

2. The process of the secularization of the papacy has, seen as a whole, been largely reversed; this happened for the most part under historical pressures, but it is a fact that must be taken into account. The development as a whole has been one from the loss of the papal

world dominion to the loss of the Papal States; from the abandonment of a *potestas directa in temporalia* [direct power in temporal affairs], via a *potestas indirecta*, down to a respecting of the independence of secular organizations; from a primacy in art and culture to a primacy of service, both humanitarian and missionary. Admittedly this abandoning of power has chiefly been connected with the relations between the papacy and secular powers in the widest sense. It has often, partly as a reaction, been associated with a development of power positions within the Church itself; thus after the loss of the Vatican State, Vatican I decided for a codification of Church law in a spirit of absolutism, and for an intensification of the process of centralization. In order to concentrate on this side of the problem, the question of power within the Church which is so much more important today, we have been considering earlier Popes rather than the medieval Popes. And for this reason a third point, the most important one, needs consideration.

3. A voluntary abandonment of spirtual power is possible; something that might seem unwise in terms of politics, and even of Church politics, may be required of a Church. Remarkably enough, and it is a very hopeful sign, this has actually happened in history. Apart from examples like Hadrian VI or Marcellus II who because of the disfavor of the time or early death were unable to have a profound influence on history, there is the figure of Gregory the Great, who followed a series of very power-conscious Popes; there is John XXIII, and the fact that Vatican I could be followed by a Council like Vatican II.

Is there a way back, or rather a way forward, to the original idea of a primacy of service? Only through the voluntary renunciation of that power which in practice has become associated with the Petrine ministry, through a long and problematical historical development, and has partly helped it but also seriously injured it. Without this renunciation of power the reunion of the divided Christian Churches is as impossible as a radical renewal of the Catholic Church according to the Gospel. The renunciation of power is by no means something that happens naturally. Why should any man, any authority or institution, give up something which it possesses, and without any visible sign of something being given in return?

The renunciation of power is in fact only possible for a man who has grasped something of the message of Jesus and of the Sermon on the Mount in particular; who has understood something of what is meant by the blessedness of the "meek" who "*shall* inherit the earth" and the blessedness of the "peacemakers" (Matt. 5:5, 9); who gives his cloak as well when only his coat has been demanded, who goes two miles with his companion who only asked him to go one (5:40f.), who does to men what he would wish them to do to him (7:12). That these demands of Jesus—and we must remember that it is not the individual examples, but the whole basic drift of a man's life which matters—are not abstract ideas, but are relevant for the Church and the governing of the Church too, is revealed by no one more clearly than by the apostle Paul in his attitude toward his Churches.

Paul knew very well that in his communities there was no higher authority than his own apostolic authority, entrusted to him by the Lord. And yet he did not try to extend or develop this authority, still less build it up into a sacral authority of jurisdiction. On the contrary, he constantly and voluntarily limited his own authority in the Church. He did this in the conviction that the apostles were not called to "lord it over your faith," but to "work with you for your joy" (2 Cor. 1:24). He did this in the conviction that his Churches belonged not to him but to the Lord, and were therefore free in the spirit, "called to freedom" (Gal. 5:13) and not "slaves of men" (1 Cor. 7:23). Paul is well aware that his Churches are immature in many ways and make mistakes. And yet he never behaves toward them as though he were a cautious pedagogue whose task it was to educate them for their freedom. Rather he presupposes this freedom as having been granted to them, he respects it, fights for it, so that his communities will not follow him under constraint, but in freedom. Of course, where Christ and his Gospel have been sacrificed to another gospel, he must threaten them with curses and judgment (1 Cor. 16:22; Gal. 1:8f.; 5:10). But the measures he resorted to with regard to an individual, temporary exclusion from the community until he should mend his ways (1 Cor. 5), he never, so far as we can tell, applied to a whole community, not even in Galatia. He always keeps his authority in the background as much as he can; he appeals rather than commands, appeals to the judgment of others and their own sense of responsibility rather than delivering prohibitions, prefers gentle admonitions to disciplinary force, prefers hortative forms to imperatives, "we" phrases to "you" phrases; instead of punishing, he speaks words of forgiveness, instead of repressing freedom he challenges it to come alive.

Paul never abuses his authority. He does not extend his powers; on the contrary, he always restricts them. In matters of Church discipline he avoids making an authoritative decision, something he could easily have done (2 Cor. 8:8–10). In moral questions, where the Lord and his Word are not at stake, he prefers to leave his communities with their freedom, rather than lay any restraint on them (1 Cor. 7:35). Even where there can be no question of what his decision is going to be, he does not offer a one-sided prescription, he involves the community (1 Cor. 5). Even in cases where he unquestionably has authority to take strong measures, he restrains himself, he seems almost to beg his community not to oblige him to use that authority; again and again we can see that from his letters (cf. 1 Thess. 2:7; 2 Thess. 3:9; 1 Cor. 4:14; 9:12, 18; 2 Cor. 13:10; Philem. 8f.) In this way Paul never confronts his communities as their lord, not even as their high priest. The apostle is not the lord, Christ is the Lord, and this Lord lays down the norms both for the Churches and for him. He can never treat his Christians simply as "children," they are his "brothers," whose servant he is in patience, generosity, and love. It is not politeness or human courtesy which is the reason why he is always ready to renounce the use of his authority; it is because he wants to be faithful to the Lord in his service. For this reason he uses his authority for building up, not for tearing down (2 Cor. 10:8; 13:10).

It would be a tremendous gain both for the Church and for the Petrine ministry if the latter could take the reflection of this apostle as its pattern, imitating Paul, who did more than any of the other apostles, even than Peter, who was the greater theologian and who, according to the oldest Roman tradition, was always seen as founding the fame and authority of the Church in Rome together with Peter. If in the course of time the Petrine ministry has become too much of a Petrine dominion, then it is not least because Paul was not regarded as highly as Peter. Paul was only quoted in selected pericopes, and was merely, if with great solemnity, "commemorated"; Galatians 1:11–20 was still quoted, but not Galatians 2:11–14—in short, "*San Paolo*" was too far "*fuori le mura.*" [This is a reference to the Basilica of St. Paul, which is the second largest basilica in Rome after St. Peter's and is geographically situated "outside the walls" of ancient Rome.]

But it was not only Paul's image which was distorted. It is doubtful whether Peter would have recognized himself in the picture that was to be drawn of him. Not only because he was no prince of the apostles, but remained to the end of his life the modest fisherman, now a fisher of men, who wanted to follow and serve his Lord. But much more because he had another side, which all the Gospels agree upon, a side which shows us the truly human Peter; misunderstanding, making mistakes, failing his Lord. It is little short of scandalizing that each of the three texts classically used to prove the precedence of Peter are accompanied in counterpoint by three passages, the dark tones of which balance, if not obscure, the bright tones of the three Petrine texts. The three great promises are balanced by three serious failures. Anyone who wishes to base his claims upon the promises cannot avoid applying to himself the three failures, which at least represent three possible temptations. And if the promises in large black letters on a golden background surround the Church of St. Peter like a frieze, it would be only right, to avoid misunderstandings, to add to them the three contrary incidents in golden letters on a black background. Gregory the Great at least, who is buried in the church, would surely have understood that as well as John XXIII.

The first temptation (Matt. 16:18f. is followed by Matt. 16:22f.) is that of knowing better than the Lord, taking the master confidently on one side and telling him how he is to act and how things are going to happen. Peter, putting himself above his master, points out a way of triumphalism which will bypass the cross. These confident ideas of a *theologia gloriae* [triumphalistic theology] are precisely human thoughts, which stand in direct opposition to what God thinks and plans: they represent a pious *theologia satanae* [devil's theology], an inspiration of the Tempter. Whenever Peter takes it for granted that he can think God's thoughts for him, whenever the confessing Peter of Matthew 16:16 becomes the misunderstanding Peter of Matthew 16:22, standing, perhaps without even noticing it, on the side of man rather than on the side of God, then the Lord turns his back on him, and delivers the hardest saying imaginable: "Get behind me, Satan! You are a hindrance to me; for you are not on the side of God, but of men" (16:23).

The second temptation (Luke 22:32 is followed by Luke 22:34) reminds us that a particular position and a particular gift imply particular responsibilities. And precisely this does not exclude trials and temptations; here again Satan appears, who has demanded the right to sift every disciple of Jesus like wheat. Peter's faith is not to fail. But as soon as he self-confidently supposes that his loyalty is beyond question and that his faith is a firm possession, beyond any temptation; as soon as he forgets that he is dependent on the prayer of the Lord and needs to receive faith and devotion over and over again; as soon as he regards his strength and his readiness to accompany the Lord as his own achievement; as soon as in his self-confidence he overestimates himself and no longer puts his whole trust in the Lord, then the hour of cock-crow is not far off. He will be ready to deny his Lord, to assert that he never knew him, not once only, but three times, that is to say, completely and totally: "I tell you, Peter, the cock will not crow this day, until you three times deny that you know me."

The third temptation (John 21:15 is followed by John 21:20ff.): the Lord three times asks Peter, who had three times denied him, whether he loves him: "Do you love me more than these?" Only under this condition can he be entrusted with the leadership of the community; he must feed the lambs and tend the sheep by following Jesus in love. But Peter, when he no longer looks at Jesus, when he turns round, sees him who had always surpassed him in love. And his unsuitable question as to what is going to happen to John, receives an answer which seems to contradict his general commission as a pastor: "What is that to you?" So there are things which do not concern Peter. Whenever Peter does not concern himself with his own task, whenever he tries to concern himself with everything, whenever he fails to see that there are things in human life that he cannot assume responsibility for, whenever he forgets that there are special relations with Jesus which do not have to pass through him, whenever he fails to accept that there are other ways apart from his way, then he will hear the word, a word of stern rebuke that is at the same time a call to renewed discipleship: "What is that to you? Follow me!"

The greater the mission, the greater the temptation. The enormous burden of responsibility, of care, of suffering and anxiety which weighs upon the Petrine ministry—provided that Peter's successor is truly a rock, a key-bearer and pastor in the service of the whole Church—is surely immeasurable. For the times in which the papacy could be enjoyed, being something given by God—as Leo X is said to have remarked at the time of Luther—are long since past. The toils and tribulations associated with this ministry, the sense of being misunderstood, and the sense of ones' own incapacity, are enough to make faith unsure (cf. Luke 22:32), to make love fail (cf. John 21:17), to make the hope of overcoming the gates of death (cf. Matt. 16:18) seem faint. This ministry, more than any other, is dependent every day afresh upon the grace of the Lord. This ministry may also expect a great deal from the brethren, more than is often given to it, and of a helpful rather than an unhelpful kind: not servile subservience, not uncritical devotion, not sentimental idolatry, but daily intercession, loyal cooperation, constructive criticism, and unfeigned love.

It is possible that even Orthodox and Protestant Christians may be able to sympathize with the Catholic in his conviction that the Church, and perhaps Christianity as a whole, would lack something if this Petrine ministry were suddenly no longer there: something that is not inessential for the Church. There is something imposing about this ministry, if it is soberly seen in the light of sacred Scripture for what it is: a ministry to the whole Church. The fully understood biblical notion of ministry goes far beyond the legal categories of Vatican I. This primacy of service is more than a primacy of honor (*primatus honoris*), which belongs to no one in a Church of service and in its passivity could help no one. This primacy of service is also more than a primacy of jurisdiction (*primatus iurisdictionis*), which, interpreted solely in terms of power and dominion, would be a fundamental misunderstanding and which, interpreted solely in terms of the words themselves, would leave out of account, if not contradict, the essential element, that of service. The Petrine ministry can be correctly and biblically described as a primacy of service, a pastoral primacy: *primatus servitii, primatus ministerialis, primatus pastoralis* [primacy of service, primacy of ministry, pastoral primacy].

> Are we here describing an ideal? Have we finally ceased to talk about the *real* Church? Is the real Petrine ministry not still, as it has always been, a Petrine dominion? With all due caution we may answer: the primacy of service is being real-

ized now once again. There are grounds for hoping that through the voluntary renunciation of power in the widest sense of the word the Petrine ministry will increasingly reveal itself as such in the near and more distant future. The way is not easy. Some things can be done at once, others will need time. At all events, a reform is in progress, and we need only indicate briefly here the things that, quite independently of current fashions, seem required in the light of the original message, in the light of the Gospel itself:

1. *Evangelical humility:* A renunciation of unbiblical titles, which are proper only to God or Christ (*Sanctissimus Dominus, Beatissimus Pater*, His Holiness, Holy Father, Head of the Church)—or alternatively are proper to all Christians, or at least to all bishops (Vicar of Christ, etc.). At the very least the title once given to pagan high priests (Supreme Pontiff) can be regarded as open to misinterpretation. Valid titles are: Bishop of Rome, servant of the servants of God, chief pastor. In early times Popes never abandoned the names given to them in baptism; only at the beginning of the present millennium did Popes regularly begin to change their names when they were elected (Hadrian VI and Marcellus II, Popes of the reform, are exceptions here). Some discretion seems called for in the use of the words "apostolic" and "holy" in connection with persons and institutions.

2. *Evangelical simplicity:* Without indulging in unrealistic and romantic poverty, a renunciation of all the pomp and luxury which stem from the early years of the Petrine dominion; above all in clothes, servants, courtly apparatus, guards of honor, and especially at times of worship. Papal orders and Roman court titles make no sense in a Church of service.

3. *Evangelical brotherliness:* A renunciation of anything that savours of absolutist government, the imperial Byzantine–baroque style of speaking and writing letters, all secret procedures, all solitary decisions without the cooperation of the Church or its representatives (collegiality, episcopate, council of bishops, council of laity); the depoliticizing of the papacy by renouncing all secular diplomacy (nunciatures).

4. *Evangelical freedom:* A furthering of the independence of the Churches and their pastoral ministries according to the principle of subsidiary; the internationalization and running down of the curial power machinery; the involvement of the relevant Churches in the election of their bishops (by means of representation both of the pastoral ministries and the communities); involvement of the whole Church in the elec-

tion of the Pope (by means of the council of bishops or possibly of a supreme senate of representatives of the pastoral ministries and the laity).

Much has happened in recent times, and the Pope has often acted more courageously than have the bishops in individual countries in changing their episcopal dominion into an episcopal ministry. Much can be achieved by the bold initiatives of individuals. Decisive changes can, however, only be brought about by a radical reform of canon law, and this in turn will require: (1) a fundamental review of the nature and the function of canon law altogether, (2) concrete reforms made not according to a particular legal tradition, but according to the Gospel itself and according to the needs of the present time; (3) a complete overhaul of individual articles which have found their way from forgeries into official canon law.

Petrine ministry or Petrine dominion: this alternative is at least equally important for any ecumenical understanding of the future as an exegetical and historical discussion. A reunion of the divided Christian Churches is unthinkable at any time with the present still centralized Roman system, and would in any case make things much too easy for the *ecclesia catholica reformanda* [the Catholic Church, which is constantly in need of reform]. The situation would immediately be different, were the bishop of Rome to draw strict lines of division between his areas of competence, according to the variety of his ministries: if, that is to say, he were to exercise the function of a bishop within the diocese of Rome, the function of a metropolitan within the Roman province, the function of a primate within the Italian Church, and the function of a servant of the servants of God, of a Pope, within the Church as a whole, while respecting the functions of the other ministries. Is it mere illusion to think that in this way in some distant future fellowship could be re-established for example between the Catholic Church and the Anglican Church? The Church of England for its part would be given the guarantee that it could retain in its entirety its present autochthonous and autonomous Church order under the Primate of Canterbury (not merely, therefore, like the Eastern "rites" in communion with Rome); and on the other hand the Church of England would recognize a pastoral primacy of the Petrine ministry as the supreme court of appeal, mediating and settling disputes between the Churches. Then instead of a Roman imperium we should have a Catholic commonwealth. In the whole early period of the Church the Petrine ministry was no more than a secondary court of appeal in extreme cases, when the authority of bishops and

> patriarchs did not suffice to settle matters. It is not clear why in such a case any more could be asked for, either in principle (dogmatically) or in practice (from an organizational point of view). A graded exercise of the pastoral primacy according to its various spheres of activity, in the light of its particular spiritual responsibility and of its active care for the welfare of the various Churches among themselves, would not only be fundamentally and practically possible, but would also correspond far better to the constitution of the Church at the time of its origins in the New Testament.

No one today can tell how the Petrine ministry, how the whole diaconal structure of the Church, still less how the reunification of the divided Christian Churches will work out in the future. The present generation has the responsibility of doing the best it can. One final point must be made in this connection: each Church, because of its individual history, has its own peculiarities which are not accepted in the same way by the other Churches; each so to speak has its own "speciality." For the Catholics this "speciality" is the Pope. But in a sense they are not alone; the Orthodox Christians too have their "Pope": their "tradition"; and the Protestants too have their "Bible," and the Free Churches their "freedom." But just as the "papacy" of the Catholics is not simply the Petrine ministry of the New Testament, so too the "tradition" of the Orthodox is not simply the apostolic tradition, the "Bible" of the Protestants is not simply the Gospel, the "freedom" of the Free Churches is not simply the freedom of the children of God. Even the best solutions are abused if they become like party political programs, and become the slogans with which one marches out to do battle for power in the Church; these programs are usually linked with the name of a particular leader, and are programs which necessarily excluded all others from the one Church.

In Corinth too there were feuding parties. Each had its program —we do not possess individual details—and had attached it to a leader whom it praised above all the rest and made more important than all the rest, at the same time denying any authority to the others. "For it has been reported to me by Chloe's people that there is quarrelling among you, my brethren. What I mean is that each of you says, 'I belong to Paul,' or 'I belong to Apollos,' or 'I belong to Cephas,' or 'I belong to Christ' " (1 Cor. 1:11). If one wished to be anachronistic here, one would without hesitation identify the party of Cephas with the Catholics, who claim to be in the right or at any rate over the others, because of his primacy, his pastoral power, and his power of the keys. The Orthodox would be the party of Apollos, who, coming from the great tradition of Greek thought, would expound revelation more intellectually, more thoughtfully, more profoundly, and therefore more "correctly" than any other. And the Protestant would certainly be the party of Paul, the father of their Church, *the* apostle, the unique preacher of the cross of Christ, who did more work than all the other apostles. And the Free Churches would be the party of Christ himself, the party which, claiming freedom from all the limitations of these other Churches, their authority, and their confessions, leans solely on Christ as the unique Lord and Master and on this basis forms the brotherly life of its communities.

And for whom does Paul decide? Of course, for Peter, since Peter is the rock on which the Church is founded? No, Paul passes over the name of Peter in silence, and equally tactfully that of Apollos too. What is most surprising is that he even disavows his own partisans. He does not wish that groups should depend on one person and make one person into their party program—a person who was not crucified for them, in whose name they were not baptized. Paul brought baptism to the Corinthians. But they were not baptized in his name, but in the name of Jesus, the crucified; and they belong to him in whose name they were baptized. Hence even the name of Paul, the founder of the community, is not to become a party slogan.

We can learn from this that however much the Petrine ministry may be a rock for the Church, its unity, and its coherence, it cannot be turned into a criterion for deciding what is Church and what is not Church. Tradition, however valuable it may be as a guideline for the Church, its continuity, and its consistency, cannot be a dividing line beyond which orthodoxy ends and heterodoxy begins. The Bible, however fundamental it may be for the Church, its faith, and its creed, cannot be turned into a quarry, the stones from which, instead of being used for building, are used for stoning others. But this is not all: it is no solution to appeal directly to Christ instead of appealing to the apostles. Even for this fourth party the question is still valid: "Is Christ divided?" (1 Cor. 1:13). Even Christ the Lord may not be used as a banner for a party which wants to make a frontal assault on others who belong to one and the same Church.

The Bible as a helpful and liberating message, faithful tradition of the original testimony, the Petrine ministry as selfless pastoral service of the Church, the free gathering of brothers in the Spirit: all this is good if each is not taken exclusively, to be used against the others. Each must be subordinated to the service of Christ, who is and remains the Lord of the Church and of everything which goes to make up the Church. No Church in the last analysis can judge itself. All are tested in the refining fire of the Lord. Then will be made clear what part of its peculiarities, what parts of its unique tradition, what parts of its special doctrine are wood, hay, and stubble, and what are gold, silver, and precious stones; it will then be made manifest what is valueless and transient, and what will survive and be saved (cf. 1 Cor. 3:12–15).

Footnotes

[1] [*Editor's note:* Denz. refers to H. Denzinger, *Enchiridion Symbolorum* (Freidburg-Barcelona, 30th ed., 1955). Many of these statements can be found in *The Church Teaches: Documents of the Church in English Translation,* John F. Clarkson, *et al.,* eds. and trans. (St. Louis: B. Herder Book Co., 1955).]

[2] [*Editor's note:* This translation is taken from Johannes Quasten, *Patrology*, Vol. I (Westminster: Newman, 1957), p. 303.]

STANLEY E. KUTZ

Public Opinion in the Church

The author of this article attempts to ascertain how the Christian community arrives at statements of belief. He tries to uncover the role of the various members of the community in arriving at these statements.

What does he mean by "unity" in the Christian community? The author describes the concept of collegiality; what is that concept? Why are all Christians both listeners and teachers? What is the role of the theologian in the Christian community? What is the role of individual conscience? What does the author mean by "responsibility"? What does he mean when he states that "the Church teaches infallibly what the Church already believes"?

Stanley E. Kutz was a Professor of Moral Theology at St. Michael's College in the University of Toronto.

The following words of an eminent theologian offer the best explanation of why an article such as this can be written by a priest of the Catholic Church; they perhaps even explain why it must be written:[1]

> Are we really allowing the formation of that public opinion in the Church which Pius XII declared was an unconditional necessity for her? Is it clear to everybody that if such a thing is to be formed, the Church, even in her public life, is going

Reprinted from *Contraception and Holiness*, ed. Thomas D. Roberts (New York: Herder and Herder, Inc., 1964), pp. 23–42, with the permission of the publisher.

> to have to be tolerant and patient in letting individuals speak out, even if the immediate effect is that the chorus of voices is no longer harmonious? Or are we always scared that any difference of opinion in the life of the Church is automatically a sign of weakness and damaging "disunity"? Or, again, are we always afraid of "giving scandal" by letting people see (as the "others" have known for a long time, anyway) that even the Church does not have a ready-made store of the best prescriptions for all concrete problems, and that therefore we have to argue with each other and thus slowly reach agreement, not just *any* agreement but as good a practical decision as we can manage?

The Church can well be described as a network of gifts. For before one speaks of the Church as society and as institution, one must speak of the Church as the gift of God, the extension in time and space of God's redeeming love made visible and available to men in the incarnation, death, resurrection, and glorification of Christ. The salvation accomplished in Christ is communicated to men through the gift of the indwelling Spirit of adoption, who apportions his gifts not in some uniform and univocal manner, but in variety and multiplicity, so that the Church is made up not simply of many individuals cast in a single mold, but of many persons, each of whom is called by name to incarnate in his life in a unique way the redeeming love which all have received from the same Spirit. The distinction between Christians is qualitative, rather than numerical. Taken collectively, Christians do not make up simply a multitude, but a body in which each part must first be *itself* before it can be of service to the whole organism. "If all were a single organ, where would the body be?" (1 Cor. 12:19). In the light of modern physiology, we can carry St. Paul's argument one step further: it is precisely when one type of cell begins to be multiplied in a purely quantitative fashion, without qualitative distinction (as happens in cancer), that the whole body is in the gravest danger.

Now in this one body of Christ, unified by the one Spirit of love, God "has appointed first apostles, second prophets, third teachers, then workers of miracles, then healers, helpers, administrators, speakers in various kinds of tongues" (1 Cor. 12:28). St. Paul felt at home in a Church constructed out of a diversity of gifts. He expected to find spontaneity and variety in the Churches, because he knew that the Spirit breathes where he will, and cannot be constrained by the small-minded plans of men. We may even postulate that he would have been surprised to find a Church in which all was in a state of quiet, where a very few spoke and none responded, for he believed that "the spirits of prophets are subject to prophets" (1 Cor. 14:32). He would have been surprised at a Church in which nothing was tested, for he believed that everything must be tested. "Do not quench the Spirit, do not despise prophesying, but test everything; hold fast what is good, abstain from every form of evil" (1 Thess. 5:19–22).

Paul placed only one condition on the manner in which the gifts of the Spirit were to be manifested: "That all things be done decently and in order" (1 Cor. 14:40), "for God is not a God of confusion, but of peace" (*ibid.* v. 35). And the one test by which the various manifestations of the Spirit were to be judged was simply this: do they contribute to the "edification"—i.e., to the building up—of the whole body? Now this is a very delicate point. We are always tempted to reject out of hand that which is new or unusual, that which challenges traditional convictions or customs. We tend to look no further than the immediately disquieting effect which a new attitude may have on customary ways of thinking and acting, and to assume that this new approach is therefore destructive of the unity of the Church. But is this not to take too narrow a view of life? Very often that which is initially disturbing and strange may ultimately have a very salutary effect. Unity is never something given, whole and complete; rather, it is always something being sought, something being realized anew. And if the unity of the Church is to have always that dynamic, expanding quality which is synonymous with life, then it will only be because there is room also for diversity, for the free expression of the manifestations of the Spirit of life.

Unity must never be confused with that type of acquiescent uniformity which is satisfied so long as all the voices are chorusing the same refrain, even though there be no unity of conviction. Such uniformity may satisfy the needs of a totalitarian state, but it has nothing to do with the unity of the children of God, whose submission is meaningless unless it is *free*. The canticle of the sons of God must be a harmony of many parts, not a loud and brassy monotone. It must be of such a range that even discordant voices are gathered together into a transcendent theme. If such a harmony is to be realized, we must have the patience and humility to wait and see whether the discordant notes can be reconciled into a new theme. We cannot afford to reject them out of hand, simply because we do not at first see where they might fit. If we were to judge too hastily, we might find ourselves rejecting the voice of the Holy Spirit from the very choir which claims to be singing his praises. We can always afford to take seriously the admonition of Gamaliel to the Sanhedrin.

> Men of Israel, take care what you do with these men . . . for if this plan or this undertaking is of men, it will fail; but if it is of God, you will not be able to overthrow them. You might even be found opposing God!" (Acts 5:35–39).

This is surely the attitude which corresponds to St. Paul's advice to the young Churches: do not snuff out the Spirit, but test everything, holding fast to that which is good—i.e., to that which proves itself of value for the building up of the Church.

Now it is of Catholic faith that it pertains to the office of the bishops, in communion with the Pope who is the sign of their collegial unity, to make the final determination of what is and what is not an authentic manifestation of the Spirit, of what does or does not contribute to the building up of that community of faith and love which is Christ's body. What is often not sufficiently stressed, however, is the manner in which the bishops, with the Pope, arrive at these judgments. There is a temptation to think of them as *sources* of Catholic faith and practice, as persons who no longer have to listen for the voice of the Spirit in the Church. In fact, of course, the very opposite is true. It is the Father who, through the communication of the Spirit, draws all men to Christ, who is the only *source* of faith. And it is for this reason that bishops, even more than other Christians, must first of all be listeners. It is they who have received a special charism, and with it the corresponding obligation, to discern the voice of the Spirit of the Church—the Spirit who is given to all of Christ's faithful, who breathes when and where and how he will, and who wishes to lead Christians to an ever-deeper understanding of the meaning for them of God's love in Christ. The teaching authority of bishops should always be seen first as a gift of God for the service of the people of God, and only thereafter as a right pertaining to an office. Let it be noted that this way of considering the Church gives rise to no title by which Christians might justify disrespect or disobedience to their bishops. Rather, it says something about the obligation of bishops to listen everywhere, attentively, patiently, and with humility (recognizing that no one is exempt from the dangers of self-delusion) to the voice of the Holy Spirit, who is the only final source and guarantor of the unity of the Church.

What we have said of the teaching office of bishops (i.e., that it is primarily a gift and a service, and only derivatively a "right") must also be said of the "witnessing office" of all Christians. Those who begin by ostentatiously "claiming their rights" succeed only in provoking others to claim contrary rights: and that which should have been a dialogue of love issuing in understanding becomes a strident chorus of conflicting monologues in which brute force is the victor (even "moral" force can be brutal), and truth is the loser. This is to act "after the manner of the Gentiles," forgetting that with us it must be otherwise (see Mark 10:35ff.). The Christian who has learned how to listen to the voice of the Spirit in his heart, who has learned that what is noble and generous and expansive in himself is not of his own doing, but is the gift of the Spirit of love who is given to him: such a Christian will know how to witness to his experience of God's love without threatening or reviling those who disagree with him. He will not be anxious about what he ought to say, he will not need to store up angry words in his heart, for the Holy Spirit will teach him, at the right time, what he must say (see Luke 12:11–12). And such witness will be received in the spirit in which it is offered—as a gift and a service, not as a threat.

The Church, so long as she is a pilgrim awaiting the final coming of her Lord, will never attain to that state of peace in which the relations of all her various members to one another are governed by perfect love. Just as truly as the gift of the Spirit is diffused in the hearts of all, so also is the malice of selfish and arbitrary whim. There will always be members of the flock who will noisily claim their "rights," forgetting that they have nothing to boast of except the Lord (see 2 Cor. 10:17); and there will always be shepherds who, with a myopic view of what edifies the Church, will be more inclined to tyrannize over those in their charge than to become true models to their flocks (see 1 Peter 5:3). These failures of individuals will not be decisive, so long as we recognize them as failures.

The matter would only become tragic if, in our search for the easy, one-answer solution, we were to deny the very right to existence of one of the poles of this dynamic tension: if the flock were to imagine it had no need of shepherds who exercise true authority, or if the shepherds were to imagine that the flock had no further purpose for existing than to be ruled over.

The Church has not entirely escaped the effects of that functionalization which has tended to depersonalize so much of contemporary existence. There is the temptation to define ourselves and others in terms of our functions within a given structure, rather than in terms of the persons that we are. This has led to a way of thinking which would see some members exclusively as teachers in the Church, and the rest as listeners or learners. What must be said, without equivocation, is that every Christian (and those in authority all the more so precisely because they are in authority) is first of all a listener, one who is open to the voice of the Spirit wherever it may be heard; and every Christian is a teacher, a witness to the meaning of the love which has been poured out in his heart. The fact that it is given to bishops to discern and to judge with authority among the manifestations of the Spirit will not lead other Christians to imagine themselves absolved from the obligation of witnessing to their convictions; much less will it lead bishops to think it dangerous for that witness to be heard. For Christians believe that it is the *truth* that will make them free (see John 8:32), and they have no fear of the outcome of the search for truth because they know that their Redeemer lives (see Job 19:25).

So sacred is the Christian's respect for the truth of the faith that he may be required to witness to it in embarrassing and painful circumstances—namely by public protest against his fellow Christians and even against prelates. When St. Thomas treats of the question of fraternal correction, he points out that there may be instances where a subject would be obliged, in humility and reverence, to rebuke an ecclesiastical superior. Because of the respect due to the office of the superior, this will always be done privately, except in the case where there is danger to the faith itself. In that instance, says St. Thomas, prelates should be corrected even publicly, as was the case when Paul confronted Peter at Antioch.[2] One does not expect that such a situation will arise so long as subjects have confidence in the guidance which the Holy Spirit exercises in and through their pastors, and pastors are attentive to the voice of the Spirit as it may be manifested in the sincere convictions of those who are in their charge.

The Role of the Theologian

Among the multitude of voices which, throughout the whole Church, bear joyous witness to the meaning of the love which God has shown for man in Christ, the voice of the theologian surely enjoys a special status. Like every other Christian, his first testimony is one of gratitude for the redemption which he has received. But beyond that, he has devoted his life in a special way to the effort of discerning and interpreting for others the direction in which the Holy Spirit is leading the whole of the convenanted people. For the Church is historical not only inasmuch as she takes her origin in an historical event, but also inasmuch as she is a pilgrim Church, *still on the way* to final consummation with her Lord. As such, she is subject to the laws of growth and organic development; and like any conscious organism, she must seek to understand the meaning of her past so that she may play a relevant and vital role in the present, and prepare at least the next step into the future. It pertains to the theologian to serve the Church in this task of discovering and elaborating her true nature. In fulfilling this role, he is not so much one who hands on "timeless truths," nor one who "proves" something about God and man; rather, realizing with what difficulty and after how much conflict of opposing convictions man actually comes to a limited insight into the truth, he seeks to discover the point at which many probabilities (no one of which is probative if taken singly) converge in such a way as to elicit an assent that is in keeping with the mystery of man's freedom. From this vantage point, the theologian is in a position to interpret to his fellow Christians the possible significance of the present moment of grace, and to indicate the options which open out into the future.

To accomplish so delicate a task, it is necessary that the theologian be a man who possesses the courage of his beliefs, and that he be as free as is possible in our human condition from external constraint. The confidence which the Christian people place in him would be betrayed if it became apparent that he was afraid to speak the truth as he has been given to see it in the light of his faith and study, or if he were seen to be merely a functionary who repeats without conviction someone else's understanding of the truth. And, as Daniel Callahan has pointed out, the hierarchy must, precisely in order to ensure the authenticity of its own teaching, allow freedom of expression to the theologian. "Otherwise, it could never have confidence that he was not simply fawning on authority or that a purported theological consensus was the real one." [3] We do not trust a man who makes a point of saying only the things we expect him to say.

All of the preceding has been preamble to the following section on the meaning of conscience. And that in turn will be preamble to our main concern: conscience and contraception. This development should not surprise the reader, for what is at issue here is much more than an isolated ethical problem. To quote again from the essay of Callahan cited above: "The birth control question is, above all, a test case of the Church's understanding of itself and especially of its understanding of the development of doctrine." We concur in this judgment, and it is for this reason that it is necessary to treat of many other issues before coming to the main question.

The Meaning of Conscience

It may be safely asserted that conscience is, if not a new word in the vocabulary of Catholics, at least a new dimension in their existential wrestling with ethical problems. As Bishop John J. Wright has pointed out: "Conscience is one of those words which everyone uses readily enough and which most think of as not only basic but also very simple, though an invitation to define it usually reveals confusion and embarrassment." [4] And it seems that no one is exempt from the danger of this confusion. In the second session of Vatican II, when Bishop de Smedt presented the schema on religious liberty (which is but one aspect of the problem of conscience), he thought it not superfluous to warn even the Council Fathers against four possible misinterpretations of this very carefully prepared document.[5]

To speak of conscience is to speak of that mysterious reality which every person experiences at the innermost core of his self-awareness, at the center of his being where he is most himself. Pope Pius XII bore eloquent witness to the profundity and inviolability of this mystery in a radio broadcast on March 23, 1952. He spoke of conscience as "the innermost and most secret nucleus in man. It is there that he takes refuge with his spiritual faculties in absolute solitude: alone with himself, or rather alone with God—whose voice sounds in conscience—and with himself. . . . [Conscience] is a sanctuary on the threshold of which all must halt, even, in the case of a child, his father and mother. . . ." [6]

The dimensions of conscience are thus proportioned to the dimensions of man himself. Respecting the complexity and sacred character of this mystery, we do not expect in these few pages to solve or prove anything about conscience, but only to reflect on some of its manifold aspects. In attempting to articulate our own insights, we hope to stimulate others to make their contribution to the dialogue on this subject.

We think it is futile to begin speaking of conscience unless we possess a fundamental intuition of what it means to exist as a *person*. We use the word "intuition" advisedly, because it seems to us that we are here in the realm of "total knowing" where the truth must impress itself on the mind in a direct encounter with concrete reality (with the "other"), rather than be deduced from some prior principle.

The problem is complicated by the fact that so much of our understanding of the meaning of personhood is still in an emerging state. Whereas in the past man was studied primarily as part of a whole (the universe, the Church, the state, the family, etc.), with a consequent emphasis on what is common and general to all men, today the primary emphasis falls on man as we actually encounter him in the concrete, as a unique person, an individual, a subject of rights, a source of creative initiative and energy; in short, an image of that God who is pre-eminently person, pre-eminently creator, pre-eminently free. Instead of understanding himself as deriving his meaning simply from the fact that he is a single unit in a larger structure, man now sees himself as responsible for the shape and direction of the evolving structures and patterns of his existence. Needless to say, this does not imply a denial of his social nature, or of the need for structure and pattern in his life; it rather means that community will attain its fully human significance only when it is a community of *free persons.*

I believe that these reflections help us to understand the insights to which Pope John gave expression in *Pacem in terris* [*Peace on Earth*]. What is original in this encyclical is not that it introduces some entirely new value or concept, but rather that it orders and relates traditional values and concepts in a new way. Whereas it had been customary for Catholic theology to speak first of nature, and only derivatively of person, first of duties and then of rights, Pope John chooses to invert this order and to treat of persons and rights as the more immediate and evident realities. He speaks of natural law as do his predecessors, but it is a natural law that reveals itself to the conscience of a free person; it is an order that unfolds itself in the course of existential encounter with persons and events.

This is an approach to order in human affairs which is quite different from the one which (rightly or wrongly) is commonly attributed to Catholics—i.e., an order that is deduced with inexorable logic from a few abstract principles about the nature of man. The universal acclaim with which *Pacem in terris* was received by men of the most divergent convictions is incomprehensible unless we appreciate how profoundly Pope John responded to the emerging sense of personhood which characterizes the best philosophical and theological thought of our day.

Creative Responsibility

For many people conscience seems to be simply a reminder of laws to be kept, or worse, some kind of casuistical gymnastic whereby one minimalizes his obligations when the demands of law are not clear. It should be apparent that these misconceptions have nothing in common with the doctrine of conscience implied in *Pacem in terris*, where the role of conscience is as positive and as comprehensive as the consequences of existence as an "image of God." The term "creative responsibility" perhaps best sums up the implications of Pope John's thought.

Now when we speak of responsibility we must not think of it in narrowly moralistic terms, as though responsibility meant no more than imputability. "Responsibility" is derived from "response"; it implies the process of a subject opening himself to reality, perceiving reality as offering itself to him, and responding in gratitude and joy to the mystery of existence of which he finds himself a beneficiary. To describe this response as creative is equivalent to saying that it is personal—i.e., that it proceeds from a subject who exists once for all, who will never be repeated, who is called by a name that is his and his alone. He is called to actualize the implications of his unique existence, in a certain sense to create his own personhood, by making a response to reality which no one else can make for him. If he does not make it, it will never be made, and all of reality will be poorer because a center of freedom, a source of creative love, a person who might have been, has failed to flower. In this sense, every person is a creator; he fashions meaning and beauty where, but for the response by which he affirms and augments his personhood, there would be only silence and void. And it is conscience which sums up and gives urgency to this invitation to creative responsibility.

The dynamics of conscience can thus be described in terms of a dialogue between man's spirit and the whole of reality which somehow presents itself to him as a "thou," as a partner who helps to reveal to man the depths of his own creative potential and the expanding meaning of his own existence. And for the Christian, this becomes a fully personal dialogue between his own spirit and the Holy Spirit, the Spirit of adoption, who is poured forth in his heart to interpret for him the meaning and the personal consequences of the love which the Father has shown for him in the death and resurrection of the Son.

It will be evident from the foregoing that to follow conscience is in no sense the same as following one's arbitrary and self-seeking whims. Our God is not a God of confusion, but of peace, and his Spirit is poured out upon all flesh for the very purpose of leading us out of the isolation and alienation of self-gratification into that community of love which is the Church. By the very excess of God's love which is implied in the gift of his own Spirit, we are impelled toward unity and communion, the very opposite of arbitrary whim. Thus, when one asserts the doctrine of liberty of conscience, one asserts human autonomy from *external coercion*, but not from the internal consequences of the love of which a person knows himself to be the recipient. In this context, we can do no better than to quote from Bishop de Smedt (*loc. cit.*):

> The human person endowed with conscious and free activity, since he can fulfill the will of God only as the divine law is perceived through the dictate of conscience, can obtain his ultimate end only by prudently forming the judgment of conscience and by faithfully carrying out its dictate.
>
> From the nature of things, in forming this judgment, whereby man tries freely to conform to the absolute demands of God's rights, neither any other man nor any human institution can take the place of the free judgment of man's conscience. Therefore, the man who sincerely obeys his own conscience intends to obey God himself, although at times confusedly and unknowingly, and is to be considered worthy of esteem. . . . The greatest injury is to prevent a man from worshiping God and obeying God according to the dictates of his own conscience.

Conscience and the Magisterium

It seems to us that much conflict between conscience and the authoritative teaching of the Church arises from a misconception of the nature of that teaching. Many people speak as though this conflict were practically inevitable, for the voice of conscience arises in the innermost spirit of the believing Christian, whereas the official teaching is presumed to originate with "them"—i.e., Popes, bishops, theologians. "They" are rarely thought of as believers, and it is presumed that they obtain the content of their teaching from some esoteric source or other—in any case, not from the witness of the conscience of simple, down-to-earth people like "us." (This misconception is of course particularly pernicious when it is applied to the problems of conjugal morality, where "they," by definition, have no direct experience.)

Such a view completely misconstrues the teaching function of the Church. The magisterium does not produce truth; rather, it delineates the degree of certainty which a particular expression of the truth has attained in the consciousness of God's people. The Church teaches infallibly what the Church already believes. And this belief is the gift of the Holy Spirit, who recalls to the minds of all the faithful the things that Christ taught and guides them into all truth (see John 14:26). This action of the Spirit on the conscience of the faithful, guiding them into an ever more profound understanding of the implications for them of the death and resurrection of Jesus, finds its fullest expression in the celebration of the liturgy, where all listen to the Word, proclaimed with authority, and respond to it in a manner that is at once personal and communal (see the Constitution on the Sacred Liturgy, Section 33). We may well hope that a revitalized liturgical practice will diminish the area of conflict between conscience (still conceived too individualistically) and authority (still conceived too impersonally).

When the teachings of the Church are thus understood as authoritative declarations of those insights into the divine mysteries which the Spirit has already produced in the Church through his action on the consciences of all believers, and when it is realized that these declarations are always capable of being more adequately formulated in proportion as the Spirit leads the covenanted people to a new and deeper understanding, then the whole problem of conscience versus authority will be seen in a different perspective. Conscience will realize that it needs the guidance of authoritative teaching, for without it there could be no growth or progress in understanding, but only an endless agonizing over first questions. And authority will discover that it can only be true to itself as Christian authority by a scrupulous respect for the existence and freedom of conscience. If God governs his free creatures in a way that always respects their freedom (and surely religion has no meaning in any other context), then those who govern in God's name —even when they are absolutely certain that they act with his authority—can do no less. Dostoyevsky's Grand Inquisitor thought that he was able to "correct" the work of Christ by replacing man's free response to the Gospel with a sterile conformity to a system of ecclesiastical rules. We may hope that he speaks for no contemporary Churchman.

If our reflections on the nature of conscience are valid, it will mean that we have to make room in our understanding of Christian existence for an element of tension, and even of uncertainty. The individual conscience may often find itself one step ahead of (or one step behind) that conscious articulation of the faith which the whole Church has attained at a particular moment in her history. The tension which results does not exist for its own sake, but only as a step toward a new harmony, a new synthesis, a new *consensus fidelium* [consent of the faithful] which will be richer and more dynamic as a result of the tension out of which it grew.

In this dynamic interplay of tension and harmony, we must leave room for the free exercise of even those consciences which we must regard as erroneous—provided always that the genuine demands of the common good, particularly the integrity and liberty of the consciences of others, be respected. Cardinal Newman, on the basis of his own experience, always insisted that habitual obedience to a sincere conscience (even when it was erroneous) would ultimately lead to objective truth. The man who adheres to a sincere conscience intends to obey God himself, and all others must have the wisdom and patience to let God bring him to the fullness of truth in his own good time.

Footnotes

[1] Karl Rahner, S.J., *The Christian Commitment* (New York, 1963), p. 111. I should add that although this essay is written by a priest-theologian, it is not the type of theological treatise in which a mass of evidence is brought to bear upon a carefully delineated problem for the purpose of arriving at a conclusion. Rather, it seeks to register the personal convictions of the author with respect to a problem which is of such urgency and complexity that the voices of as many consciences as possible must be heard if it is to be resolved in a manner consonant with Christian responsibility. Finally, it is written in a spirit of service to the Church, and dedicated to those Catholic couples whose burdens I may have increased by my own confusion and lack of clarity about this subject in the past. I hope that they will read these pages and understand.

[2] *Summa Theologica,* II–II, 34, 4, ad 2.

[3] "Authority and the Theologian," *The Commonweal,* June 5, 1964, p. 322.

[4] "Reflections on Authority and Conscience," *The Critic,* April/May 1964.

[5] *Council Speeches of Vatican II* (New York, 1964), pp. 237–53.

[6] *Acta Apostolicae Sedis,* XLIV, 1952, p. 270.

GREGORY BAUM, O.S.A.

Vatican I, Infallibility, and Doctrinal Renewal

In reading this article we should ask the following questions. What is the difference between inerrancy and infallibility? Does the Pope ever act "alone" or is he always acting as head of the college of bishops? How does infallibility depend on Holy Scripture; tradition; the faith of the bishops; the faith of the entire community? What is the meaning of ordinary magisterium, ordinary and universal magisterium? Is doctrinal development merely an unfolding of that which was given at the beginning? How does doctrinal development relate to death and resurrection? What obedience do Christians owe to the magisterium? In what circumstances can we espouse a position that contradicts that of the magisterium?

Gregory Baum, O.S.A. is a Professor of Theology at St. Michael's College in the University of Toronto. This is Father Baum's second article in this volume.

One of the most interesting contributions to the growing Catholic literature on birth control is the discussion among various commentators published in several American diocesan papers.[1] One commentator explains that his Catholic education has supplied him with four arguments proving that contraception is intrinsically evil: arguments from Scripture, from natural law, from the Fathers of the Church, and finally from papal teaching. After reading modern

Reprinted from *The Problem of Population,* ed. George N. Schuster, Vol. III (Notre Dame, Ind.: University of Notre Dame Press, 1965), pp. 111–35.

critical studies on the question, this commentator tells us, he is left with a single argument, namely, that of papal authority.

This is the position of many Catholics who have written on birth control. Their discussion of family morality is, in the first place, a study of papal documents and an evaluation of their respective authority. In the present crisis, when minds are divided on a matter of human wisdom, this shift away from the examination of the real situation to the preoccupation with ecclesiastical authority seems to me an inversion of the order of reality. Any examination of the natural values of human life (or natural law) must, first of all, be concerned with the truth of the matter. A proper respect for the ecclesiastical magisterium does not prevent us from doing so. Only a false one does. Someone has maliciously suggested that in the issue of birth control Catholics are at this time not really concerned with the integrity of marriage but with the integrity of Pope Pius XI. We may think such a joke in poor taste, but we do have to admit that an exaggerated and, therefore, undogmatic veneration of the magisterium is often found among our theologians. Without attending to the limits which the Councils have defined in regard to the Church's and the Pope's infallibility, many authors, sometimes encouraged from on high, tend to attach the aura of infallibility to papal teaching in general and regard the official teaching of the Holy See, taken in its entirety, as an unchanging body of truths. There is good evidence that the true Christian understanding of the papal magisterium is thus often replaced by a myth or legend of the papacy.

The Catholic theologian deeply attached to the teaching authority of the Church will consider it his duty to vindicate the true value of papal teaching and thereby separate the Christian reality from the myth. An exaggerated veneration of her teaching authority is always dangerous to the Church, for when the faithful discover that their high expectations in regard to the magisterium were not justified, they may be so deeply disappointed that they will abandon not only the myth, but with it the Christian reality. The teaching authority of the Church is undermined by an overcritical outlook on the part of men who are unwilling to be led, as well as by a credulous and officious attitude on the part of those who attribute inerrancy to every statement of the magisterium, thereby arresting the development of doctrine.

The myth of inerrancy is sometimes encouraged by certain institutions. A tone, a gesture, a form of expression can creep into the exercise of the magisterium, suggesting that truth has been totally mastered. This may even take on extraordinary proportions. The Vatican daily, *L'Osservatore Romano*, never admits an error in its reporting. A number of years ago, it reported by mistake that Archbishop Seper of Yugoslavia (the present Cardinal) had died. Notified of the good health of the prelate, *L'Osservatore Romano* refused to rectify the error. It was only when the Archbishop had his next visit with the Pope that his name appeared again in the Vatican daily.

In what follows we want to examine the Christian reality of papal infallibility and to distinguish it from the legend which has developed around it.

Vatican I

The Church has always believed that, thanks to the written Word of God and the Spirit animating the community, the gift of the Gospel is protected in her. The Church announces the Gospel in all truth, infallibly—i.e., without error. The Spirit speaking in each member also makes use of particular organs or institutions within the community to assure the infallible proclamation of the Good News. These institutions speaking in the name of the whole Church are (a) the college of bishops in union with the Pope or (b) the Pope exercising his office as universal teacher. We regard, therefore, the Pope's or the Council's infallibility as a service of truth offered to the whole Christian community.

The First Vatican Council defined infallibility. During this Council some of the bishops tried to introduce a wide dogmatic formula attributing to the Pope an infallibility the limits of which were not clearly spelled out. This attempt did not succeed. The definition of papal infallibility that was finally adopted drew clear boundary lines specifying the conditions under which the Pope enjoys the unfailing assistance of the Holy Spirit. The formula used has become familiar to Catholics: Vatican I defined that the Pope exercises his infallible teaching ministry when he speaks *ex cathedra* [from the chair (of Peter)].

We do not wish to study here what Vatican I tells about the way in which the Pope's teaching office is exercised, how the Pope depends on Holy Scripture, tradition, and the faith of the bishops and the faithful. We simply wish to study what is meant by the term "speaking *ex cathedra*." In order to have an *ex cathedra* pronouncement of the Pope three conditions must be fulfilled: he must speak as supreme teacher, he must use his apostolic authority, he must teach on faith and morals.

1. The Pope must teach as supreme teacher. If the Pope teaches simply as the Bishop of Rome, or as a preacher in worship, or as a speaker in a congress, then his teaching is not *ex cathedra;* and however authoritative it may be, it is not infallible teaching (unless it belongs to the Church's ordinary preaching of the Gospel).

One of the reasons why speaking *ex cathedra* was so carefully defined was the insistence of the historians among the bishops that in many instances in the past the Popes had actually erred. The case of Pope John XXII was frequently recalled. Against the theological conviction of his day, Pope John XXII (fourteenth century) had preached that the faithful who die in the Lord will not enjoy the beatific vision until after the general resurrection. This position was regarded as heretical by many teachers of that day. The Pope retracted his views on his deathbed. His successor, Pope Benedict XII, issued a solemn teaching document on the entry of believers into the joy of God prior to the resurrection on the last day.[2] Since Pope John XXII had not taught as supreme teacher of the Church, but simply as preacher in public worship, his error did not create any difficulty for the doctrine of papal infallibility. The conditions for *ex cathedra* speaking do not apply here.

2. The second condition necessary for *ex cathedra* teaching of the Pope is that he is exercising his apostolic power. He must invoke his intention to teach with supreme authority; he must be conscious that he is now defining a truth of faith which will bind Catholics for all time.

According to this requirement it is conceivable that a Pope teaches with authority on matters affecting the faith of all Christians and yet does not involve his gift of infallibility. This is, in fact, his usual way of teaching. This does not mean that then the Pope is not teaching the truth but simply that his authoritative teaching does not make any claims to infallibility.

One case played a considerable role at Vatican I. This was the case of Honorius I, the Pope who was condemned for heresy. Pope Honorius I, in the seventh century, did not condemn a Christological error, but protected it, unwittingly, in two letters to Sergios, the Patriarch of Constantinople.[3]

In these letters Honorius regarded the controversy over one or two "energies" in Christ as a useless quarrel and suggested that, if the party insisting on one energy in Christ abandoned its stand, then the opposing party asserting two energies should also withdraw the newly coined expression. In 681 the sixth Ecumenical Council condemned the doctrine of one energy of Christ as heretical, and among the list of heretical authors Pope Honorius was named as protector of heresy.[4] Pope Leo II acknowledged the acts of the Council. He softened the formula in which Honorius was condemned without, however, changing the meaning. These condemnations were repeated by the seventh and eighth Ecumenical Councils. In later centuries Catholic apologists have sometimes tried to refer to the whole affair as a libel action on the part of the Greek Orthodox, yet today there is general agreement among historians about this doctrinal episode of the seventh century.

Though Honorius intervened in a Church-wide controversy dealing with matters touching upon Christian faith, he did not invoke his supreme authority in his letters to Sergios. The Pope did not manifest his intention to bind the faithful to a definitive doctrine. In other words, he did not speak *ex cathedra*. We see, therefore, that it was for very good reasons that Vatican I was so stringent in defining the Pope's infallible teaching office.

3. The third requirement for *ex cathedra* pronouncements of the Pope is that they must deal with teaching on "faith and morals." What, precisely, does this expression mean? A certain popular understanding of this phrase suggests that "faith" stands for divine revelation and "morals" for the entire field of man's moral life. Yet this is false. "Faith and morals" is a classical term of conciliar language. Since God's Revelation is not handed on to us simply as a body of doctrines but includes norms of life—in other words, since

Revelation includes *credenda* and *facienda* (things to be believed and things to be done)—it was often referred to as teaching on faith and morals.[5] This corresponds to an expression of Vatican II: *Fides credenda et moribus applicanda* [the faith that must be believed and put into practice].[6] Faith and morals, therefore, *have to do with the Gospel and its meaning for human life.* It does *not include all of human wisdom on man's moral existence.*

Teaching concerning the Gospel involves *two* areas of doctrine. First there is the proclamation of the revealed Gospel, and second there are doctrinal positions connected with this revelation, either derived from the revealed as explanation or drawn from human wisdom to defend the Gospel. When the Councils speak of the doctrine on faith and morals, they suggest in an undetermined way, these two areas, i.e., the proclamation of the Gospel and its defense and explanation.

We must take note here that Vatican Council I did not determine the extent of the Pope's infallible teaching. The expression "doctrine on faith and morals" limits the infallibility to what concerns the Gospel of Christ, but does not indicate whether and to what extent the Pope can teach infallibly in the second area mentioned above, i.e., doctrines necessary for the defense or explanation of the Gospel. The bishops of Vatican I were divided on this issue. Some wished to restrict the Pope's infallible teaching authority to the annunciation of the Gospel and exclude from it the secondary object; others wished to extend his authority even to matters which are only remotely connected with Revelation. To side-step the controversy, the conciliar commission decided to equate the extent of the Pope's infallible teaching office with that of the Church. Thus the question remains open.

At certain periods of the Church's history, it has been necessary for the magisterium to define doctrinal positions in defense of the Gospel or to explain the meaning of the Gospel in the face of divergent schools and then to regard these definitions as criteria of fidelity to God's Word. There can be no doubt that the Church has understood her infallibility as extending beyond the primary area of announcing the Gospel to include, at times, doctrines that are intimately connected with the Gospel, as defense or explanation. One should insist, however, that the Church did not arbitrarily choose the moments when she taught with irrevocable authority in this area. Usually it was absolutely necessary to do this in order to preserve Church unity or guarantee the purity of the Gospel.

Nevertheless, there have been many instances when bishops and Pope have taught in the area of faith and morals with authority, without, however, involving the Church's infallibility. These are exceptional cases where authoritative teaching on things remotely connected with the Gospel have been wrong. We recall the famous bull *Una Sancta* of Pope Boniface VIII, in which he held that the two swords, the spiritual and the temporal, are in the power of the Church; the first is wielded *by* the Church and the second *on behalf of* the Church. The first is wielded by the hand of the priest, the second by the hand of kings and soldiers, at the wish and permission of the priest. The bull closes with the solemn sentence: "We declare, say, define, and pronounce that it is absolutely necessary for the salvation of every human creature to be subject to the Roman pontiff." [7] This papal teaching derived from the Gospel on the basis of various premises, has been rejected by the contemporary magisterium.

It would be quite important, therefore, to circumscribe the object of the Church's and the Pope's infallibility more clearly. How far into the area of the *connexa cum revelatis* [intimate relation with Revelation] does the prerogative extend? Vatican I did not answer this. Nor has Vatican II. From the history of teaching in the Church it seems to me that only what is *absolutely* necessary to explain or defend the Gospel in a given situation belongs to the secondary object of the Church's and hence to the Pope's, infallible teaching.

After Vatican I

In the years after Vatican I, the care and sobriety with which papal infallibility had been defined at the Council were almost forgotten. Catholic authors began to attack the quality of infallibility to papal teaching in a very wide fashion, as if the Council had never wrestled with the question or defined the conditions under which the Pope enjoys the charism of truth. A rather extraordinary tendency developed among Catholic writers, a tendency to expand the conciliar definition along two lines, one regarding the subject and the other regarding the object of papal infallibility.

1. Regarding the subject of infallibility: while the Council had defined that the Pope was an infallible teacher in his solemn definitions, certain writers proposed that the Pope was also infallible in his ordinary magisterium, i.e., in his regular teaching through decrees, letters, encyclicals, and so forth. The first author after the Council to propose this idea was A. Vacant, one of the main interpreters of Vatican I. Vacant knew very well, and freely admitted, that the infallibility of the Pope's ordinary magisterium was not taught by Vatican I. He believed, nevertheless, that it was a legitimate extension of the conciliar teaching. He was followed by a number of authors at the end of the nineteenth century, right into the twentieth century.

One of the arguments used by these writers was drawn from Roman documents in which the Popes insisted that their ordinary magisterium is authoritative and hence demands the respect and obedience of the whole Church. This has been a papal emphasis for a long time.[8] It is, however, one thing to demand obedience to authoritative teaching (we shall see what precisely this means) and another to claim infallibility, i.e., to make one's teaching a test of fidelity to God's Word. In the texts wherein the Popes insist on the privileged position of their *ordinary* magisterium, there is no indication that they regard this teaching as an expression of their *infallible* magisterium.

As a matter of fact, the problem had come up at Vatican Council I. There were, indeed, some bishops who favored a doctrine of papal infallibility which included the ordinary magisterium of the Pope. By restricting the Pope's infallible teaching office to *ex cathedra* pronouncements, i.e., to the solemn or extraordinary teaching, the position of the Council was made clear. The stringent description of what *ex cathedra* teaching means clearly shows that the Council wished to limit the exercise of papal infallibility to certain definite moments in history. The Council Fathers realized that the history of the Church did not give them any grounds for making a broader claim.

The intention of Vatican I to restrict papal infallibility to the

Pope's extraordinary or solemn magisterium also emerged in the discussion and the formulation of the dogmatic constitution *De Fide Catholica* [the Constitution on the Catholic Faith], promulgated by the same Council. At a fairly late stage in the development of this document, a sentence was included to define the object of Catholic faith in a precise fashion. The Council wanted to stress, against a tendency of certain scholars in Germany,[9] that the Catholic believer accepts in faith not only the solemn definitions of the Church but the Gospel message as handed on by the ordinary magisterium of the Church, that is, by the preaching and teaching of bishops and their priest. The sentence inserted into the draft was: "By divine and Catholic faith all those things must be believed which are contained in God's Word, written or traditional, and proposed by the Church to be believed either in a solemn decree or in her ordinary magisterium."

Many Council Fathers did not understand the meaning of this sentence. The notion of "ordinary magisterium" was not familiar to them. Some of the Fathers believed, in fact suspected, that this sentence was an attempt to introduce papal infallibility surreptitiously. They took the ordinary magisterium to mean the teaching of the Holy See through decrees and letters. Hence some Fathers protested against the new sentence. Other bishops felt that it should be made clearer that what the Church proposes to be believed must be contained in Revelation; the office of the magisterium is not to teach new truths but to protect the Gospel of Christ. After this discussion the responsible Deputation changed the sentence by inserting two sets of words: "By divine and Catholic faith all those things must be believed which are contained in God's Word, written down or traditioned, and proposed by the Church to be believed as *divinely revealed*, either in solemn decree or in her ordinary and *universal* magisterium.[10]

This amended sentence made it clear that the magisterium serves the Word of God and that this service is exercised either by solemn teaching (Councils, Popes) or by the ordinary teaching of the entire episcopate with their priest helpers. When it is a question of ordinary magisterium, therefore, the only subject enjoying infallibility is the Church universal. The Pope's ordinary teaching, however great its authority, lays no claim to infallibility unless it is simply an expression of the universal ordinary magisterium.

2. The second tendency apparent after Vatican I was to extend the object of the Church's infallibility. We noted that the Council had not clearly defined how widely the secondary object of infallibility is to be understood. We noticed, however, a general tendency of the Council to be careful and sober in assessing infallibility so that nothing is claimed for the teaching Church and the papacy in our age which is not verified by the facts of past history.

Examining the manuals used in Catholic seminaries for the last two generations (see those written by Tanquéry or Hervé), we find that the object of infallibility has become so wide that almost everything that is derived from the Gospel (theological conclusions) belongs to it, including the canonization of saints, the approval of religious orders, and the doctrinal substance of canon law. These authors regard the area of natural and social morality as belonging to the object of papal infallibility and attach almost an irreformable status to papal decrees of the Church dealing with biblical research.

Such an understanding of the Church's infallibility is fantastic! There is not a shred of evidence for it in Catholic doctrine. The basic confusion behind this position is between infallibility which is a definitive gift of the Spirit protecting the message of God's self-revelation in Jesus Christ, and authoritative noninfallible teaching which is a provisional gift protecting the unity of the Church and the progress of God's people toward greater insight.

The bishops of the Church teach with authority not only when they claim to communicate the Gospel infallibly but also when they teach in other areas dealing with truth derived from the Gospel, with natural morality, and with theological and biblical research. This kind of authoritative teaching has been vindicated many times in the Church's history. The Popes have repeatedly insisted on the authoritative teaching of bishops and have attributed a very special place to the magisterium of the Apostolic See of Rome. The Church has the authority to teach in these areas; she is assisted in this by the Holy Spirit for the sake of fostering and protecting the unity and formation of the Christian people. This expression of the magisterium is basically pastoral in character. Even if the assistance of the Spirit in this area does not provide irreformable statements of truth, it does assure the Church of pastoral wisdom (prudence) in keeping the Christian people together in their common quest for deeper understanding. It would be wrong to restrict the action of the Spirit to the teaching of infallible doctrine. In the whole authoritative teaching of the Church the Spirit is at work, giving us guidance, even if the insights may be partial and are destined to give way to deeper understanding at a later period.

Cardinal Journet distinguished between the "infallible assistance" of the Spirit in areas where the Church is teaching infallibly and the "prudential assistance" of the Spirit where she teaches with authority, not claiming infallibility but simply demanding obedience for the sake of truth to be possessed in unity.

In the above paragraphs we have mentioned three distinct areas of the magisterium: (1) the Gospel and what is derived from the Gospel in explaining or defending it; (2) the natural values of human life; and (3) biblical and theological research. In the first area we have a nucleus of teaching for which infallibility is claimed: announcing the Gospel and, in certain concrete historical situations, defending and explaining it. Beyond this central core the authoritative teaching in the first area is noninfallible. Since the second area does not belong to the doctrine of faith and morals, the Church's authoritative teaching here is always noninfallible; and since the third area is mainly concerned with guiding the progress of studies constantly moving ahead, the authoritative teaching is here always noninfallible and provisional.

When we call authoritative teaching noninfallible, we mean that the guidance of the Spirit helps the Church to come to a deeper understanding in matters where the search for truth continues, where we constantly need further insights, where development or progress is the proper mode of truth, where there is no last word. In this area no teaching is irreformable. The advance of biblical research, science, and theology, as well as the new situation of men in history, may lead the Church to transcend the positions she taught with authority in the past.

We admit, of course, that even the infallible teaching of the Church is not the last word on God's mystery. Even here deeper insight is possible and, in many situations, pastorally necessary. But the deepening of the Church's infallible teaching will never invalidate it, will never lead to a negation of something that was affirmed before. The development taking place in noninfallible authoritative teaching may, under certain circumstances, be more far-reaching, question positions of the past, and, under the guidance of the Spirit, proceed through negation to a positive formulation of truth.

By confusing and identifying the Church's authoritative teaching with her infallible magisterium, the theological trend after Vatican I has created the legend of the inerrant Church. By extending the subject of infallibility and by widening its object, there has been created a mythical understanding of the papacy. A Catholic theologian deeply convinced of the necessary role of the magisterium in the Church will regard it as his duty to refute the legend of an inerrant papacy in order to bring to light the Christian reality of the magisterium as proposed to us by Catholic dogma.

Doctrinal Reform

There is a tendency in religion, in all religion, to create legends. While the Christian faith is threatened by people who are skeptical, who do not want to accept the teaching of the Gospel or not enough of that teaching, the Christian faith is also threatened on the other side by people who are credulous and believe too much, who add all kinds of beautiful but untrue stories to the truth revealed by God. Faith is threatened on both sides, by the skeptics and by the myth-makers. Usually the magisterium is more worried about the threats to Christian faith coming from the skeptically inclined than about the danger to Christian faith arising from man's myth-making tendency. This danger is nevertheless great, even if it usually leads to a crisis only after a long period of time. If legends become attached to the Gospel, Christians may mistake the legend for the reality; and when their experience proves to them that what they held to be a truth of religion is simply untrue, then they may abandon the legend and with it the Gospel which, though distinct, was seen as forming a unity with it.

If Catholics have a legendary understanding of the magisterium, if they believe that the Church which announces the Gospel infallibly is, in fact, inerrant, they will be profoundly shaken in their faith when they come in touch with doctrinal development and even, at rare moments, with errors in the Church's noninfallible authoritative teaching. This might well be for them the end of their Christian faith.

The Christian reality is that the ecclesiastical magisterium which, thanks to the Spirit, always announces, and at certain moments defends and explains the Gospel infallibly, is beyond this, the authoritative teacher of Christians in the fields of doctrinal conclusions, natural morality, and theological research, where development and progress belong to the essence and where, despite the prudential assistance of the Spirit, it has sometimes upheld inadequate and erroneous positions.

Catholic theologians are used to the idea of development of doctrine. Yet until now the theories of development that have been proposed describe the process to understanding as a passage from the implicit to the explicit, from truth to greater truth. Or they speak in an analogy to the growth of a living organism, the growing tree, which, in some sense, contains the riches of future stages in its initial form. Whether this development be logical or organic, it is a process of unfolding of that which is given at the beginning. One may wonder, however, if such an understanding of development is sufficient to explain the doctrinal reforms that have taken place in history and that we are witnessing in our own day.

We could easily choose examples from the three areas indicated above, doctrinal, natural values, and theological or biblical research, where the development that took place was not simply the passage from the implicit to the explicit but involved a change of position, the correction of former tenets, and the discovery of a new insight. If, in the first area, we study the history of the Church's teaching on the possibility of salvation outside the Church, we discover a basic change of outlook. It may be true that even the severe documents of the magisterium, confining salvation to the Catholic Church,[11] intended to leave the door open for the exceptional case where a man has access to salvation beyond the Church, and in this way provided for a future development expanding this exceptional case to be the situation of mankind in general. But even if we find documentary evidence that such an extension of the exceptional case to the many has actually been made by some theologians, this theological advance does not really describe the development that has taken place in the Church. It seems to me that what has happened is a change of attitude, something of a conversion, a more Christian approach to our brothers outside the Church. God has not simply stirred up some logical development to take place in his Church, permitting us to pass peacefully from one position to the next. No. He has led us to repentance. He has taught us how to look at other men in the light of faith. Development in this case is not simply a passage from truth to greater truth but includes a change of heart, the acknowledgment that we must abandon a position of the past and pass on to a new insight created in us by the living Gospel. Doctrinal development in this case has a Paschal dimension of death and resurrection.

As an example belonging to the second area of teaching, that of natural values of human life, we choose the Church's position on religious liberty. We realize that there has been impressive development. Bishop de Smedt in his conciliar speeches has admirably demonstrated that there has been a logical development from the position of the papacy of the last century to the present position, a logical development made possible through some new insights and the evolution of modern society. And yet, is this explanation sufficient to render an account of what has happened in the Church? Whatever the theological basis of the development may be, we must admit that what has happened implies a real change of attitude in the order of faith, a willingness to look in a new way on the followers of other religions, and to make legislation guaranteeing their religious freedom. This is not simply a development from truth to truth, but also a change of heart, a conversion to an attitude toward others which is more wholly determined by God's will. Here again development implies a dimension of Passover, of repentance and renewal.

From the third area of authoritative teaching, that of biblical and theological research, we choose as example the norms proposed by the Biblical Commission at the beginning of this century.[12] As biblical science advanced and new positions became capable of demonstration, Catholic biblical scholars entered into a period of great suffering. They wanted to be faithful to the Church's authority and faithful to their human integrity as scholars. Scholarship and science eventually prevailed, and the magisterium abandoned the positions of the past and approved the methods and approaches of contemporary biblical science. But is it true to call the evolution of the magisterium simply a logical development or an organic growth? Must we not admit that it included an element of Passover, of dying to the past and living to a new truth, of a passage from error to truth? As God leads the ecclesiastical magisterium into greater truth, is this not sometimes accompanied by repentance for past positions, especially when they have caused great suffering? I am convinced that understanding doctrinal renewal of the Church simply in terms of development is inadequate; we must acknowledge the dimension of Passover, *nova et vetera* [new and old], some negation of the past and some new affirmation. Death and resurrection are the law of all Christian growth. Despite the Church's infallibility in teaching the Gospel, it is meaningful to speak of the blindness and fallibility of the Church and assert confidently that God's merciful action always present within her will open her eyes, produce a clearer understanding of the Gospel and its implications for human life. The growth in understanding the Gospel in the Church is conditioned by our humility, by our willingness to learn from God, by our readiness to abandon past positions when we see their inadequacy and to accept deeper truth from the Spirit.

The magisterium which announces and, at certain historical moments, defends and explains the Gospel infallibly, is not an inerrant magisterium; it is the teaching authority of a pilgrim people, walking not by sight but by faith, which eagerly listens to God's Word and continues to be taught by it. In this context it is possible to assert that the magisterium has made mistakes. This is the Christian reality revealed in Christ which must be carefully distinguished from the myth of an omniscient teaching authority.

We do not have the space here to examine in detail what doctrinal renewal means in the Catholic Church. In each of the three areas indicated above, it means something different. In the area of Christian doctrine, doctrinal renewal is a quest for deeper insight into, and fresh formulation of, the Gospel of salvation, which would be in greater conformity with God's Word and at the same time be closer to the needs of men today. In this area, therefore, the twofold movement of doctrinal renewal is towards greater authenticity and greater relevance. Despite the unfailing protection provided by the Spirit for the annunciation of the Gospel (infallibility), the Church's doctrinal renewal in certain contexts is not simply a passage from truth to greater truth but, at times, also involves conversion or the victory of the Gospel over our hardness of heart. In the area of natural morality, renewal would mean greater sensitivity to real or objective values and a greater awareness of the changes in man himself, that is, of the deeper layers of his personality that are being discovered in our age. In the third area of biblical and theological research, the reform of teaching implies an assimilation of the progress which the various sciences have made in our day.

Authority and Obedience

This understanding of doctrinal renewal and the development of official teaching does not betray the doctrinal authority of the hierarchy in the Church. The bishops of the Church (magisterium) may propose with authority even its noninfallible teaching. We believe that Christ has equipped the shepherds of his Church with this power. For the sake of growing in truth, for the sake of Catholic unity, for the sake of pastoral guidance, the bishops of the Church may teach with authority doctrines and doctrinal positions which are binding for Catholics even when they are not intended to be the final Christian answer in these matters. Since the Church is a people, Catholics must grow into truth and sanctity together. For the sake of this dynamic unity the hierarchy has the power to teach with authority in a very wide area beyond divine Revelation. The Catholic trusts that, in the Providence which God established for the Church, the bishops, led by the Holy Spirit, adequately provide guidance in this quest for greater truth. In ecclesiastical documents we repeatedly read that Catholics must faithfully acknowledge the authoritative teaching of the ecclesiastical magisterium.

What precisely is the act of the mind by which a Catholic accepts the noninfallible authoritative teaching of the Church? It is certainly not an act of divine faith. Faith we have in God revealing himself in Christ and addressing us through the witness of the Church. Faith we have in the divinely revealed message preached to us by the Church. The acceptance of the Church's noninfallible teaching in the three areas indicated above is the acknowledgment of a human teacher, albeit a very special human teacher. The ecclesiastical documents describe it as a religious assent (*assensus religiosus*) or an obedience of the mind (*obsequium intellectus*). What precisely does this mean?

In the proper sense obedience is not of the mind but of the will. We are obedient to laws and precepts. Obedience is an act of the will whereby we decide to do the will of another. Obedience has to do with action. But when we speak of the mind and of knowing, it is at first not clear what obedience could mean here. While we are free to conform our action to the will of another person, we are not free to conform our mind to the mind of another, unless certain factors are given. Here good will alone is not enough. The mind is able to accept an idea only when there is evidence for it, or when there are good arguments for it, or when the teacher of the idea is credited with knowing much about it. Many things that we learn we accept on the authority of the teacher. If, therefore, obedience has any meaning when applied to the life of the mind, then it must refer to the willingness of the learner to acknowledge the authority of the teacher. In other words, the religious assent given to the ecclesiastical hierarchy exercising its noninfallible teaching ministry is an act of docility, a readiness to be taught.

The obedience of the mind called docility is constantly practiced by men, children as well as adults, in the process of learning. As we begin to study a new subject, we must put our trust in the teacher. We must be willing to learn from him, even when we are unable to verify what he tells us. We may not see the connections of various statements and we may even find some of the positions strange or difficult to grasp, yet we accept them easily and uncritically, in order to assimilate the subject the teacher is communicating to us. If a student were critical too soon, if he wanted to understand before he had a certain familiarity with the subject, he would never be able to assimilate all that the teacher has to give him. Learning, for instance, a foreign language from a teacher, we may occasionally have the impression that what we learn in one lesson contradicts what we have learned in a previous one, but if we are docile we trust the teacher and try to make our own what he offers us. If we are critical too soon, we will never learn the language. Only after many years, having achieved a real proficiency in the language, may the learner become critical. He may then discover that some of the details taught him by his teacher were untrue, but he is able to correct the errors precisely because he was then willing to assimilate with trust and readiness everything the teacher had to offer. Only the docile student is ever able to correct the teacher.

The obedience of the Catholic to the magisterium is the exercise of docility. The Catholic accepts the teaching of the Church in all simplicity trusting that in the order established by Christ, the Holy Spirit instructs the faithful first and foremost, though not exclusively, through the ministry of Popes, of bishops, and their priests. The Catholic does his best to assimilate this teaching. He embraces the revealed Gospel with an act of faith in Christ and seeks to make his own the entire teaching of the Church, whether it is closely or only remotely connected with this Gospel. If after years of study and reflections, a Catholic docile to the Church and formed by the Gospel preached by the Church should find that he cannot reconcile this or that particular doctrinal position, taught authoritatively but noninfallibly by the magisterium with the total message of the Church or with the established results of human wisdom, then he need not do violence to his mind. He may then wait until he sees more clearly how this position may be integrated into the whole of Catholic teaching or perhaps until the official teaching of the magisterium has undergone an evolution.

If he is a theologian, he may be able to contribute to this evolution through his research.

In the past it was, often, very difficult for obedient Catholics to express their difficulties with the official noninfallible positions of the magisterium. It was difficult because of the way in which teaching authority was conceived and administered. Many of the great theologians of our generation prior to the convocation of the Vatican Council were exposed to a great deal of suffering because of this. According to the teaching of Vatican II, the Church is being led to a deeper understanding of the Gospel through the Spirit speaking in the entire people. The magisterium is therefore not simply a teaching body; it is also and first of all a listening body, listening to the Spirit speaking in the Gospel, in the Spirit-guided tradition, and in the contemporary Church.

One of the unhappy results of the authoritarian manner in which the ecclesiastical teaching ministry was exercised was that it prohibited Catholic theologians from studying many doctrinal and moral questions with an open mind. This has produced a kind of crisis in the Church's teaching authority, making our Christian people suffer. We must hope that after Vatican II the ecclesiastical magisterium, more conscious of episcopal collegiality and the divine dialogue within the Christian people, will find methods of teaching with authority, protecting the Gospel and preserving unity of faith and action in the Church, without preventing the examination and responsible discussion among theologians, episcopal, sacerdotal, or lay, of those doctrinal positions which by their nature are stages to further insight rather than definitive verdicts.

The Catholic theologian, also taught anew by Vatican II, realizes that the gift of wisdom is never simply personal but is always given for the sake of the people. He will learn to speak with great responsibility to the brethren. He will propose his own insights in a tentative way, unwilling to engage himself fully in his own convictions unless they are confirmed by the community and ultimately by the shepherds appointed by the Spirit. In this way, the infallible Church will be a humble Church trusting that the Spirit will lead her into the truth of the Lord while she is on pilgrimage.

Footnotes

[1] See *The National Catholic Reporter,* February 24, 1965. [*Editor's note:* It is necessary to point out that not all these commentators would today take the positions that they took when this was written. Dr. John Cavanaugh is one of the 21 theologians at the Catholic University of America who signed the Theologians' Statement which took a position against *Humanae Vitae.*]

[2] Denz. 530. [*Editor's note:* This refers to H. Denzinger, *Enchiridion Symbolorum* (Freiburg-Barcelona, 30th ed., 1955). Many of these citations can be found in *The Church Teaches: Documents of the Church in English Translation,* John F. Clarkson *et al.*, eds. and trans. (St. Louis: B. Herder Book Co., 1955).]

[3] Denz. 251, 252.

[4] Denz. 550–52.

[5] Cf. Council of Trent, Denz. 783–85.

[6] *De Ecclesia,* Section 25. [*Editor's note:* This refers to the Dogmatic Constitution on the Church.]

[7] Denz. 469.

[8] See Denz. 1684, 2113, 2313.

[9] Denz. 1679–84.

[10] Denz. 1792.

[11] Cf. Council of Florence, Denz. 714.

[12] Cf. Denz. 2113.

AVERY DULLES, S.J.

Dogma as an Ecumenical Problem

This article affords insight into one of the most vexing questions facing the Christian today: What must I believe? Why does Father Dulles disagree with what he labels "the prevalent concept of dogma"? What is the importance of Vatican II's concept of Revelation? What is the relation between Revelation and dogma? Can Revelation be contained in a verbal articulation? On what grounds does the author claim that dogmatic discourse has an almost sacramental function? Is change in dogma merely a change in words to describe the same concept? How does a sociocultural situation affect our conception of reality, our articulation of the conception? What is doctrinal pluralism? Should there be any limits on doctrinal pluralism?

Avery Dulles, S.J., is a Professor of Systematic Theology at Woodstock College in Maryland. He has recently published *Revelation and the Quest for Unity*.

If there is any validity in the familiar dictum that "doctrine divides but service unites," it might well be expected that dogma would be an obstacle to reconciliation among the Churches. Experience seems to show that this is the case. According to Edmund Schlink, "At any ecumenical gathering it may be observed that members of divided Churches find it much easier to pray and witness together

Reprinted from *Theological Studies*, Vol. XXIX (1968), No. 3, pp. 397–416, with the permission of the publisher and author.

than to formulate common dogmatic statements." [1] At the Roman Catholic–Protestant Colloquium held at Harvard five years ago [1963], Cardinal Bea addressed himself quite forthrightly to this point. With regard to the future possibilities of the ecumenical movement, he felt obliged to warn:

> First and foremost the fundamental teaching of the Catholic Church will not be changed. Compromise on points of faith which have already been defined is impossible. It would be quite unfair to our non-Catholic brethren to stir up false hopes of this nature. Nor is there a possibility that the Church —even in its zeal for eventual union—will ever be content with a recognition only of "essential dogmas," or that she will reverse or withdraw the dogmatic decrees drawn up at the Council of Trent. Again it would be simply dishonest to suggest that there is any likelihood that the dogmas of the primacy or the infallibility of the Pope will be revised. The Church has solemnly proclaimed all these doctrines to be of faith, that is to say, truths revealed by God himself and necessary for salvation. Precisely because of these solemn declarations made under the guidance of the Holy Spirit, the action of the Church in this field is severely limited. She must guard these truths, explain them, preach them, but she cannot compromise them. For the Church founded by Christ cannot tamper with the Word of God which he preached and entrusted to her care. She must humbly subject herself to him with whom she is inalterably united.[2]

The Prevalent Concept of Dogma

These remarks of Cardinal Bea are predicated on a concept of dogma which has been for some time, and is today, widely accepted in Catholic theology. In current Catholic usage, the term "dogma" means a divinely revealed truth, proclaimed as such by the infallible teaching authority of the Church, and hence binding on all the faithful without exception, now and forever. To doubt or deny a dogma, knowing that it is a dogma, is heresy; it involves an implicit denial of the teaching authority of the Catholic Church, and therefore automatically excludes one from the Church.

Nobody has ever undertaken to draw up a complete list of the

Church's dogmas, and the effort would be futile, because there are many borderline cases. Any such list would presumably include the declaration of Nicaea that the Son is consubstantial (*homoousion*) with the Father; the definition of the First Council of Constantinople that the Holy Spirit is worthy of divine adoration; the affirmation of Chalcedon that Jesus Christ has two complete natures, divine and human; the listing of the seven sacraments by the Council of Trent; papal infallibility as defined by Vatican I; and the two Marian dogmas of 1854 and 1950—the Immaculate Conception and the Assumption. This is not a complete list, or even a selection of the most important, but a mere sampling to indicate the kind of thing we are talking about when we speak of dogmas.

Although many Protestants would recognize some of these dogmas as unquestionably true, and perhaps as divinely revealed, dogma does raise serious obstacles to Christian unity; for the various Churches do not agree about what the dogmas are. The Catholic Church, in particular, has defined a number of dogmas since the great divisions between the Eastern and Western Churches in the Middle Ages and between Protestantism and Catholicism in the sixteenth century.

The problem of dogma, as an ecumenical issue, arises chiefly from the side of the Catholic Church, since it would seem that the Catholic Church must require, as a condition for reunion, that the other Churches accept the Catholic dogmas. Having taken irreversible steps on its own, Catholicism must demand that others take the same steps. If Christian reunion is conceived in this light, it seems to be a one-sided affair. The other Churches would have to come to where the Catholic Church now is, while Catholicism, apparently, would not have to make any corresponding concessions. No wonder that many Orthodox, Anglican, and Protestant Christians are suspicious that Roman Catholic participation in the ecumenical movement is merely a disguised effort to convert other Christian bodies to the Catholic version of Christianity.

If this impression is allowed to stand, the ecumenical progress of the past few decades may lead to a dead end. It is imperative, therefore, to take a new look at the Catholic understanding of dogma. Catholic theology in the past few years has been radically reassessing the status of dogma, with the result that the Church's position appears far less inflexible than is generally thought to be the case.

The concept of dogma underlying Bea's remarks, though widely prevalent, is of relatively recent vintage. Neither in the Bible, nor in the writings of the Fathers, nor in medieval Scholasticism does the term have this technical meaning.[3] In ancient and medieval times "dogma" sometimes denotes simply an opinion or tenet of some philosophical or religious group—not necessarily true, let alone revealed. The term was used also in a juridical sense, to designate an official edict or decree. Even in the sixteenth century, as Piet Fransen points out, the Council of Trent "could 'define a dogma' while remaining perfectly conscious of the fact that the content of this *dogma* was not necessarily immutable." [4]

While there were obviously anticipations in earlier centuries—especially perhaps in the medieval concept of the *articuli fidei* [articles of faith]—the current notion of dogma was forged in the controversial theology of the Counter Reformation. Walter Kasper attributes the emergence of the term, in its precise modern significance, to the Franciscan Philipp Neri Chrismann. In his *Regula fidei catholicae* (1792), Chrismann declares "that a dogma of the faith is nothing other than a divinely revealed doctrine and truth, which is proposed by the public judgment of the Church as something to be believed by divine faith, in such wise that the contrary is condemned by the Church as a heretical doctrine." [5] Chrismann's narrow definition of dogma was assailed by many as too minimalistic, and his work was placed on the Index of Forbidden Books in 1869;[6] nevertheless it continued to exert great influence.

In the latter part of the nineteenth century, when the faith was threatened by the attacks in the name of reason, Chrismann's authoritarian view of dogma was found to be a handy weapon. At least in substance, it reappears in the official Roman documents of the period, such as the Syllabus of Errors of 1864, the Constitutions of Vatican I, and the anti-Modernist documents of 1907–10.

The notion that there could be doctrines immune to historical limitations and capable of being imposed by the sheer weight of extrinsic authority reflects the nonhistorical and juridical type of thinking prevalent in the Church of the Counter Reformation. The roots of this mentality may be traced to Greek intellectualism and Roman legalism. More proximately, the absolutistic view of dogma reflects the characteristics of Catholic theology in a rationalistic era. To ward off naturalistic rationalism, orthodox theology adopted a supernaturalistic rationalism in which Revelation was conceived as a divinely imparted system of universal and timeless truths entrusted to the Church as teacher.

Vatican II, to a great extent, broke with the concept of Revelation that had been prevalent in the previous century. The Constitution *Dei verbum* [the Dogmatic Constitution on Divine Revelation], without turning its back on previous Church pronouncements, depicted Revelation primarily as a vital interpersonal communion between God and man.[7] In so doing, it paved the way for the reconsideration of dogma that has been going on in the theological literature of the past five years. Postconciliar theology calls into question at least four important features of the Neoscholastic notion of dogma: its identity with revelation, its conceptual objectivity, its immutability, and its universality. Let me comment briefly on each of these four points before I proceed to the question of ecumenical applications.

The Reconsideration of Dogma

Dogma and Revelation

Regarding the first point, contemporary theology is conscious of the need of re-examining the relationship between Revelation, considered as a salvific event, and those propositional formulations we call "dogmas." It is commonly conceded today that Revelation does not actually exist except when it is being apprehended by a living mind. Dogmatic statements serve an important, and in some ways indispensable, function in the "self-becoming" of the individual believer and in the creation of Christian community; they bring to explicit realization essential aspects of man's prepredicative encounter with God. But Revelation itself cannot be limited to spoken or written words, nor do such words of themselves constitute Revelation.

To illuminate the paradoxical relationship between Revelation and dogma, some modern theologians have made use of the Heideggerian analysis of truth. The term "revelation" (*apo-kalypsis*, unveiling) has close affinities with the Greek term for "truth" (*a-lētheia*, unconcealment). According to Heidegger, truth is the event of the luminous self-donation of the mystery of Being. He therefore comes close to the theologian's notion of Revelation as the attesting Word of uncreated Truth.[8] If truth itself is, as Heidegger insists, at once the revealment and the concealment of the plenitude of Being, the theologian might well look upon divine Revelation as the gracious self-disclosure of the immeasurable Plenitude which faith calls God.

Following this line of thought, several modern theologians have sought to clarify the relationship between dogma and Revelation by applying analogously what Heidegger has to say of the relationship between beings and Being. Being itself, according to Heidegger, is interior to all beings, lighting them up for what they are, and yet is not itself a being. This paradoxical diversity within unity Heidegger calls the "ontological difference." Kasper, extending this concept, speaks of a "theological difference" between gospel and dogma.[9] The truth of Revelation, he maintains, is neither separate from dogma nor, without remainder, identical with it. Dogma has the value of Revelation if, and only if, it is grasped by a mind presently influenced by God's active self-bestowal. (In classical terms, we may translate: there can be no Revelation, and hence no faith, without the interior illumination of grace.) When the event of Revelation occurs, there is a kind of dynamic identity between Revelation and dogma. The revelatory truth is present in the dogmas through which it comes to expression, and yet continues to exceed them insofar as it surpasses man's powers of comprehension. In the words of William Richardson, "Every human effort to utter the ineffable is constricted by the law of finitude and therefore leaves something un-said." [10]

This notion of truth is modern but, as Kasper shows, it bears close analogies with the biblical conception of God's truth as his life-giving presence in and through his word. Even Scholasticism preserved something of this dynamic notion of revelatory truth. According to the well-known axiom, fruitfully exploited by Albert the Great, Thomas, and Bonaventure, "*articulus fidei est perceptio divinae veritatis tendens in ipsam*" [an article of faith is an indivisible truth concerning God, exacting our belief].[11] In the formulas of faith we catch fleeting glimpses of the divine truth toward which our whole being is tending. The truth of the revealing God cannot be reduced to the dead letter of any doctrinal affirmation, yet such an affirmation may become God's revelatory word. Because Revelation is eschatological, dogma always points to a future disclosure beyond all history.

Conceptual Objectivity of Dogma

The second question raised by contemporary theology has to do with the supposed objectivity of dogmatic discourse. Some have depicted the definitions of Popes and Councils as if they were capable of exactly circumscribing the content they affirm. But from what we have already said it is evident that the content shatters our ordinary framework of discourse and demands a unique type of assent. From the form of dogmatic language it can easily be shown that this is the case. Schlink, in the study already referred to, calls attention to the structural complexity of creedal and confessional statements.[12] They combine elements of repentance, faith, worship, and witness. The creed is composed with a view to being uttered in the presence of God, and as a testimony before men. The recitation of the creed aims to bring about a situation in which believers, gathered in worship, can better apprehend and respond to the revealing presence of the divine. Most of the early Christian confessions, which form the basis of later dogmatic statements, were framed in a liturgical context and are doxological in form.

Ian Ramsey shows the futility of treating dogmatic statements as though they were intended as descriptive or scientific statements. Building on analogies from various types of nonreligious discernment, Ramsey establishes beyond doubt that "the language of Christian doctrine is likely to bristle with improprieties" and "logical oddities." [13] In this connection he points out that in titles used of Jesus (e.g., the eternal Son, the only-begotten of the Father), the adjectives are not further descriptions of something previously designated, but intrinsic modifiers which enable the notion of sonship to "do justice to what is 'disclosed' in worship." [14] The norm of correct usage is derived from a situation in which the mystery of the divine is efficaciously evoked and encountered. It would be a fatal error, says Ramsey, to imagine that the dogma of the hypostatic union describes some fact in the way that ordinary language describes its objects. This would lead to such absurdities as the equation "Godhood + manhood = Jesus Christ."

On this point the Catholic Karl Rahner adds his testimony to that of the Lutheran Schlink and the Anglican Ramsey. The realities of God and his grace, according to Rahner, do not permit of any simple objective presentation.[15] Dogmatic discourse, therefore, must somehow contrive to point the way to an existential confrontation with the mystery itself. Theological dogmatic language, he asserts, is "mystagogical," insofar as it conjures up the gracious presence of the divine. It has an almost sacramental function, transmitting not the idea but the reality of God's generous self-outpouring. The truth of symbol is existential insofar as it transcends the subject–object schema of ordinary propositional discourse, and cannot be rightly apprehended without personal appropriation.[16]

Nothing here said about the peculiarities of creedal language ought to be taken as undermining its truth-value. On the contrary, these peculiarities stem from its task of conveying a truth greater and more serious than ordinary language is able to bear. Thus dogmatic speech, while it is irreducible to scientific or descriptive language, is by no means equivalent to mere subjective fantasy. The propositions of dogma, as Hans Urs von Balthasar has remarked, "are true insofar as they are a function and expression of the Church's understanding of the Christ-mystery, as given to it by the Holy Spirit. They cannot be taken out of this setting; therefore, they do not have any *purely* theoretical (i.e., nonexperiential, nonexistential) truth." [17]

Immutability of Dogma

A third development in the Catholic understanding of dogma has reference to its supposed stability. Once a dogmatic formula is hammered out, it must, according to the popular conception, remain forever. If it states a revealed truth, why should it ever be changed?

One answer, of course, is that the meaning of words shifts according to varying circumstances of time and place. When the original language ceases to be well understood, it may prove necessary or expedient to change the words for the sake of conveying the original ideas more effectively. This much is obvious and may be abundantly illustrated from the history of dogma.

Surprising changes in the verbal tests of orthodoxy have occurred in the course of time. For example, a local Council of Antioch, in 268, ruled that the Son was not *homoousios* (of one substance) with the Father.[18] Half a century later the Council of Nicaea declared that he was *homoousios*. Had the Church changed its mind? By no means. The term *homoousios* taken in one context implied Unitarianism, and in another context became a touchstone of the Church's authentic Trinitarian faith.

Many similar lessons may be culled from ancient history. The Councils of Nicaea and Sardica accepted the view that there was but one hypostasis in God. Constantinople I and Chalcedon, however, took the view that there were three divine hypostases.[19] Once again, neither formula is necessarily better than the other. What is vital is the meaning, not the choice of words. The term "hypostasis" does not have some one pre-established meaning, but receives its precise meaning from general usage and from the particular context in which it is used.

All this has evident applications for the faith of Christians today. Many of them recite the orthodox formulas with so little understanding that their thoughts may well be heretical. When the modern Christian declares that there are three divine persons, he may well have in mind the modern psychological concept of person as an autonomous subject endowed with its own proper consciousness, intellect, and will. Such a concept, consistently followed out, would lead to tritheism. God might be conceived as Siamese triplets! To safeguard Trinitarian orthodoxy, one might raise the question whether it would not be preferable to call God a single person with three modes of being. Whatever may be thought about this particular case, the principle of variability in language seems unassailable.

Many Christians, neglecting the lessons of history, fall into the error of imagining that orthodoxy consists in adhering rigidly to consecrated formulas. To reject these is considered heresy, as is suggested by the familiar expression "*si quis dixerit* . . ." [if anyone says . . . (then let him be anathema)] in the conciliar canons. But the more one studies language, the more obvious it becomes that words are a poor test of right thinking. What most people call "orthodoxy" really ought to be called "orthology" or "orthophony"; it has to do with right speech rather than right ideas. While right speech has its value, the rightness of speech depends on a great variety of circumstances, some of which are not within the control of the Church. Thus the Church may be forced to change its canons of right speaking.

It would be a gross oversimplification, however, to imagine that the reformulation of dogma consists simply in changing words. Revelation always comes to men within some definite sociocultural situation, and this necessarily affects the manner in which they articulate the Revelation conceptually. The biblical peoples inevitably expressed their experience of God in terms of their own central concerns, with the help of concepts derived from their own physical and cultural world. The content of the Bible is therefore permeated with ideas and images borrowed from the agricultural and patriarchal society of the ancient Israelites. The subsequent history of doctrine in the Christian Church has been deeply affected by the societal forms, the customary attitudes, and the philosophical heritage of the Greek, Roman, feudal, and baroque worlds.

In interpreting biblical and ecclesiastical pronouncements, therefore, we must be alert to distinguish between the Revelation itself, which is coming to expression in human concepts and words, and the culturally conditioned manner in which the Revelation is expressed. A competent interpreter of any doctrinal statement will have to examine the entire historical and cultural context out of which it arose in order to discern its true significance. The modern believer cannot and should not be asked to accept the world view of ancient or medieval Christians. He should be encouraged to think as a man of his own day. To the extent that traditional statements of the faith are conditioned by a cultural situation no longer our own, they must be reinterpreted for modern man. Otherwise they will inevitably seem meaningless, incredible, or at least irrelevant.

This process of reinterpretation cannot be a matter of stripping away the human conceptual vesture until one reaches some timeless and unquestionable kernel of pure divine truth. The pursuit of such an unconditioned grasp of Revelation is an illusion, betraying a serious ignorance of man's fundamental historicity. We ourselves are just as historically conditioned as our ancestors, and hence cannot hope to achieve supracultural formulations. The hermeneutic process by which we reinterpret past dogmatic formulations will involve a concrete logic of proportionality. We begin by noting that the Revelation (R) was expressed in a certain way (a^1) by men in a cultural situation (a^2). Our problem is to devise a new statement (b^1) appropriate to our own cultural situation (b^2). The process of finding the right formula involves more than mere deductive logic. It calls for a living sense of the faith and for a realistic grasp of the world in which we live. To validate new and appropriate expressions, suited to the mentality of the times, is primarily the responsibility of the Church's magisterium. But the theologian has the function of exploring new possibilities and of seeking in this way to be of service to the Church.

Such reconceptualization has been occurring throughout the history of the Church. It may be illustrated, sufficiently for our purposes, by the axiom "Outside the Church no salvation" (*Extra ecclesiam nulla salus*). This ancient maxim, with a venerable patristic pedigree, was affirmed in the strongest terms by Popes and ecumenical Councils in the Middle Ages.[20] And there can be little doubt but that those who proclaimed the principle understood it in a harshly literal sense. In our time the ancient understanding of the formula is repugnant to practically all Catholics. As Gregory Baum has written, "the conciliar documents . . . make it quite clear that this sentence is no longer taught *eodem sensu eademque sententia* [in the sense in which it was originally understood]. According to the repeated teaching of Vatican Council II there is plentiful salvation outside the Church." [21] Many contemporary theologians would prefer to see the formula used as little as possible in preaching, since it will almost inevitably be misunderstood.[22]

What is here in question is no mere change of words. The formula must be changed because in the mental and social structures of the contemporary world there is no longer any room for an exclusivist concept of the Church. The old formula was not totally wrong. It was based on a valid insight into the ecclesial character of all Christian salvation; it called attention to the inseparability of the grace of God from the Church of Christ. But the modern conception of the relationship between the Church, as a visible community of believers, and the saving grace of God must be more nuanced than the axiom, "Outside the Church no salvation," would suggest.

It is an oversimplification, therefore, to say that dogmas are irreformable. In principle, every dogmatic statement is subject to reformulation. At times it may be sufficient to reclothe the old concepts in new words which, for all practical purposes, have the same meanings. But in other cases the consecrated formula will reflect an inadequate understanding. In order to bring out the deeper and divinely intended meaning, which alone is inseparable from faith, it may be necessary to discard the human concepts as well as the words of those who first framed the dogma. When men acquire new cultural conditioning and mental horizons, they have to reconceptualize their dogmas from their present point of view. There are signs that this process is now going on with respect to many Catholic dogmas, such as original sin, transubstantiation, and perhaps the virginal conception of Jesus. This prompts us to ask whether those doctrines that have traditionally divided the Churches might not be capable of an equally radical reinterpretation.

Universality of Dogma

Before developing the ecumenical implications of this point, let me make my fourth and last remark about the emerging concept of dogma. Modern theologians have generally taken it for granted that a dogmatic formula, once it is sufficiently validated, ought to be professed by all believers everywhere. But this has not always been assumed. The New Testament displays a proliferation of creedal affirmations traceable to various segments of the primitive Church. And in the early centuries, as a glance at the opening pages of Denzinger's *Enchiridion* will show, the several Churches were content to possess their own local creeds. At least until the conversion of Constantine, when Christianity became the general law of the Empire, the recitation of identical creedal formulas was not considered essential to Christian fellowship. The Churches had other ways of testing the genuineness of one another's apostolic faith.

In the Middle Ages the Latin West, excessively isolated in its own theological world, began to make additions to the ancient creeds and to formulate new dogmas without regard to the rest of Christendom. The addition of the *Filioque* [and from the Son] to the Nicene Creed, of course, was one of the major factors leading to the tragic schism between East and West. The Council of Florence, which in the fifteenth century temporarily patched up this schism, showed an exemplary breadth of understanding.[23] It affirmed that the unity of the Church should be built not on particular doctrinal formulas but rather "on the cornerstone, Christ Jesus, who will make both one." In the union then decreed, there was no question of compelling either Church to accept the devotional practices of the other. The Western and Eastern Churches were allowed to follow their own liturgical calendars and to worship their own saints (which might seem to imply the validity of each other's canonizations).

More importantly for our purposes, an agreement based on mutual tolerance was reached regarding the crucial question of the procession of the Holy Spirit. Both East and West were permitted to follow the long-standing tradition of their own Churches. The Latins, therefore, could continue to declare—and to recite in their Creed—that the Spirit proceeded from the Father and the Son, while the Greeks could omit the *Filioque* from the Creed and subscribe to the formula "from the Father through the Son."

The primary issue, on the surface of the discussion, concerned the legitimacy of the use or omission of certain words. One might read the Decree of Union as if it meant that both verbal formulas had the same meaning. But in reality, as Kasper notes, the dispute was rooted in irreducibly diverse forms of thought.[24] The decision amounted to a recognition that the revealed truth was so rich that it could not be captured by either of the two formulas. Although verbally they seemed contradictory, and could hardly be combined in a single unified system, they were seen as expressing different aspects of the same divine mystery. Thus the Council of Florence implicitly rejected the equation "one faith = one dogma." It acknowledged that there can be a dogmatic statement which is, from a certain point of view, valid and orthodox, but which need not be imposed on believers who look at things from another angle.

The valid principle of dogmatic pluralism, after prevailing at Florence, became obscured during the Counter Reformation, and even more so in the past century, when the Church felt obliged to take stringent measures to stave off various forms of relativism. But in Vatican Council II pluralism managed to reassert itself, as several passages from the Decree on Ecumenism[25] will attest:

> The heritage handed down by the apostles was received in different forms and ways, so that from the beginnings of the Church it has had a varied development in various places, thanks to a similar variety of natural gifts and conditions of life. (no. 14)
>
> In the investigation of revealed truth, East and West have used different methods and approaches in understanding and proclaiming divine things. It is hardly surprising, therefore, if sometimes one tradition has come nearer than the other to an apt appreciation of certain aspects of a revealed mystery, or has expressed them in a clearer manner. As a result, these various theological formulations are often to be considered complementary rather than conflicting. (no. 17)
>
> After taking all these factors into consideration, this sacred Synod confirms what previous Councils and Roman Pontiffs have proclaimed; in order to restore communion and unity or preserve them, one must "impose no burden beyond what is indispensable" (Acts 15:28). (no. 18)

A similar regard for pluralism may be found in the Dogmatic Constitution on the Church, which strongly emphasizes the value of the distinctive contributions of individual local Churches to the many-splendored spectacle of Catholic unity. The unity of the faith, we are told, is all the more radiant when refracted in the variety of many traditions (cf. no. 13).

Ecumenical Applications

As a result of the current reassessment of dogma, briefly surveyed in the preceding paragraphs, we may be in a position to moderate somewhat the apparent rigidity of Cardinal Bea's statement quoted at the beginning of this essay. It is far from obvious that the dogmas of the Church, having been "revealed by God himself," cannot be revised by the Church, or that they are unconditionally "necessary for salvation," or that they can in no sense be subjected to compromise. Our findings suggest that the Catholic dogmas as presently formulated and understood may be significantly changed, and that positive acceptance of all the dogmas may not be absolutely necessary for communion with the Roman Church. Let me explain each of these two points in greater detail.

With regard to the "irreformability" of dogma, I have endeavored to show that, as our total fund of knowledge increases, and as our perspectives change, dogmatic formulations must be kept under constant review. Without failing in due reverence for the past, we may frankly admit that an increasing number of dogmatic statements are showing the kind of inadequacy already noted in the axiom "Outside the Church no salvation." This may be readily illustrated regarding several ecumenically disputed dogmas.

If the Church were today in a position to speak for the first time about the institution of the sacraments, it would not be likely to declare without qualification, as Trent did, that the seven sacraments of the New Law "were all instituted by Jesus Christ our Lord" (Denz. 1601).[26] A contemporary scholar familiar with modern biblical and historical studies would see the need of important distinctions that would scarcely have occurred to a sixteenth-century theologian.

So too, in speaking of the origins of the papacy, we should be unlikely to use the concepts and terms of Vatican I, which forbade anyone, under pain of anathema, to deny "that Blessed Peter the Apostle was constituted by Christ the Lord prince of all the apostles and visible head of the entire Church militant," or that Christ invested him "directly and immediately with the primacy not of honor alone, but of true and proper jurisdiction" (Denz. 3055). These statements embody important principles regarding the unity of the Church, and to these the contemporary Catholic feels strongly committed. But the formulation reflects the religious "style" of the baroque Church and the exegesis of an age less sensitive to historicity. If someone were being asked to become a sharer in the belief of the Church as of 1968 rather than 1870, it would not be desirable or necessary to hold him to anachronistic or triumphalistic declarations of this kind. The path toward Christian unity would be greatly facilitated if Catholics abandoned any thought of obliging other Christians to submit to outmoded and admittedly deficient expressions of the faith, even though these expressions are to be found in documents of the highest authority. To demand this type of submission would contravene the principle of Florence, reaffirmed by Vatican II, that one must "impose no burden beyond what is indispensable."

Not only must outworn formulations from previous centuries be clearly distinguished from Revelation itself; the same must be said of contemporary statements which may have to be corrected at some future date. As stated above, we never receive the revealed truth except in fragile human vessels. Thus even the most current dogmatic utterances must be questioned. The true test of orthodoxy is not whether a man accepts the official statements at their face value, but whether he has sufficient confidence in the tradition to accept its formulations, in spite of all their human deficiency, as vehicles of a divine truth that lies beyond all formulation. The Catholic may accept in substance the conjectures of the Lutheran Carl Braaten;

> . . . we cannot now foresee the terms on which our churches might agree on those important doctrines which now divide us. It seems likely, however, that the dogmas concerning papal infallibility and Mary will have to be so reinterpreted that many people will scarcely recognize their continuity with the older traditions. Mere traditionalists who cling to ancient formulae will be unhappy. Equally radical reinterpretations of those protestant affirmations which give offense to Roman Catholics will be demanded. We cannot say *a priori* that this is impossible or improbable. Dogmas are things of history; they arise in history, they have a history; and they generate a history of interpretation in which earlier meanings are transcended through incorporation into new and quite dissimilar formulations. . . . Neither the trinitarian and christological dogmas, which we share with Roman Catholics, nor the papal and mariological dogmas, which we do not share, are exempt from new interpretations in an age of radical historical consciousness.[27]

The current ecumenical dialogue imposes a task upon all the Churches engaged in it. The effort to explain our positions to others compels us to re-examine what we ourselves have been saying. At many points we shall doubtless find that our views have not been accepted because they are in some respects unacceptable. This should accelerate the process of dogmatic development which history, to some extent, forces on us anyway. It should help us to amend the distortions in what we have hitherto been saying and thinking about our own faith. In this way divided Christians who are committed to the same gospel, and who invoke the same Holy Spirit, may hopefully converge toward greater solidarity in confession.

The question still remains whether total unity in confession is a prerequisite for full ecclesiastical communion. From what precedes, it should be clear that simultaneous dogmatic pluralism is sometimes admissible without prejudice to Church unity. If one and the same faith can be differently formulated for different historical epochs, a similar variety may be tolerated for different cultures in a single chronological period. In view of the literary form of confessional statements, as described above, creeds may be regarded as resulting from the inner exigencies of a lived faith; they should not be forcibly imposed, by external authoritative action, upon peoples not prepared for them by their corporate historical experience. The Christians of the early centuries were orthodox in their faith, but they probably could have made no sense of some of the dogmas which Bea would regard as "necessary for salvation." Why could not the same liberty be granted to culturally diverse peoples living contemporaneously? In line with the teaching of Vatican II, it might be fairly asked whether Christianity would not even stand to gain from a greater diversity in its creedal formulations.

The unity within difference permitted by the Florentine Decree of Union might prove paradigmatic for Protestant–Catholic relations. The Reformation Churches, if they were ever to enter into communion with Rome, could contribute many riches from their own traditions. In this connection one thinks especially of the great Reformation watchwords, such as *sola fide*, *sola gratia*, *sola Scriptura*, *soli Deo gloria* [faith alone, grace alone, Scripture alone, the glory of God alone], and of phrases such as *simul iustus et peccator* [at once justified and yet a sinner] and *ecclesia semper reformanda* [the Church in constant need of reform]. These are the nearest Protestant equivalents to the new dogmas of post-Reformation Catholicism. Just as Protestants would do well to try to find some religious value in these Catholic dogmas, so Catholics should seek to relate themselves positively to the key principles which have sustained Reformation Christianity for the past four centuries.

Until recently it was common for Catholics to polemicize against the Reformation slogans, which can surely be understood in ways incompatible with the Catholic vision of the Christian dispensation. But in the past generation many Catholic theologians, including some of the most eminent (Rahner, Küng, Bouyer, van de Pol . . .), have been pointing out that these formulas admit of a Catholic interpretation. Vatican II practically adopted the last two of these expressions. In the Decree on Ecumenism it declared: "Christ summons the Church, as she goes her pilgrim way, to that continual reformation of which she always has need, insofar as she is an institution of men here on earth" (no. 6). And in the Dogmatic Constitution *Lumen Gentium* [the Dogmatic Constitution on the Church] *simul iustus et peccator* is in effect applied to the Church, which is described as being "at the same time holy and always in need of being purified" (no. 8).

As in the case of the Catholic–Orthodox discussion about the procession of the Holy Spirit, so with regard to these Protestant slogans, we should not imagine that words alone are involved. Behind the formulas lies a very definite style of thought, characteristic of Evangelical Christianity. The question is whether Catholicism can absorb this without diluting its own witness.

Otto Pesch, O.P., in a lengthy treatise on the subject,[28] has shown that the Lutheran formula *simul iustus et peccator* rests upon a mode of thought that may be called "existential"—one that corresponds to what the believer is prompted to utter in a situation of prayer, when he comes into the presence of his God. No matter how just or holy he may be, he still has to declare "Lord, have mercy upon me, a sinner." Normative Catholic theology, as represented by Thomas Aquinas, for example, has taken a more objective or, in Pesch's term, a more "sapiential" point of view. It therefore seeks to analyze the process of justification from a more detached standpoint. These two theological styles, according to Pesch, lead to verbally contradictory formulas. Aquinas will have to say that once a man is justified, he is no longer in a state of sin; Luther will have to say the contrary. These statements cannot be harmonized; yet they are not strictly contradictory, any more than are the theologies of Paul and James, or John and the Synoptics. Since they stem from different points of view, the same words do not have identical meanings. Thus Pesch can conclude:

> If one does not antecedently give absolute value to Luther's form of existential theology and exclude every other form as deceptive, then there is a presumption that the difference we have discussed, and likewise all other differences traceable to it, can find a home within the same walls; that the two modes of theology need each other as critical insurance against falling into mistaken forms, and that the Church of all times needs both, in order to preserve the full tension of the Christian reality.[29]

Can logically irreconcilable dogmas, as Pesch here suggests, be admitted within one and the same Church? If one recognizes the logical anomalies of religious language, to which reference has already been made, it is difficult to see why not. It would be a bold man who would try to make a neat logical system out of the dogmas of a single Church. Catholic theology today abounds in logical antinomies, such as, for example, the twofold assertion that God's dominion is absolutely sovereign and that man remains free in working out his salvation. The affirmations seem to be mutually repugnant, and no one has really succeeded in showing why they do not conflict, but Catholics are convinced that in the real order both truths are compatible. In the same way it might be possible to hold with St. Thomas and Trent that in justification the sinner is truly cleansed of his fault, and yet, with Luther, that he remains in some real sense guilty and sinful. At every point religious language has to do with truths which it cannot fully comprehend.

I do not wish to imply, of course, that in religion anything goes, or that all the formulas of all the Churches can be thrown together into some great theological mishmash. There are statements which suitably express what Christian faith perceives, and others which fail to do so. Before Christians with irreducibly diverse confessions can acknowledge their mutual solidarity in faith, they must find a way of ascertaining that neither group has substantially departed from the gospel. As Schlink points out, it is uncommonly difficult to decide under what conditions to give recognition to a formula that we do not appropriate as our own.[30] He recommends a careful study of the literary forms, and a reinsertion of the disputed formula into the precise confessional context out of which it arose. The tools of exigetical and hermeneutical science must be skillfully brought to bear.

In the last analysis, I suspect, there are no adequate extrinsic norms for measuring the validity of confessional statements. They cannot be tested against other biblical or creedal utterances by merely syllogistic logic. The norm must be to some extent existential. It is necessary to enter into the spiritual world of the other Church with true empathy, and in this way to assess its declarations in relation to one's own sense of the Christian reality. Christian reunion therefore presupposes a certain sharing of religious experience on the part of believers of different denominations. It also presupposes that the Churches themselves assess and ratify the judgments of individual Christians.

For those who with sufficient preparation engage in the task, religious contact with another tradition cannot fail to be immensely rewarding. It affords a new perspective on both the other tradition and one's own. While one must keep open the possibility that either or both traditions may be found to have forsaken the pure wellsprings of divine truth, one will probably find, more often than not, that the different confessions are surprisingly near in spirit. The manifest diversity of their confessions often conceals an inarticulate unity at a deeper level.

The aphorism "doctrine divides but service unites" is therefore not the last word. Dogma is not in the first instance a source of division but rather a badge of unity. It expresses what some relatively large body of Christians see together, and find the strength to affirm in unison, by the light of their common faith. The fact that the dogmas of different Christian groups seem to conflict should not turn us against dogma itself. The conflicts are partly due to the faultiness of the ecclesiastical statements, many of which are in urgent need of reformulation, and partly also to the ineffable richness of Revelation, which defies compression into compact formulas. Ecumenical confrontation can serve the double function of making us critical of the formulations we accept from our own tradition, and of awakening us to the authentic values in other confessional families.

Conclusion

No attempt has been made in these pages to solve any of the substantive doctrinal issues presently dividing the Churches. My concern has been only with method. If my thesis is correct, it may take decades of ecumenical experience before any far-reaching doctrinal consensus between the Catholic Church and other Christian bodies can be achieved. But it should be clear at least that the objection put in the opening pages is not fatal. Christian reunion should on no account be conceived as if it were a mere matter of convincing Protestant, Anglican, or Orthodox believers to adopt all the Catholic dogmas presently "on the books." Nor can it consist in a simple abrogation of distinctively Catholic dogmas, or in a passive acceptance by Catholics of the present views of other denominations. Each participant in the ecumenical discussion must be seriously critical of its own traditions and genuinely anxious to receive enrichment from the heritage of the other Churches. Through this process of mutual teaching and learning we can progressively rediscover one another—and deserve to be rediscovered by one another—in Christ. As we do so, we shall undoubtedly find Christ himself in a new and richer way. For he wills to be found not simply as the head of various separate sects and denominations, but as the bond of mutual union among all who have life in his name.

Footnotes

[1] E. Schlink, "The Structure of Dogmatic Statements as an Ecumenical Problem," in *The Coming Christ and the Coming Church* (Edinburgh, 1967), p. 16.

[2] S. H. Miller and G. E. Wright, eds., *Dialogue at Harvard* (Cambridge, Mass., 1964), pp. 63f.

[3] For the history of the term "dogma," see the brief survey, with many references to scholarly literature, in W. Kasper, *Dogma unter dem Wort Gottes* (Mainz, 1965), pp. 28–38. Similar shifts have of course occurred in the meaning of the terms "faith" and "heresy," which have only recently acquired the technical significance they bear in modern Scholastic theology and modern Church documents.

[4] P. Fransen, S.J., "The Authority of the Councils," in *Problems of Authority*, ed. J. M. Todd (Baltimore, 1962), p. 74.

[5] "*Quod dogma fidei nil aliud sit, quam doctrina et veritas divinitus revelata, quae publico Ecclesiae iudicio fide divina credenda ita proponitur, ut contraria ab Ecclesia tamquam haeretica doctrina damnetur*" (quoted in W. Kasper, *op. cit.*, p. 36).

[6] *Acta Apostolicae Sedis*, IV (1868–69), p. 508.

[7] The theological thrust behind the document is clearly apparent in the *relatio* prepared by the Theological Commission and presented in the aula of St. Peter's by Archbishop Florit. Cf. G. Baum, O.S.A., "Vatican II's Constitution on Revelation," *Theological Studies*, XXVIII (1967), pp. 58–61.

[8] W. J. Richardson, S.J., "Heidegger and Theology," *Theological Studies*, XXVI (1965), p. 91; cf. R. Latourelle, *Theology of Revelation* (Staten Island, N.Y. 1966), p. 308.

[9] Kasper, *op. cit.*, pp. 101–6.

[10] Richardson, *loc. cit.*, p. 98.

[11] Cf. Thomas Aquinas, *Summa Theologica*, II–II, q. 1, ad. 6, *sed contra.*

[12] Schlink, *op. cit.* (n. 1 above).

[13] I. T. Ramsey, *Religious Language* (New York: The Macmillan Company–paperback edition, 1963), p. 191.

[14] *Ibid.*

[15] K. Rahner, S.J., "What Is a Dogmatic Statement?" *Theological Investigations*, Vol. V (Baltimore, 1966), pp. 58–60.

[16] In this connection one is reminded of all that Tillich has to say about symbol as the bearer of the power of that for which it stands. See the texts cited in C. J. Armbruster, S.J., *The Vision of Paul Tillich* (New York, 1967), pp. 156–59, 228–30.

[17] H. U. von Balthasar, "Truth and Life," in *Concilium*, Vol. XXI (Glen Rock, N.J.: Paulist Press, 1967), p. 90.

[18] J. N. D. Kelly, *Early Christian Doctrines* (New York, 1958), pp. 117–19.

[19] Cf. H. Küng, *Structures of the Church* (New York, 1964), pp. 386f., with references.

[20] See especially the affirmations of Lateran Council IV (Denz. 802), the Bull *Unam sanctam* (Denz. 870), and the Decree *pró Iacobitis* of the Council of Florence (Denz., 1351). [See note 26 below.]

[21] G. Baum, O.S.A., "The Magisterium in a Changing Church," in *Concilium*, Vol. XXI (Glen Rock, N.J.: Paulist Press, 1967), p. 69.

[22] So, e.g., H. Küng, *The Church* (New York: Sheed & Ward, 1968), p. 318.

[23] In the following several paragraphs I am profoundly indebted to G. Dejaifve, S.J., "Diversité dogmatique et unité de la révélation," *Nouvelle Revue Théologique*, LXXXIX (1967), pp. 16–25. For the history of the debate on the procession of the Holy Spirit, see J. Gill, S.J., *The Council of Florence* (Cambridge, Eng., 1959), Chap. 7.

[24] W. Kasper, "Geschichtlichkeit der Dogmen?" *Stimmen der Zeit*, CLXXIX (1967), pp. 401–16, esp. 410f.

[25] English translation in W. M. Abbott, S.J., and J. Gallagher, *The Documents of Vatican II* (New York, 1966), pp. 341–66.

[26] [*Editor's note:* Denz. refers to H. Denzinger, *Enchiridion Symbolorum* (Freiburg-Barcelona, 30th ed., 1955). Many of these citations can be found in *The Church Teaches: Documents of the Church in English Translation*, John F. Clarkson, *et al.*, eds. and trans. (St. Louis: B. Herder Book Co., 1955).]

[27] C. E. Braaten, "Reunion, Yes; Return, No," *Una Sancta*, XXIII (1966), pp. 32–33.

[28] O. H. Pesch, O.P., *Theologie der Rechtfertigung bei Martin Luther und Thomas von Aquin* (Mainz, 1967), esp. pp. 935–48.
[29] "Existentielle und Sapientiale Theologie," *Theologische Literaturzeitung*, XLII (1967), pp. 741–42.
[30] Schlink, *op. cit.*, pp. 80–84.

ROSEMARY RUETHER

Schism of Consciousness

The author of this article speaks in favor of a position that is finding an increasing number of advocates in the Christian community. In reading, we should try to keep in mind the following questions. What does the author mean by "schism of consciousness"? Is the Christian community being separated into factions? What is the author's definition of "Church"? What does she mean by "radical pluralism" in the Church? Is this the same as the position taken in the article reprinted here by Avery Dulles? What are the two revolutions going on in Roman Catholicism today? What is the "Free Church" movement?

Dr. Rosemary Ruether is a married Catholic theologian. She is a member of the faculty in the School of Religion at Howard University, Washington, D.C. She has written *The Church Against Itself*.

In the euphoria of the Second Vatican Council, it appeared that the Roman Catholic Church was accomplishing what historical experience and the laws of institutions would seem to rule out as impossible; namely, an established and highly bureaucratic institution revolutionizing itself through the channels of constituted authority. It appeared that, after centuries of inbred fear and stagnation, a renewal was taking place that was to catapult the Roman Catholic

Reprinted from *The Commonweal,* LXXXVIII (1968), No. 11, pp. 326–31, with the permission of the publisher, Commonweal Publishing Co., Inc.

Church into dialogue with "modern times." There was to be balanced assimilation of the best of contemporary thought, but without schism or breaking of ranks on any side.

But as the impact of the Council has had an opportunity to develop, and many of the theories of the Council, enunciated with such calm assurance at that time, are in process of being lived out, this optimistic judgment is by no means so certain. We find that it is one thing to define a noble theory of collegiality on all levels of the Church, and quite another to seek to put it into practice when this means a concrete challenge to the power structures which have hitherto prevailed. We find that it is one thing to outline an inspiring concept of the liturgy as the celebration of community, but quite another to scrutinize the present life of the parish in the light of these ideals.

The extraordinary aspect of the Council is that the bishops, led on by theological *periti* [experts] who often delicately underplayed the revolutionary possibilities of what they were saying, allowed themselves to say far more than they had intended to say. In so doing, they seemed oblivious to the changed situation in the Church created by mass media of communication (as their decree on this subject so amply demonstrated). They still assumed that the implications of what they were saying could be worked out in secret, high-level meetings, and then passed down to the "listening church" through regular ecclesiastical channels exactly as though there were no television or world press at work already interpreting what they were saying to the world.

It did not seem to occur to the bishops that Catholics, in great numbers, all over the world would be reading and interpreting for themselves all these ideas without waiting for official guidelines; that Catholics all over the world, reading the decrees on the liturgy, on the meaning of the Church, on the need to modernize the religious orders, would take all this quite literally, would believe exactly what they read, and would proceed to act upon these things as though they themselves were the Church.

Thus it came about that a revolution begun by a Pope rapidly got out of hierarchical hands altogether and became a popular movement, and the bishops found themselves in the strange position of being picketed in their chanceries by people carrying signs covered with words from conciliar decrees and papal encyclicals.

But this revolution in mass communication which suddenly revealed another and very different kind of teaching authority in the Church is only a part of the situation that has brought about our present tensions. This would mean little without the total historical context in which it operated. Culturally speaking, the conciliar decrees tried to span an abyss created by all the revolutions in thought and society from the Latin Middle Ages to the twentieth century with one magic thread of the development of doctrine.

The span of thought between Trent and Vatican II was, in fact, far too great to be so easily assimilated. History is not cheated. One cannot retreat before historical development for five centuries and then expect to take it all in with a three-year cram course. Much blood has flowed under the bridge in that time (to quote a line from *Who's Afraid of Virginia Woolf?*). A revolution in consciousness has taken place which assumes an autonomy, secularity, historicity, and a democratic structure of society. None of this did the Roman Church gather to itself during that long period of crisis and change. Now the Church optimistically throws open long-closed windows but expects these winds to circulate through much the same Renaissance structures with perhaps a partition knocked out or a new door installed here and there. The results should have been predictable.

We have then a schism of consciousness in the Roman Church, a schism of profound depth and complexity. It is a schism which touches upon the basic ways we understand God, man, history, and community; the whole relationship between man and man in the world and before God. This schism touches on the fundamentals. It is more than a matter of cultural forms, or if it is only a question of forms, then the question of forms itself cannot be separated from substance.

In other words, faith cannot be separated from its cultural dress and clothed in another dress and pretend to be still the same. The change of culture changes all the ways we interpret the data of our existence. The old mold of thought, formal, legal, and paternalistic, defining all power in a Platonic manner, as proceeding from the apex of the hierarchy downward, this mold of thought is so far removed from the historical and equalitarian culture of today that their interpretation of Christianity differs not only in conclusions, but in their understanding of almost all the premises as well. Even when they use the same symbols, they mean very different things by these symbols. When an heir of the Counter-Reformation and a disciple of the theology of secularity use the words Christ, Church, *diakonia* of *koinonía* [service of the fellowship], the meaning of these words are so divergent as to be in direct contradiction. It is unfair to say that never in the history of Christianity has there existed, within the formal boundaries of a single ecclesiastical institution, poles of interpretation which share so little of what is termed "a common faith."

If the unity of the Church rests on some broadly common ethos and consensus on the meaning of faith, then there is no unity in the Roman Catholic Church, but only a formal collective based on cultural lag. Nor is there any prospect for creating a new consensus within the immediate future. The conciliar documents, far from being a focus for such a consensus, are simply a center-boundary marking preconciliar from postconciliar. If we are to continue to speak of Roman Catholicism as a "community," therefore, we are faced with a real problem of what such a phase means when applied to such a disparate aggregate. Roman Catholicism as a definable identity embracing all these in this institution has ceased to exist. The formal boundaries remain as historical accidents which temporarily contain people of the most divergent views.

By the same token, the old question of joining the Church or leaving it is being relativized out of all relevance, so that the person who publicly makes a thing out of leaving the Church becomes almost a reactionary who insists on clinging to the old boundaries' markers between in and out. Since no group in the Church any longer has the power to impose its identity upon all or expel dissenters, no particular identity is fixed as mandatory any more, and those who, by historical accident, find themselves in this organization can choose various positions from among a spectrum of possibilities.

In other words, the whole contradiction between a Church which claims universality and yet has made its identity through sectarian tactics has now broken down at all the vulnerable points. All the possibilities available in Western and perhaps even in world culture have now become possibilities for Catholics, and in the process the identity of Catholics as a distinct group becomes impossible to define. What we have instead is an intramural struggle of factions. It is a struggle because we have not yet accepted the radical pluralism which is becoming our reality.

But even the word "radical pluralism" is no magic phrase to resolve our multiplicity because our differences are real and to no small degree contradictory. We might look to Anglicanism as a smaller model of the multiform Church which Roman Catholicism might become. But the spectrum of plurality relating an Evangelical and High Church Anglican is small compared to the vast distances of life with which we have to deal. What can unite an aristocratic Spanish Trentine Cardinal who sips sherry with the landholders, and a revolutionary, Marxist-oriented priest who shares the wineskin of the insurgent peasantry? Here is no mere difference in life style, but a conflict of principle so deep that one wonders on what ground they can honestly call each other "fellow Christians." The conflict is real, because it does not admit of a neutrality which would not itself be a form of taking sides. No mere eclecticism or mutual toleration of pluralism can subsist when the differences are such as to point in prophetic judgment against the other. It is the kind of difference that calls men to choose sides.

This is schism in the most profoundly moral sense of the word. It is the sense in which we say that the Gospel brings not peace, but a sword; the schism which divides those who have ears to hear from those who do not or will not. It is very dangerous to speak of the schism in these terms, and especially to identify who is who, for ultimately only God can make this final judgment. Yet we must see that this is the ultimate dimension of the schism that divides the Church against itself. Here the question of the lack of a community which can be existentially affirmed shows up at the crucial point, and we see that Roman Catholicism as a "communion" is a legal fiction. Our schism then is not merely one of culture but of faith. It is an estrangement of the deepest existential commitments pitted against each other, where the word forgiveness is stilled by the word of wrath, where compromise is ruled out on principle and only conversion could effect reconciliation. The Church therefore contradicts itself. In hope it would stand for the community of reconciliation, but its historical existence is rather that of man's self-estrangement and his alienation from his fellowman.

The Free Church Movement

The Free Church movement is the reflection of this schism. It bespeaks clearly that we are not in communion, not merely sociologically, but in our fundamental interpretation of what the Gospel is. For those most serious about their commitment, this has become an intolerable situation, and the worship of the official Church a deeply alienating experience. This is not simply because they would like to replace organs with guitars or wafers with real bread. All this is surface, although it represents the deeper issues. Fundamentally they want the Church to witness to and celebrate their faith, and it does not.

This is why the official worship is so distressing, and why it becomes intolerable to sit through the typical parish liturgy. I have heard people say that they wanted to scream and run out of the church, that they had to dig their nails into the pew to keep from crying out in frustration. The sermon was a parable of incredibility, the whole format screamed out a preposterous concept of faith. If the faith celebrated here was really anyone's faith, it was not their faith. It was all the worse because it used symbols they accepted, but systematically gave them meanings they must reject as hollow, superficial, or even antithetical. It is therefore no wonder that such people seek other assemblies outside the official Church worship. Sooner or later one wakes up to the fact that one does not have a Sunday obligation to destroy one's soul.

In seeking other assemblies, fundamentally what is sought is a gathering that will do what a liturgy is supposed to do, namely renew the soul and not blast it further into Hell. One seeks a Christian community, a community which will sustain you in common faith, not tear you apart in alienation. The Free Church is then nothing else but the quest for the authentic Christian community, and a protest against the Church whose reality mocks the symbols it professes to exemplify. Unless it is clearly seen that the Free Church is an issue of faith, and a search for a community which can authentically celebrate this faith, then all that is going on in this movement will be superficially understood, and its real import will be overlooked entirely.

The break with the official Church reflects the fact that those who control the official Church themselves have become a faction; one might almost say that the official Church in general has become a faction within the body of those who call themselves Christians. A faction which no longer represents the whole of the people, particularly those who are thinking of Christianity in radical terms, places its stamp on the official policies of the parish and diocese. The people of the new Church, consequently, are homeless. They are interlopers at the parish, not at home there. This is the immediate occasion for their departure to seek a community where they can be at home among fellow believers.

We might for a moment focus on this question of lack of representation. Can the organization itself be enlarged and structurally redesigned so that the new Church can also be represented in its councils? We might imagine a democratic reorganization of the Church on a representational basis, such as presently exists in modern Protestant denominations. Such an organization does not banish a hierarchical structure, but it organizes the community on many levels of responsibility from a communal basis upward, rather than from the top downward.

The Episcopal Church might be taken as a model of such a hierarchical yet communally based Church. Each congregation selects lay members to represent it at a diocesan council. This, together with priests from the diocesan council and the bishops, makes up the governing synod of the diocese. Such a synod elects the bishop and makes basic legislative decisions. In a similar way representative councils of both clergy and laity meet on the national level. Here then is a hierarchical, episcopally governed Church, but one in which there is a balance and interrelation between administrative power and representative power. Such a structure does not eliminate all tensions and differences by any means, but it allows representation to various positions and provides channels of recourse and appeal. The feeling of unjust and arbitrary procedures and lack of representation and participation in decision-making so characteristic of Roman Catholicism is significantly altered in a democratically organized Church.

Institutional Reform?

Here then would seem to be one focus for Catholic reform, a basic reform of the institution itself, so that it becomes representational rather than dictatorial. The theoretical framework for a concept of ministry which evolves from the people upward rather than from the apex of the hierarchy downward is already available in current theology. One has only to clarify it and put it into practice. But how do we do that? There seem to be precious few handles for a constitutional reform of the ecclesiastical structure, since the only persons empowered to make such changes have both theoretical and practical vested interest in the old regime. How do you create a revolution in an autocratic regime which has no constitutional or ideological means of democratization?

Historically, the solution to that problem was the French Revolution. The Catholic Church, in effect, is the last surviving institution of that ancient regime that was toppled in the liberal revolutions of the eighteenth and nineteenth centuries. The counterpart of this revolution in the Church is, in fact, long overdue. It is a little hard to visualize this taking place by rushing the barricades, yet it is also fairly certain that it will not take place without some kind of force, since those in power seldom yield power voluntarily unless they are put in a position where they have practically no other alternative.

There is perhaps one way this could happen by nonviolent methods of revolution. One might create autonomous, representative councils of both clergy and laity for each diocese. Such councils will have to be distinguished from the parish and clergy councils which are set up within the limits allowed by the present power structure. To be truly revolutionary councils, such organizations must be autonomous, gathered and organized by the people represented independently. Such councils will have to rival the puppet councils set up by the hierarchy and will have to establish themselves as the true voice of their constituency. Such groups should affiliate on a national basis and hold national synods which would coincide with and rival the bishops' councils. By gathering organizational strength and economic power, and through use of communications media to set forth their program, such revolutionary councils could ultimately succeed in negotiating with the hierarchy to reform the whole structure, and amalgamate with it, so that such representative councils become the main body of the new organization. Such movements are already in progress, and deserve support.

However, I find a marked lack of interest among the more *avant-garde* Catholics and especially Free Church Catholics in efforts to reform and democratize the structure. Part of their indifference seems to me illegitimate, in that these people seem naïvely anti-institutional and are unable to realize both what a democratically organized Catholic Church might do for the good and also what harm it can do if left to be run as it is. Nevertheless, there may also be a legitimacy in their indifference, in this respect: they instinctively recognize that the issues involved in the Free Church movement go beyond what even a democratically organized Church institution could be. The outlook that guides the Free Church people goes far beyond the boundaries of intramural ecclesiastical reorganization, and for this reason the most creative and involved people tend to feel that they have more important things to do than to play Church structure games.

We have to distinguish two very different revolutions going on in Roman Catholicism and in historical Christianity as a whole today. These two movements may ultimately meet at some point in the future, and I believe they are both necessary, but for the time being they are quite distinct. One is the movement for reform of the Church institution itself. It includes the efforts to democratize unrepresentative institutions like our own and bring then into closer proximity to the organizational procedures which people today feel to be mandatory for minimal justice. It also includes the official ecumenical movement which seeks to compare official positions and ultimately to effect ecclesiastical corporation mergers. At its best this movement recognizes that it is not enough merely to compare and synthesize the old, but there must be renewal and reconstruction at the same time. Such an attempt is presently underway in the Consultation on Church Union which seeks to unite the major American Protestant denominations in a single united Church. This Consultation presently has ten member denominations participating.

But the time for such internal housekeeping seems to be running out fast. Church reforms are having a hard time keeping the interest of the most creative people. A whole new revolution is upon us, urgently calling our attention to its services and rendering churchly revolutions pale by comparison. This shift of interest away from the Church institution comes through the realization that the Church, for all its formidable structure and real estate, has become a sideline in human experience, and Church-going has been relegated to a small and increasingly insignificant corner of man's total life.

If the Gospel is really to be a good news for the whole man, then it has to break out of that corner created by the secularization of society and the retreat of the Church into the private umbilical sector of man's life. It must move into the fullness of man's existence, but it cannot do this as a churchly institution, but only in some new and entirely different form which abrogates the distinction between sacred and secular institutions, a distinction that has been created by the self-mythologies of Church and non-Church institutions alike. It must decisively alter the very meanings of communion and ministry, Church and mission, to break these realities out of the corner where they are but are not, and reveal them where they are though not to be and yet are. It is precisely to this task that the Free Church, the Church which is conscious of being the Christian community and yet decisively breaks out of the mold of historic Church organizations, is now called.

Dissolving All Boundaries

These needs to which Christians are responding are such as to strain and dissolve the boundaries of all previously known Church organizations, not only hierarchical, but even loose, congregational type organizations. The very idea of the Church as an identifiable sacred organism, the very idea of Christianity as a specific historical culture is being thrown into question. For many people who live in this breach, interest in the Church can continue only if it is understood in ways which radically transcend these cultural and institutional limitations.

If ministry is not something we can find in the street as well as the sanctuary, if communion is not something we can find around a kitchen table, if the Church is not something about all mankind here and now, then we can scarcely be interested anymore in what is called the "Church." There then comes about a scattered, floating Christian people who don't find Church realities happening in churchly places, but carry ecclesial consciousness into unchurched places to discern there these realities in the flesh. This diaspora Church is only partly to be identified with experimental communities. Basically it is the site of a new consciousness of what the Church is and where it is really happening.

Once this consciousness emerges into maturity, it will become, not the underground, but the Free Church. It is better understood as the Free Church both because of its affinities with the traditional Free Church position in the left wing of the Reformation, and because the reasons for dissolving the institutional reference of the word "Church" have become even more compelling today. In some ways the Free Church parallels other movements, such as the "free press" and the "free university" which are similarly moving outside present power structures to find more authentic ways of doing things.

We should not think that these outside communities are produced simply by imbalances of power within the present organization which make it difficult for innovating groups to get a hearing. It is true that the power lies with a conservative group who try to hold back the pace of change and balk at the prospect of autonomy and diversity, but even if these conditions were somewhat rectified, it would not abolish the conditions which make for the free, noninstitutional community. After all, the Shalom communities did not appear in Spain or Italy, but in Holland. More freedom to experiment with the liturgy might keep a few people in the parish instead of sending them into rebel communities, but the conditions which are creating the Free Church are much larger than that. No amount of broadening the rules of the liturgy within the present structure of the Roman rite could encompass the style of the Free Church, because the Free Church is already living out beyond the presuppositions upon which the present concept of the liturgy is based.

The difference might be summed up in one word: secularity. The liturgy of the Church organization remains a sacral rite which only those empowered with the sacred power of the institution can perform, which produces a certain sacred substance which is ontologically distinct from our daily bread. The Free Church is tending in a direction which inevitably if not already has dissolved that magic circle of the sacred. Its priest is the charismatic leader of its community, the one whose toil and integrity earn him the place of prophet in its midst. Its sacrament is not transsubstantial bread, but our own daily bread in its fullness of meaning and its Church is not of another world, but of the hopes of this very world upon which we stand. It feels no need for the ministrations of the sacred institution because its symbols, its doctrine, priesthood, and sacraments have been demythologized, brought back from never-never land and returned to this earth, to that humanity with its covenant and its premise which is now seen to be the only place where these symbols really exist and have meaning.

The authentic theology of the Free Church, then, I would suggest is a secular theology, that worldly interpretation of the Gospel toward which Bonhoeffer was groping during his last days in prison. Secular theology is not a passing fad, but it is indeed, as Bonhoeffer perceived, the theological interpretation of the present historical modality of our existence in the world. Not everyone lives contemporaneously with his own times, and for those who can live bodily today but spiritually remain in the mythological or metaphysical forms of the past, it may be possible to continue to abide in the presuppositions of sacred societies. But for those who live existentially in the present era, it is impossible to live in these presuppositions.

Secularity, as the way of understanding Christian existence today, is shaking the foundations of the sacred institution. It is at the heart of that disturbance among the monks and nuns, the traditional representatives of the "religious" life in the Church. These people discover that they can no longer believe in the idea of being "religious" as distinct from being Christian, because, more profoundly, they can no longer believe in being Christian in any way that is distinct from being authentically human. In Bonhoeffer's words, "to be a Christian is not to be a religious man, but to be a man."

Behind the fracas over nuns' habits and priestly celibacy lies this more fundamental perception. All the movements to dissolve these badges of the past lie in the dissolving credibility of the sacral as such. One wishes to break down these boundaries and distinctions, these ways of being set apart from the community of the Church and the community of man because, more fundamentally, one no longer believes in being a sacred person as distinct from being a person, a person standing before God and one's fellow man, to repent and respond to one another and to break bread together. In that lies all there is to say about priesthood, community, Church, and sacrament.

Church Life and Human Life

Therefore, it seems to me that the true significance of the Free Church does not lie in some demand for updated liturgies or more democratic structures for Church institutions. Rather it is a sign of an entirely new way of understanding the Church itself which simply and in the last analysis dissolves any need for the sort of Church idea which would interpret itself as something more or something else than the life of man in the world.

This does not mean, however, that the Church becomes the religion of present culture or that it simply dissolves into the world, in the New Testament sense of "this world"; that it loses itself in the social status quo or the present power structure. This is, in fact, exactly what the Church did in so-called Christian civilization, and the Free Church is also rescuing the Church from "worldliness" in this other sense of the word. Here secularity, in the sense of a creational perspective, must be sharply distinguished and contrasted to secularism or even sacralism, or whatever view may endorse a closed system of powers and principalities.

Secularity does not mean settling for things as they are because the dialectic of man's existence cannot settle for things as they are, but rather the dialectic of man's existence forces him to stand out against the powers and principalities of his own history and to move in a constant élan of self-transcendence. The community which witnesses and points to the place of this transcendence is the Church, but this community must be sought wherever, in fact, it is being lived. Only there do we find the true Church, while the sacred institution has become a part of those powers and principalities which have been overthrown by the power of the Gospel.

The dialectic of grace and judgment to which the Gospel points is just as real as ever, but we now see that it points, not to some mythic rite carried on in a sacred space, but to the dialectic of man's real, everyday existence. The Free Church, therefore, deserts the sacred space in order to follow the Spirit where he is really at work. It wishes to be with Christ where he is really renewing the world. It gathers, now here, now there, not in temples, but in tents, in pilgrim communities which group temporarily and on the roadside. These communities gather wherever men find they touch each other and find some communication. They celebrate, not as a scheduled rite, but on the occasion of some real victory, to acclaim and commemorate some real breakthrough in the currency of man's existence.

Does this mean that ecclesiastical institutions ought to disappear? I think they will diminish, but they will remain, and I suspect they will do both mostly for the wrong reasons.

Institutionalization of the Christian community is a function of historical perpetuation of a particular tradition and should remain relative to that purpose. The Church institution has a function as a relative and provisional instrument for the transmission of a message, for engaging in an experiment in community, and for reflecting upon and handing down this reflection on this message and experiment. But the gospel upon which it reflects is not exclusively about itself.

The Holy Spirit is not simply its own *zeitgeist*, but the Spirit which underlies the creation and renewal of all the world. Christ is not simply its body, but the body which takes shape as the destiny of mankind in history. The covenant and its promise are not confined to what people called Christians do in buildings called churches, but these are the reality of man's life together and the future hope of the world. Therefore, while explicitly Church structures can play a role in this mission, they can do so with theological integrity only by strictly relativizing the application of these references to themselves. They can really be the Church when they know that they are in no special sense the Church, but only one place where, by the grace of God, the Church might be happening.

The importance of the Free Church, the nonecclesiastical community, is that it makes this worldiness of the Gospel and this secularity of the Church clear and explicit. The Free Church overruns the false boundaries between Church and non-Church institutions and thus helps us to see more clearly what and where the Church really is.

GREGORY BAUM, O.S.A.

Church as Movement

The foundation of this article is a new view of what man is, that is, theological anthropology. Does Father Baum describe man as the reader knows him? Why does the author choose as a new model for the Church the outer-oriented movement rather than the other possible forms that he mentions? Is the outer-oriented movement or Open Church the same as the Free Church of the previous article? What is the mission of the Church? Is the concept of the "third man" merely a rationalization to get us off the hook if we dislike something in the Church? What is the institutional part of the outer-oriented Church? Does Father Baum advocate that the Church become something like a social agency?

Gregory Baum, O.S.A. is a Professor of Theology at St. Michael's College in the University of Toronto. This is Father Baum's third article in this volume.

It seems to me that the restlessness in the Catholic Church is due to a new self-understanding that is emerging among Christians. Our theological anthropology has undergone a significant development. Through the biblical movement, through dialogue with contemporary philosophy, and through man's participation in the new conditions of the modern world, a theological understanding of man has

Reprinted from Gregory Baum, O.S.A., *The Credibility of the Church Today* (New York: Herder and Herder, Inc., 1968), pp. 181–85, 193–210, with the permission of the publisher.

evolved in Catholic literature that was able to express itself in the documents of Vatican Council II, especially in the Constitution on Divine Revelation and the Pastoral Constitution on the Church in the Modern World. What is happening at the moment is that the anthropology proposed in the conciliar documents as a doctrine, is being assimilated by Christians as personal knowledge and hence is beginning to determine their own self-understanding.

How can this new anthropology be described? I will attempt a brief sketch of it, a schematic description to convey the idea to the reader who, from his reading and his own personal experience, knows what I am talking about.

Man Is a Listener

As God reveals himself as the One who addresses man in his Word, so he reveals man to himself as one who is meant to listen. Man is open to what others communicate to him, and he will never cease to be a learner. Man listens to other people; and through these others he is able to listen to the world, to history, and even to God. According to biblical teaching, God communicates himself to men through human speech and human gestures: Word and sacrament as mediated by men are the matrix of man's relationship to God.

Saying that man is a listener is different from saying that he is a knower. When man is called a knower then his vis-à-vis is truth, possibly abstract, impersonal truth. When man is called a listener then his vis-à-vis is always a person. We listen to someone. Listening relates us to someone who has something to say to us.

As a listener man realizes that he is only beginning to understand what life is all about. He is always ready to learn more. He enters every situation expecting to learn something new. He wants to be sensitive to the summons that comes to him from his relationship to people and from his situation in the world. He is even ready to listen to the unconditional call that comes to him as God's Word. For this reason man is unwilling to tie himself to any position that will prevent him from being a listener. Deep religious convictions are acceptable to him only if they allow him to remain open to other people. Today we distinguish clearly between faith and fanaticism. Religious convictions are regarded as fanatical when they prevent a man from being open to others, block his ears, and always make him misunderstand what others are saying.

The Personal Structure of Man Is Dialogical

Man comes to be a person through dialogue with others. Man is a listener summoned to respond, and his responses constitute him in his personal being. Man is not a finished substance whose life simply actualizes what is potentially contained in him. . . . Man is an open-ended being. He is involved in an unending dialogue which makes him to be who he is. Man is forever led into new situations, he listens to a summons that does not come from himself and by responding to it he determines his existence as a person.

In Jesus Christ, God has revealed his purpose to enter into a dialogue of salvation with every single human being.[1] Wherever a man is, in the Church or outside of it, he lives in a situation that is salvational. He is addressed by a call or challenge, the absolute character of which betrays its transcendent origin. God is Word, eternal Word: God is always One who addresses himself to men. For this reason we affirm that human life is supernatural. Human life is not simply the living out of man's nature; it is the realization of man's dialogue of salvation with God.

The man who is open to dialogue is nourished by God. God redeems man, sanctifies or humanizes him, through dialogue. God acts in the world through the conversation and association of men.

Man Grows Through a Process of Conversions

A man does not want to remain as he is. He always wants to change and grow. He seeks to become more truly himself. For this reason he desires to come to self-knowledge. He wants to know who he is. He wishes to face all that is in him, even the destructive, even the sinful, with utmost sincerity. He realizes that he cannot change himself by his own will power. He might be able to force himself to do this or that, but he cannot give himself the freedom to forget himself and be concerned about others. The important changes in a man's life will have to happen to him, happen as the result of his listening and his involvement with others.

Man is not simply an intelligent agent who comes to knowledge by learning objective truth. Coming to a knowledge that counts always implies a reorientation of a man's life. Insight comes through a process of conversion. This is true for Christians and non-Christians alike. Wherever people are, they are summoned to growth, to leave their childish past behind, and to assume greater responsibility for themselves and for their environment. This repeated reorientation of a person's life toward reality demands a great price. Conversion always hurts. It demands the abandoning of many things that are dear to us. At the same time, conversion is always experienced as a reply to a call that comes from beyond ourselves. The important changes in human life are never experienced as being self-initiated. They are grace.

Man Is in Need of the Community to Become Himself

The dialogical personal structure of man indicates that his inner reality has been received by him from others. His speech, his feelings, his knowledge would never have developed without mother, father, and other people who came close to him. What is true of early childhood is true of later life. Man needs the community to fulfill his destiny. Without the help of his brothers, and ultimately of the whole human family, man cannot exercise his divine vocation of reconciling and humanizing life on earth. Man must therefore be politically involved.

This personalistic understanding of man is quite different from the individualism that we find in some authors of the past. Man is not an individual who grows by focusing on himself. Man does not achieve well-being by straining narcissistically after self-fulfillment. Man is a person, and hence he becomes more truly himself through communion with others. The center of man is outside of himself.

This community aspect of the human person also discloses a new understanding of the human body. Man is inserted into the community through his body. His body is the instrument of communication with people. The body may not simply be regarded as a physical substructure of the spiritual soul; it must be understood as a more truly human reality. It is the locus of man's presence to other people and to the world. The new self-understanding of man leads him to a new way of experiencing his bodiliness, its meaning and role in his life.

Man's Life Is Constantly Threatened

Man is exposed to forces that could undo him. These forces could prevent a man from being a listener; they could keep him from entering deeply into dialogue and from growing up through repeated conversions; they could prevent him from entering into communion with others. Man is threatened by the outer and inner situation of his life to become unfaithful to the divine call of becoming truly human.

The task of the Gospel is to reveal to man the forces that threaten his human existence and to offer him access to a communion, a divine communion, that enables him to be faithful to his call and destiny. The Gospel does not offer a ready-made blueprint of the good life. It does not solve all of man's problems in advance. It leaves many moral and intellectual questions unsolved. What the Gospel lays bare are the forces that could destroy man and what it offers as a remedy are the sources that enable a man to become a listener, to enter into dialogue, to be ready for conversion and growth, and to participate in the life of the community. This is the present salvation brought by Christ.

. . .

How will the new self-understanding of man affect the social organizations of the Church? Are we able to foresee in which direction the Church will move? Catholics have begun to speculate on this question.

Among some Catholics deeply concerned with reform and renewal we find the desire to introduce into the ecclesiastical institution the democratic processes developed in modern society.[2] They foresee a vast conciliar system, parish councils, diocesan councils, national councils, and more universal councils, in which the representatives of various groups in the Church can make their voices heard and contribute to the making of public policy. The final decisions will be made by the bishops and the Pope through processes that involve the lower clergy and the people and at the same time preserve the special role and power of the episcopal college. Foreseen is a legislation in the Church protecting the rights of individual Christians and their societies against undue interference by higher superiors. The principle of subsidiarity will be guaranteed by law. For the better functioning of the Church there will be law courts to which Christians may appeal if they have not been justly treated according to the common law of the Church.

Canon law societies and individual canon lawyers have already worked out various projects for the institutional Church of the future, and outlined the nature and the form which constitutional law should take in this Church.[3] In all of these, modern concepts of government play a great role. These projects may vary as to the amount of independent action they ascribe to the hierarchy in the process of decision-making. Some canonists think it desirable, and possible, that the Catholic Church adopt a constitution, parallel to civic society, which limits the power of the ecclesiastical government according to common law. In other words, there are Catholic theologians and canonists who believe that it is in harmony with the Catholic understanding of the Church's divine foundation and the apostolic succession of the episcopal college (Pope and bishops) to advocate the creation of a constitutional papacy and constitutional episcopacy.

This interpretation of the structural development taking place in the Church is clearly based on the historical experience of Western society. From a highly diversified and many-leveled feudalism, Western society passed into the age of the absolute monarchy. Then, under the pressure of national life, the king created councils or parliaments and permitted the people or their representatives to have an increasingly greater share in the making of his own decisions. Eventually the affirmation of the citizens' power transformed deliberative councils into legislative assemblies. This was the common road of Western society to constitutional monarchies and the republican state.

There are undoubtedly signs that a similar kind of development has taken place in the Churches. The Catholic Church has resisted this development and until recently her methods of government reflected political institutions which are no longer with us. In particular, there is in the Catholic Church no separation between the legislative and judicial offices. The desire for a constitutional Church, then, is born of the conviction that the experience of Western society is being relived in the Catholic Church, and that what is happening at this time is the structural perfection of the Church as a spiritual republic.

What are we to think of this interpretation of the structural development in the Church? There are many Catholics, among them bishops, who regard the perfections of the Church as a replica of a well-functioning modern state as the ideal for which to strive.

I have great difficulties with this view, both as an ideal and as a description of what is happening at this time in the Catholic Church. I have great difficulties in thinking of the Church as a spiritual replica of political society. In other words, I wonder whether in the present age the political society is the "sociological model" for describing the Church's institutional reality. In the first place, I do not think it would be desirable to have a Church that is a spiritual republic in which all members are involved in policy-making and the perfection of the ecclesiastical organization. In such a situation every Christian would be involved in ecclesiastical life—he would spend much of his time and ingenuity in making decisions regarding the organizational life of the Church. Every Christian would become a kind of ecclesiastical person. It seems to me, however, that the task of the Christian is to live in the world and to give his time and intelligence to the transformation of the civil society to which he belongs—and of the whole of mankind. The Gospel and its celebration in the Church should not withdraw the Christian from his involvement in secular society but should free him to serve his community in new ways and with greater dedication. If the Church were the ideal spiritual republic which we have described, she would face the civil society as a kind of spiritual duplication of itself, she would face civil society as another society. This has been true in the history of the Church for a long time. But one may wonder whether a structure which makes the Church face the secular society as a parallel sort of society, even though spiritual, does not create many undesirable effects today. A Christian then belongs to two societies and his loyalties will be strained, if not divided. In such a situation the Church would take him out of his secular life into her own, rather than intensify his participation in the society to which he belongs. In such a situation the institutional Church may become a drain in the lives of men: it would demand intellectual, personal, and financial resources for the building up of the spiritual replica of society, which would become an enormously complex ecclesiastical bureaucracy.

I wish to propose another sociological model for the institutional life of the Church which corresponds more faithfully to the contemporary understanding of the Christian involvement in secular life and describes more realistically, I think, what is beginning to happen in the Catholic Church. This new sociological model is the movement.

There are many kinds of movements in society and it may not be easy to find a single set of characteristics which define what a movement is. Some movements are inner-oriented. Some movements, that is to say, have the purpose of transforming the people who belong to them. The life and action of such a movement are designed to affect those who participate in it. Alcoholics Anonymous, for instance, is such a movement. Its purpose is to heal people with an alcoholic problem. Other movements are outer-oriented. Their purpose is to transform the society in which they exist. The life and action of such movements are designed to affect the whole of society. An outer-oriented movement also affects its own members but this effect is subordinated to the wider aim of influencing the entire community of men. An outer-oriented movement cannot be defined with reference to itself. Its essence cannot be described simply by indicating the interrelationship of the people who belong to it. In order to define an outer-oriented movement one must speak of the whole of society and indicate the role which the movement is designed to play in it. In other words, an outer-oriented movement is defined by its mission. The movement may educate its members, create fellowship among them, organize them in various groups and associations, but this inner activity is subordinated to the purpose of the movement which is to have a transforming effect on the whole of society. A political party, to give one example, is such an outer-oriented movement. It can be defined only with reference to the whole of society. While it has an effect on the people who are variously associated with it, its main purpose is to transform the political life of the entire country.

It seems to me that the outer-oriented movement may be a useful sociological model for the Church of tomorrow. The Open Church, as understood by Vatican II, is not a segregated people. The Spirit-created fellowship in the Church extends to other people, to the baptized generally, and to people wherever they are, who are led by the Spirit. The Open Church is a reconciler in society. The Open Church wants to involve the whole of society in conservation. The Open Church is in solidarity with the human community in which it lives; it wants to bear the burden with others; it wants to help solve the problems from which people suffer; it realizes that the redemptive mystery—"the kingdom"—which it serves is a gracious reality that pervades human life and that gains a deeper hold on people everywhere as they enter more deeply into conversation, cooperation, and unity. The Open Church, therefore, cannot be defined in terms intrinsic to itself. It must be defined in terms of the whole human race and of its role in it. The fellowship the Open Church creates among her members and the holiness into which she initiates them are subordinated to the transforming effect of the Christian community on the society in which it lives.

An outer-oriented movement is defined in reference to the society in which it exists. A movement may want to grow and become stronger, it may want to attract more members; but it does not envisage including all people and identifying itself with society. A movement wants to be a lively, intelligent, and active group within society, having a profound effect on the well-being and growth of the entire social life of people.

The sociological model of the outer-oriented movement seems particularly apt to describe the Open Church of Vatican II and the changing concept of the Church's mission. However varied the concept of mission may still be in Catholic theology, all theologians agree that the Church's mission cannot be defined in terms of the salvation the Church offers to men who, without her, would be eternally lost.[4] Vatican II has affirmed God's redemptive involvement in human life everywhere. This mission of the Church is to unify and reconcile the human family in the power of the Gospel. There is disagreement among Catholic theologians as to what precisely this means. It is possible to understand this mission as the witness of the Church in dialogue and cooperation by which she serves the redemptive mystery present in others, and in doing so mediates to them as well as to herself the freedom to enter more deeply into man's divine destiny. Since the Gospel reveals the sickness of society and makes available the sources of well-being, the Church's mission is a movement of humanization. The Gospel is a critique of human life. The mission of the Church, therefore, is to serve mankind with this Gospel and to help the redemptive presence of God among people to triumph in terms of unity, reconciliation, social justice, and peace. The Church wants to be a strong movement. She hopes to attract people to join her in faith and dedicate themselves with her to serve the kingdom mysteriously present in human society. But the Church after Vatican II also acknowledges the pluralistic world in which we live as good and has no intention of becoming coextensive with the society in which she lives. She wants to be an outer-oriented movement in society.

Another characteristic of a movement is that there are many ways of belonging to it. People involve themselves in a movement in different ways, depending on their gifts and interests, on their situation in life, and on their ideals at the particular time. They may become active and assume responsibility in it; they may attend all the meetings and read the literature; but they may also choose to have a rather limited contact with the institutional center of the movement and simply follow its thinking, reflect on its wisdom, and endorse its ideals in their association with other people. A movement does not have a clearly defined membership. People choose their own way of being involved in it. Some people who have little organizational contact with the movement may, nonetheless, be deeply touched by its ideals which have a profound effect on society and thus, in their own way, promote the purpose for which the movement exists.

In this a movement differs from a society. A society has a clearly defined membership. You always know whether you belong to it or not. You are a member of a society, not by a particular function or by the work you do, but simply by being assigned a particular place in the society, by having your name written into a book. If you are a member of a society you remain a member, even if your involvement becomes minimal—as long as you do not take your name off the list. A society is sociologically visible in all of its members. A society has clearly defined boundaries. A movement does not have visible boundary lines.

It seems to me that the Catholic Church, in these days of evolution, is becoming a social movement. People involve themselves in the life of the Church in different ways and in different degrees. At a time when the teaching of the Church encouraged Catholics to believe that divine grace was operative principally within the Church, an attitude was generated that produced clearly defined boundary lines around the Church. Either you belonged to it or you did not. You always knew whether you were in it or out of it. But today when we teach that the redemptive mystery is present to human life and communicated wherever people are open to one another, the boundaries of the Church are not so clearly visible. The Church is still a visible community, the community of those who announce and celebrate this mystery, but since she extends her fellowship to others and wants to identify herself in solidarity with the whole community, she no longer generates the attitude that draws up strict boundary lines. People have begun to involve themselves in ecclesiastical life in a variety of ways. It is not always as easy as it was in the past to know whether a man is a member of the Church.

There may be good reasons for regretting this development. It seems to me, however, that this shift from society to movement is already taking place in the Catholic Church. This is the Open Church in the making.

In this connection we must examine a wide-spread phenomenon in the Catholic Church that has been called "the third man." The term goes back to François Roustang's article "Le troisième homme," published in the French Jesuit review *Christus*,[5] which has been widely acknowledged in the Catholic Church. The article describes the creation of a new kind of man in the Church. There are in the Church progressive Catholics who wish to renew Catholic life according to Vatican II, then there are conservative Catholics who prefer the preconciliar Church, and finally there is "the third man." Who is this third man? The third man believes that God has acted in Jesus Christ on behalf of all men and that this divine salvation is available in the Spirit in the celebration of the Catholic Church. The third man is a Catholic. He regards the Church as his spiritual home. He is deeply attached to the Catholic tradition. At the same time, he takes the institutional Church with a grain of salt. He loves Catholic teaching when it makes sense to him, when it gives him access to new life and enables him to respond to the demands the world makes on him; but if the teaching does not make sense to him, he does not bother with it. He does not wish to argue with other Catholics about it. It would not occur to him to argue with the bishops or the Pope. If these teachings make sense to other Catholics, the third man thinks they should accept them wholeheartedly. Similarly, the third man loves the sacramental life of the Church. He participates in the sacraments when they make sense to him, when they deepen his awareness of God's presence and strengthen him in his involvement with other people. But when they do not make sense to him, when they become barriers to worship and to community, then he does not bother with them. Again, he does not feel like arguing about it. He makes his own choice; he does not feel guilty about it. He wants to leave other people free to make up their own minds. The third man, moreover, acknowledges the law of the Church. He is no rebel. He believes in law and order. At the same time, he realizes that human life is complex and that there are situations in which ecclesiastical law does not promote the spiritual well-being of persons. In those cases he feels free to act apart from canon law and, if necessary, move to the margin of the ecclesiastical institution.

What are we to think of the third man? The question is an important one since the ecclesiastical phenomenon is very widely spread in the North American Church. The third man, as first analyzed by François Roustang and then acknowledged in Catholic literature, differs from the Christian who is losing his faith. Some people move away from the Church because they find it increasingly difficult to accept that there is a redemptive mystery in human life. Life is identified by them simply with what they see; they find it impossible to believe in the mystery of God present to men. The third man differs also from the Christian who loses interest in the Church because he gives in to his selfish desires. A Christian may become so self-centered that the community of faith and love becomes a burden to him. He may stay away from the Church because he finds the Gospel a hard road to follow. Again the third man is different from the confused Christian who does not know what to believe anymore. Because of the changes in liturgy and doctrinal emphasis and because of the uncertainty in regard to much of traditional morality, some Catholics may simply be confused. They want to follow the Church but they no longer know exactly what this implies. The third man, as analyzed by François Roustang, we conclude, is neither the unfaithful man, nor the selfish man, nor the confused man. Who, then, is he?

The third man wants to be faithful to the divine presence revealed in Christ and mediated in the Catholic Church. He wants to be sensitive to the Spirit who creates the Church. The third man, it seems to me, is an inevitable phenomenon accompanying the Church's entry into a new spiritual–cultural environment and the refocusing of the Gospel which this entails. We have shown that Vatican II has begun to refocus the self-identical Gospel and that the reinterpretation of the Church's teaching in the light of the new focus is a gradual process. While we pass through this process we are all more or less third men. As Catholics we accept the Church's teaching, but as we adjust to the new focus of the Gospel, there are many doctrinal positions to which we are, at this time, unable to assign a clear meaning. These doctrinal positions were formulated with a reference to a previous focus. Because the focus has been shifted, these positions no longer make the sense they once did; and because the process of reinterpretation is a gradual one, it may happen that these positions cannot yet be related to the new focus. These positions seem to hang in the air. What is required is more reflection, more dialogue, more theological research, more vital engagement in Christian life. This will speed up the process of reinterpretation. In some important cases, what may be required is the endorsement of the reinterpretation by the ecclesiastical magisterium.

Let me give a simple example. The attitude of the Catholic Church to infant baptism made sense in terms of the restrictive understanding of Church. Baptism is man's saving contact with Jesus Christ, the one mediator. Children can be saved only through baptism. We thought, therefore, that it was a matter of great urgency to baptize babies that were dying, whether they came from Christian families or not. We thought that without baptism a child could not enter the glory of God. This doctrinal understanding determined the baptismal practice of the Church. Catholic priests, for instance, were not permitted to give liturgical burial to babies that had died without baptism, even when they came from Christian parents. Or, to extend the influence of baptism, Catholic hospitals would perform intrauterine baptisms in cases where the life of the embryo was threatened before birth. Today, after Vatican II, the Church teaches that God is redemptively involved in human history. To be born into the human family means to be born into a sinful community and to become a sinner oneself; at the same time, it means to belong to a community that has been oriented once for all toward divine salvation. To be human—in this history—means to be summoned to salvation. For this reason our attitude to baptism is bound to change. We no longer want to defend infant baptism in the Church on the theory that without it little babies are excluded from salvation. We no longer want to be overanxious about the baptism of babies. A Catholic who is not theologically trained may not be able to express these insights in correct theological propositions; he may not be able to work out a theology which explains the positive meaning of infant baptism in the Church and at the same time acknowledges the salvation of babies who die without baptism. The old doctrinal position no longer makes sense to the Catholic; he no longer accepts the anxious practice of the past; at the same time he may not be able to reinterpret the old position in the light of the new focus and come to a satisfactory doctrinal position. He becomes a third man. This is a slight example of a phenomenon which is wide and reaches deeply into the doctrinal life of the Church.

I wish to mention in this connection that Charles Davis is not a third man. He left the Catholic Church and took up a doctrinal position against her. In the view of Charles Davis, a Catholic is ignoble and insincere if he puts a question mark behind a doctrinal position defined by the Catholic Church. He interprets such a question mark as a sign of doubt or disbelief. Such a Catholic, Davis feels, ought to leave the Catholic Church. In our view, the entry of the Church into a new spiritual–cultural environment leads to a refocusing of the Gospel and to a process of reinterpreting traditional teaching in which open questions are removed only gradually. In this state of transition every Catholic is more or less a third man.

Let us return to the thesis that the sociological model for the institutional life of the Open Church is the outer-oriented movement. We saw that a movement is characterized—and differs from a closed society—by the fact that people belong to it in various ways and varying intensities, according to their own choice. While the official concept of the Church, expressed in canon law and the diocesan–parochial structure, is still that of a closed society, the doctrinal development of Vatican II and the experience of the Catholic people have produced a shift in the sociological reality of the Church

—a shift, we add, in keeping with her divinely given hierarchical structure. The widespread phenomenon of "the third man" makes the Church a movement in fact, even while this may not be acknowledged by the ecclesiastical government.

This leads us to the next characteristic of an outer-oriented movement. A movement is institutionally visible at the center. A society, we have said, is visible in every one of its members. Since membership is clearly defined, the boundary lines of a society can be clearly drawn. Yet the social organization of a movement is visible only at the center: the movement is visible in its regular meetings and the on-going committees that plan these meetings. A movement assumes clear and often powerful visibility when the people variously associated with it gather for different purposes: to affirm their self-identity as a movement, to strengthen one another, to discuss and decide orientation and policies, to be educated and to plan education, to meet one another and become friends, to exchange ideas and learn from the experience of others, and so forth. The movement is, therefore, an institution. Its institutional life is embodied in the meetings and the on-going committees responsible for them. At the same time, the institutional part of an outer-oriented movement may not be the place where it is most vitally concentrated. The movement is most itself in the exercise of its mission.

It seems to me that, also from this viewpoint, the sociological model of movement fits the postconciliar Church. The Church is institutionally visible at its meetings, especially at worship; it is visible at the other meetings, be they decision-making or simply educational. The variety of ways in which Christians associate themselves with, and come to be, the Catholic Church does not make her what in the old Protestant–Catholic polemics was called an "invisible Church." Regarding the Church as a movement does not weaken her institutional character. It simply assigns the institution a different role in the total life of the Church. In the Church the meetings are the institution. The hierarchical ministry in apostolic succession—in association with other Christians according to the evolution of canon law—organizes, serves, and directs these meetings. The divinely appointed ministry exercises their authority in the teaching, worship, and policies of the Church—not, indeed, to enforce uniformity but to promote diversity in the unity of faith. The apostolic authority remains with the episcopal college (including papal primacy) to protect and enliven the tensions implicit in the Gospel between the local and the universal, and between past and present. The Church as outer-oriented movement preserves the apostolic authority at its institutional center to achieve the doctrinal consensus, accepted by all, for the refocusing of the Gospel in ever-new environments.

In the Church that has become movement the authority of the hierarchical ministry will have to do mainly with the establishment and formulation of consensus. It will be power to promote the Gospel. The Church of tomorrow will no longer understand the power which Jesus gave the apostles and which is exercised by her ministers in terms of jurisdiction over people. The people will associate themselves in the movement freely and responsibly, as they decide in the Spirit.

What will the Church look like if she becomes a movement? Here is an example. Let us assume that a large North American city has 40 parishes. Parish means closed society. A parish has geographical boundaries. The pastor is in charge of the parish; he is appointed over the people. Then let us imagine that instead of these 40 parishes we have 10 or 15 centers of Christian life, conveniently spread over the whole city, without any territorial rights. At these centers, worship is celebrated on Sundays and throughout the week. Every day there are activities of various kinds in which people can involve themselves. There are talks, discussion groups, action programs, adult education, catechesis for children . . . the action at the centers can be shared in by people. It stimulates them, makes them ask important questions, impresses on them the meaning of faith, and encourages them to reach out for the answers to new questions. People involve themselves in what happens at these centers, as they choose. When they go there no one has authority over them. If they want to participate on the organizational level, they will be able to do so and eventually influence the making of policy regarding the center. But what counts is not so much what happens at the center but what happens in people's lives as the result of their contact with these centers.

What would happen if the Church became a movement visible at the center? We may find that at first there may be a numerical decrease. At the same time, I believe that the effect of the centers on the lives of people would be greater and hence the total influence of the Church on the society, even though through fewer Catholics, would be greater. The Church would be able to influence the social conscience of the city; it would stimulate programs of social reform, it would make people generally more sensitive to what is precious and important in life. The Church in this situation would not face the secular society as a spiritual replica of itself, the Church would not inspire people to become members of her own societies and organizations, the Church would enable Catholics to become more dedicated members of the secular society in which they live. The Church as movement would intensify the people's involvement in the life of society. Through conversation and common action, the Church would draw men more deeply into the mystery of redemption present in human life. And if the participation in the worship and the programs at these centers makes people more alive and more sensitive to what is real in life, then others will join them in their faith and worship God in union with them. The whole movement will remain strong enough to exercise the mission that makes it Church.

There are signs that in the big cities the Church is already taking on the form of a movement, even though this is not yet acknowledged by the ecclesiastical government. Where in the cities do people become deeply involved in Catholic life? Where do they learn about Christ? Where do they meet one another and become friends? Where do they learn to assume wider responsibility in the community? It would be unrealistic to say that this is happening in the city parishes today. The Catholic life of a city is often mediated through other institutions. There may be a Catholic center or school or college that reaches out for the public; there may be special pastors and groups of priests who organize pastoral projects. There may be radio programs and religious news that touch people. There may be religious congregations or individual parishes that have an influence on people. The vitality of Catholic life, the new ideas people have, the ardent aspirations they entertain, the social impact they have on society . . . these things are not communicated through the parish system in the big cities. Sociologically speaking, the Catholic Church in big cities is already becoming a movement.

If this observation is correct, then the effort of the ecclesiastical government must eventually turn to a totally new pastoral approach. What must be created are ways of involving people in thinking and acting as Christians. Radio and television may turn out to be major sources of grace in the community. What we need is not new institutions in which people can be assigned their place; what we need are words and actions that move people, educate them, and make them live out their new life in the secular society. To use the terminology of Marshall McLuhan, the Church must become a "cool" Church: it must become a medium that invites participation.

It seems to me that understanding the Church as movement is in harmony with the sacramental and collegial structure of the Church. Is it also in harmony with the teaching that Church is community? Since the community created by the Church extends beyond her boundaries to others it seems to me that the outer-oriented movement is the only sociological model that does justice to this inclusive character of the Church. The Church as movement makes people conscious of what community means in the lives of men. At the institutional center of the Church, Christians learn the mystery of community in the Eucharist and in the teaching of Christ; they learn this, not to form a closed community about the visible centers but, rather, to become community-creators themselves and move into society, the places where they live and work, to form community with people there. The Open Church is the community of the faithful; but more than that, it initiates Christians into the redemptive role of community in human life and renders them capable of being friends with others and of making the people with whom they live a community. The Open Church, moreover, is community because through Christians it seeks to reconcile the human race as a community of men who are open to one another and willing to promote the well-being of all. In this action God is graciously present to men.

We conclude that the new self-understanding of man has a profound effect on the institutional structure of the Catholic Church. There is some evidence that the Church is being transformed from a closed society into an outer-oriented movement. The Open Church is defined in terms of the whole human family and her role in it. The Open Church is no spiritual replica of the political society. She is a movement, visible at the institutional center, involving people in various ways, according to their own choices. This will eventually demand an adaptation of the Church's sacramental and collegial structure. Yet throughout this transition the Church remains herself, once for all founded by God in Christ, and forever re-created by his living Word, in the identity of God's gift of himself to men.

Footnotes

[1] Cf. Constitution on the Church, articles 2 and 16; Constitution on the Church in the Modern World, articles 16 and 22.

[2] Cf. the proceedings of the Canon Law Society of America, 1965, 1966, and 1967. Cf. also F. Klostermann, "Structures of the Church of Tomorrow," IDO-C [*Information Documentation on the Conciliar Church*] (North America), 1967, doss. 28, 29.

[3] Cf. H. Heimerl, "Outline of a Constitution for the Church," *Concilium,* Vol. XXVIII, pp. 59–68, and the conclusions of the Canon Law Society of America, 1967, "Towards Constitutional Development in the Church," IDO-C (North America), 1968, doss. 1.

[4] Decree on the Church's Missionary Activity, article 3: "This universal design of God for the salvation of the human race is not carried out exclusively with a kind of secrecy in the souls of men. Nor is it achieved merely through those multiple endeavors, including religious ones, by which men search for God. . . . For these attempts need to be enlightened and purified, even though, through the kind disposition of divine providence, they may sometimes serve as guidance toward the true God or as a preparation for the Gospel."

[5] *Christus,* XIII (1966), pp. 561–67. Cf. M. West, "Testimony of a 20th Century Catholic," *America,* December 2, 1967, p. 681.